ITALIAN SENTENCE BUILDERS
A lexicogrammar approach
Beginner to Pre-Intermediate

Imprint: Independently Published

Edited by Stefano Pianigiani

About the authors

Gianfranco Conti taught for 25 years at schools in Italy, the UK and in Kuala Lumpur, Malaysia. He has also been a university lecturer, holds a Master's degree in Applied Linguistics and a PhD in metacognitive strategies as applied to second language writing. He is now an author, a popular independent educational consultant and professional development provider. He has written around 2,000 resources for the TES website, which have awarded him the Best Resources Contributor in 2015. He has co-authored the best-selling and influential book for world languages teachers, "The Language Teacher Toolkit" and "Breaking the sound barrier: Teaching learners how to listen", in which he puts forth his Listening As Modelling methodology. Gianfranco writes an influential blog on second language acquisition called The Language Gym, co-founded the interactive website language-gym.com and the Facebook professional group Global Innovative Language Teachers (GILT). Last but not least, Gianfranco has created the instructional approach known as E.P.I. (Extensive Processing Instruction).

Dylan Viñales has taught for 15 years, in schools in Bath, Beijing and Kuala Lumpur in state, independent and international settings. He lives in Kuala Lumpur. He is fluent in five languages, and gets by in several more. Dylan is, besides a teacher, a professional development provider, specialising in E.P.I., metacognition, teaching languages through music (especially ukulele) and cognitive science. In the last five years, together with Dr Conti, he has driven the implementation of E.P.I. in one of the top international schools in the world: Garden International School. This has allowed him to test, on a daily basis, the sequences and activities included in this book with excellent results (his students have won language competitions both locally and internationally). He has designed an original Spanish curriculum, bespoke instructional materials, based on Reading and Listening as Modelling (RAM and LAM). Dylan co-founded the fastest growing professional development group for modern languages teachers on Facebook, Global Innovative Languages Teachers, which includes over 12,000 teachers from all corners of the globe. He authors an influential blog on modern language pedagogy in which he supports the teaching of languages through E.P.I. Dylan is the lead author of Spanish content on the Language Gym website and oversees the technological development of the site. He is currently undertaking the NPQML qualification, after which he plans to pursue a Masters in second language acquisition.

Simona Gravina has taught for 15 years, in schools in Italy and the UK, both in state and independent settings. She lives in Glasgow, Scotland. She is fluent in three languages and gets by in a few more. Simona is, besides a teacher, a mum, a bookworm, a passionate traveller and a fitness enthusiast. In the last couple of years she has been testing and implementing E.P.I. in one of the top Independent schools in Scotland, St Aloysius'College, where she is currently Modern Languages Curriculum Leader in the Junior School.

Acknowledgements

Translating a book is a time-consuming yet rewarding endeavour. Simona would like to thank her family for all the support but most importantly her daughter, Giulia, for all her encouragement and for being a caring and wonderful daughter.

Secondly, a huge thanks to our editor, Stefano Pianigiani, from Rome, Italy. Stefano is a real pleasure to work with; good humoured, extremely dedicated and with an eagle-eye. His contributions have gone far beyond proofreading for accuracy, into advising on formatting and best selection of language content. Stefano holds an MA in Education. He is a committed teacher based in Leeds, England, and he has been a real asset to our team.

Lastly, thanks to Dr Mario Conti for his efforts and insight during the final rounds of proofreading. His contributions to making this book as accurate as possible and his comments surrounding usage of language have been of great help.

Introduction

Hello and welcome to the first 'text' book designed to be an accompaniment to an Italian, Extensive Processing Instruction course. The book has come about out of necessity, because such a resource did not previously exist.

How to use this book if you have bought into our E.P.I. approach

This book was originally designed as a resource to use in conjunction with our E.P.I. approach and teaching strategies. Our course favours flooding comprehensible input, organising content by communicative functions and related constructions, and a big focus on reading and listening as modelling. The aim of this book is to empower the beginner-to-pre-intermediate learner with linguistic tools - high-frequency structures and vocabulary - useful for real-life communication. Since, in a typical E.P.I. unit of work, aural and oral work play a huge role, this book should not be viewed as the ultimate E.P.I. coursebook, but rather as a **useful resource** to **complement** your Listening-As-Modelling and Speaking activities.

Sentence Builders – Online Versions

Please note that all these sentence builders will be available in bilingual and Italian only versions on the Language Gym website, available to download, editable and in landscape design optimised for displaying in the classroom, via the Locker Room section.

How to use this book if you don't know or have NOT bought into our approach

Alternatively, you may use this book to dip in and out of as a source of printable material for your lessons. Whilst our curriculum is driven by communicative functions rather than topics, we have deliberately embedded the target constructions in topics which are popular with teachers and commonly found in published coursebooks.

If you would like to learn about E.P.I. you could read one of the authors' blogs. The definitive guide is Dr Conti's "Patterns First – How I Teach Lexicogrammar" which can be found on his blog (www.gianfrancoconti.com). There are also blogs on Dylan's wordpress site (mrvinalesmfl.wordpress.com) such as "Using sentence builders to reduce (everyone's) workload and create more fluent linguists" which can be read to get teaching ideas and to learn how to structure a course, through all the stages of E.P.I.

The book "Breaking the Sound Barrier: Teaching Learners how to Listen" by Gianfranco Conti and Steve Smith, provides a detailed description of the approach and of the listening and speaking activities you can use in synergy with the present book.

The basic structure of the book

The book contains 19 macro-units which concern themselves with a specific communicative function, such as 'Describing people's appearance and personality', 'Comparing and contrasting people', 'Saying what you like and dislike' or 'Saying what you and others do in your free time'. You can find a note of each communicative function in the Table of Contents. Each unit includes:

- a sentence builder modelling the target constructions;
- a set of vocabulary building activities which reinforce the material in the sentence builder;
- a set of narrow reading texts exploited through a range of tasks focusing on both the meaning and structural levels of the text;
- a set of translation tasks aimed at consolidation through retrieval practice;
- a set of writing tasks targeting essential writing micro-skills such as spelling, functional and positional processing, editing and communication of meaning.

Each sentence builder at the beginning of a unit contains one or more constructions which have been selected with real-life communication in mind. Each unit is built around that construction but not solely on it. Based on the principle that each E.P.I instructional sequence must move from modelling to production in a seamless and organic way, each unit expands on the material in each sentence builder by embedding it in texts and graded tasks which contain both familiar and unfamiliar (but comprehensible and learnable) vocabulary and structures. Through lots of careful recycling and thorough and extensive processing of the input, by the end of each unit the student has many opportunities to encounter and process the new vocabulary and patterns with material from the previous units.

Alongside the macro-units you will find:

- grammar units: one or two pages of activities occurring at regular intervals. They explicitly focus on key grammar structures which enhance the generative power of the constructions in the sentence builders. At this level they mainly concern themselves with full conjugations of key verbs, with agreement and preposition usage. Note that these units recycle the same verbs many times over by revisiting at regular intervals but in different linguistic contexts;
- question-skills units: one or two pages on understanding and creating questions. These micro-units too occur at regular intervals in the book, so as to recycle the same question patterns in different linguistic contexts;
- revision quickies: these are retrieval practice tasks aimed at keeping the previously learnt vocabulary alive. These too occur at regular intervals;
- self-tests: these occur at the end of the book. They are divided into two sections, one for less confident and one for more confident learners.

The point of all the above micro-units is to implement lots of systematic recycling and interleaving, two techniques that allow for stronger retention and transfer of learning.

Important *caveat*

1) This is a **'no frills'** book. This means that there are a limited number of illustrations (only on unit title pages). This is because we want every single little thing in this book to be useful. Consequently, we have packed a substantive amount of content at the detriment of its outlook. In particular, we have given serious thought to both **recycling** and **interleaving**, in order to allow for key constructions, words and grammar items to be revisited regularly so as to enhance exponentially their retention.

2) **Listening** as modelling is an essential part of E.P.I. There will be an accompanying listening booklet released shortly which will contain narrow listening exercises for all 19 units, following the same content as this book.

3) **All content** in this booklet matches the content on the **Language Gym** website. For best results, we recommend a mixture of communicative, retrieval practice games, combined with Language Gym games and workouts, and then this booklet as the follow-up, either in class or for homework.

4) An **answer booklet** is also available, for those that would like it. We have produced it separately to stop this booklet from being excessively long.

5) This booklet is suitable for **beginner** to **pre-intermediate** learners. This equates to a **CEFR A1-A2** level, or a beginner **Y6-Y8** class. You do not need to start at the beginning, although you may want to dip in to certain units for revision/recycling. You do not need to follow the booklet in order, although many of you will, and if you do, you will benefit from the specific recycling/interleaving strategies. Either way, all topics are repeated frequently throughout the book.

We do hope that you and your students will find this book useful and enjoyable.

Gianfranco, Dylan and Simona

TABLE OF CONTENTS

THE LANGUAGE GYM

UNIT 1
Saying how I feel and talking about my age

In this unit you will learn:

- How you feel
- How to say your name and age
- How to say someone else's name and age
- How to count from 1 to 15
- A range of common Italian names
- The words for brother and sister

Ho quindici anni

Ho dieci anni

Ho sei anni

Ho trent'anni

UNIT 1a
Saying how you feel
'Come stai? - Perché?'
[How you do feel? - Why?]

					MASCH.	FEMM.
Ciao *[Hi]*		**bene** *[well]*			**arrabbiato** *[angry]*	**arrabbiata** *[angry]*
Salve *[Hello]*	**Sto** *[I feel]*	**molto bene** *[very well]*	**perché** *[because]*	**sono** *[I am]*	**contento** *[joyful]*	**contenta** *[joyful]*
Buongiorno *[Good morning]*		**così così** *[so so]*			**emozionato** *[excited]*	**emozionata** *[excited]*
Buonasera *[Good evening]*		**male** *[bad]*			**felice** *[happy]*	**felice** *[happy]*
		molto male *[very bad]*			**in gran forma** *[feeling great]*	**in gran forma** *[feeling great]*
					nervoso *[nervous]*	**nervosa** *[nervous]*
					preoccupato *[worried]*	**preoccupata** *[worried]*
					stressato *[stressed]*	**stressata** *[stressed]*
					stanco *[tired]*	**stanca** *[tired]*
					tranquillo *[calm]*	**tranquilla** *[calm]*
					triste *[sad]*	**triste** *[sad]*

Author's note: *Bear in mind that adjectives end in –o for masculine and –a for feminine. The ones ending in –e do not change.*

Unit 1a. Saying how you feel: VOCABULARY BUILDING

1. Match up

1.sono contento	a.I feel so so
2. perché	b.I am nervous
3.sono stanco	c.I feel bad
4.sono triste	d.I am happy
5.sono felice	e.I am joyful
6.sono stressato	f.I am stressed
7.sono nervoso	g.I am sad
8.sto bene	h.hello
9.sto male	i.I feel good
10.sto così così	l.because
11.buongiorno	m.I am tired
12.salve	n.good morning

2. Complete with the missing word

a. Salve _Sto_ bene perché _sono_ felice.

[Hi, I feel good because I am happy]

b. Buonasera, sto _male_ perché sono _stanco/a_

[Good evening, I feel bad because I am tired]

c. Ciao, sto_molto_ bene _perché_ sono in gran forma.

[Hi, I feel very good because I am feeling great]

molto	male	stanco
perché	sono	sto

3. Choose "sto" or "sono"

Sto/sono	Adjective
Sono	contento
Sto	bene
Sono	felice
Sto	male
Sono	preoccupata
Sto	così così

4. Complete the table

Masculine	Feminine
contento	contenta
felice	felice
stressato	stressata
tranquillo	tranquilla
emozionato	emozionata
stanco	stanca
arrabbiato	arrabbiata
triste	triste
nervoso	nervosa

5. Translate into Italian   *Buongiorno, sto bene perché sono felice*

1. Good morning, I feel good because I am happy
2. Hi, I feel very bad because I am tired (feminine)
3. Good evening, I feel very good because I am joyful (masculine)
4. Hello, I feel very well because I am calm (feminine)
5. Good morning, I feel very bad because I am worried (masculine)
6. Hello, I feel so so because I am nervous (masculine)
7. Good evening, I feel very well because I am excited (masculine)
8. Good morning, I feel well because I am feeling great.

THE LANGUAGE GYM

UNIT 1b
Talking about my age
'Come ti chiami? - Quanti anni hai?'
[What is your name? - How old are you?]

Io [I]	mi chiamo [am called]	Alessio Antonio Anna Barbara Davide Dylan Emanuela Filippo	e [and]	ho [I have*]	un [1]	anno [year]
					due [2] tre [3] quattro [4] cinque [5] sei [6] sette [7]	anni [years]
Mio fratello [My brother] Mia sorella [My sister]	si chiama [is called]	Gianfranco Giuseppe Giulia Katia Mario Paolo Simona Stefano		ha [he/she has*]	otto [8] nove [9] dieci [10] undici [11] dodici [12] tredici [13] quattordici[14] quindici [15]	

Author's notes:

*1) The number **"uno"** becomes **"un"** when it goes before a noun. E.g. " Ho un fratello".*

2) In Italian, we use the verb "to have" for age. So, we say "ho dieci anni" to say how old we are, evern though it means, literally "I have ten years". There are a few Latin languages (e.g. Spanish/French) that also do this :D

4

Unit 1b. Talking about my age: VOCABULARY BUILDING

1. Match up

1.un anno	a.seven years
2.due anni	b.four years
3.tre anni	c.five years
4.quattro anni	d.six years
5.cinque anni	e.eleven years
6.sei anni	f.ten years
7.sette anni	g.twelve years
8.otto anni	h.nine years
9.nove anni	i.two years
10.dieci anni	l.eight years
11.undici anni	m.one year
12.dodici anni	n.three years

2. Complete with the missing word

a. Ho _dodici_ anni. *[I am twelve years old]*

b. Mio fratello _si_ chiama Davide.
[My brother is called Davide]

c. Mi _chiamo_ Roberto. *[My name is Roberto]*

d. Mio fratello _ha_ due anni. *[My brother is two]*

e. Mia sorella ha _quattro_ anni. *[My sister is four]*

f. _Mi_ chiama Anna. *[My name is Anna]*

quattro	ha	si
mi	dodici	chiamo

3. Translate into English

a. Ho tre anni   I'm 3
b. Ho cinque anni   I'm 5
c. Ho undici anni   I'm 11

d. Ha quindici anni   He/she has 15 y/o
e. Ha tredici anni   " 13
f. Ha sette anni "   7

g. Mio fratello   my bro
h. Mia sorella   my sis
i. Si chiama   is called

4. Broken words

a. H_o_ *[I have]*

b. Mi chia_mo_ *[my name is]*

c. Mia sor_ella_ *[my sister]*

d. Quin_dici_ *[fifteen]*

e. Sed_ici_ *[sixteen]*

f. Und_ici_ *[eleven]*

g. No_ve_ *[nine]*

h. Quatto_rdici_ *[fourteen]*

i. Do_dici_ *[twelve]*

5. Rank the people below from oldest to youngest as shown in the example

Michele ha quindici anni	1
Giorgia ha tredici anni	2
Luca ha due anni	7
Piero ha quattro anni	6
Alex ha un anno	8
Roberta ha cinque anni	4
Benedetta ha nove anni	3
Dorotea ha tre anni	5

6. For each pair of people write who is the oldest, as shown in the example

A	B	OLDER
Ho undici anni	Ho tredici anni	B
Ho tre anni	Ho sei anni	B
Ho undici anni	Ho dodici anni	B
Ho quindici anni	Ho tredici anni	A
Ho quattordici anni	Ho undici anni	A
Ho otto anni	Ho nove anni	B
Ho undici anni	Ho sette anni	A

Unit 1b. Talking about my age: READING

Ciao, mi chiamo Leo e ho dodici anni. Sto molto bene perché sono felice. Ho un fratello che si chiama Stefano. Stefano ha quattordici anni.

Buongiorno, mi chiamo Dita e ho dieci anni. Ho una sorella che si chiama Flutura e un fratello che si chiama Bledar. Flutura ha cinque anni. Bledar ha nove anni.

Mi chiamo Tian e ho tredici anni. Sto male, perché sono arrabbiato. Ho un fratello che si chiama Cheng. Cheng ha quindici anni.

Salve, mi chiamo Marine. Sto bene perché sono tranquilla. Sono francese e ho dieci anni. Ho una sorella che si chiama Fabienne. Fabienne ha undici anni. Ho **anche** [also]un fratello che si chiama Pierre. Pierre ha otto anni.

Mi chiamo Kaori e ho sette anni. Ho una sorella che si chiama Yoko. Yoko ha tredici anni. Ho anche un fratello che si chiama Hiroto. Hiroto ha dieci anni.

Ciao, mi chiamo Moritz e ho quattordici anni. Ho due fratelli. Mio fratello maggiore si chiama Patrick e mio fratello minore si chiama Philip. Patrick ha sedici anni e Philip ha quindici anni.

1. Find the Italian for the following items in Leo's text

a. I have a brother
   Ho un fratello
b. My name is
   Mi chiamo
c. I feel very well
   Sto bene molto
d. I am happy
   Sono felice
e. Who is called Stefano
   che si chiama Stefan
f. I am twelve _Ho dodici anni_
g. He is fourteen
   Ha quattordici anni

2. Answer the following questions about Dita

a. What is the name of Dita's sister?
   Flutura
b. How old is Dita?
   _10_
c. How many siblings does she have? _2_
d. What's her brother called? _Bledar_
e. What age is he?
   _5_

3. Complete the table below

	Age	How many siblings	Ages of siblings
Tian	13	1	15
Leo	12	1	14
Dita	10	2	5 + 9

4. Moritz, Kaori or Marine?

a. Who has a 15- year-old brother? _Moritz_
b. Who has an 11-year-old sister? _Marine_
c. Who is 11? _Fabienne_
d. Who has an older brother aged 16? _Moritz_
e. Who is calm? _Marine_

un fratello/maggiore / minore

6

Unit 1b. Talking about my age: TRANSLATION

1. Faulty translation: spot and correct (in the English) any translation mistakes you find below

a. Mi chiamo Patrizia: *Her name is Patrizia*

b. Ho due sorelle: *I have two brothers*

c. Mia sorella si chiama Marta: *My mother is called Marta*

d. Mio fratello ha cinque anni: *My sister is 5*

e. Ho quindici anni: *I am five*

f. Mio fratello ha otto anni: *My brother is seven*

g. Non ho fratelli: *I don't have a sister*

h. Ho diciotto anni: *I am 17*

i. Ho dodici anni: *I am 13*

j. Si chiama Gianni: *My name is Gianni*

2. From Italian to English

a. Mio fratello si chiama Dario.

My bro is called Dario

b. Ho quindici anni.

I'm 15 y/o

c. Mio fratello ha sei anni.

My bro is 6 y/o

d. Mia sorella si chiama Marina.

My sis' called Marina

e. Ho sette anni.

I'm 7

f. Sto bene

I'm well

g. Mia sorella ha quattordici anni.

My sis he is 14

h. Ho un fratello e una sorella.

I have a bro + a sis

i. Marta ha dodici anni.

Marta is 12 y/o

j. Annamaria ha nove anni.

Anna is 9 y/o.

3. English to Italian translation

a. Hello, my name is Guido. I am six. *Salve, mi chiamo Guido. Ho sei anni*

b. My brother is fifteen years old. *Mio fratello ha quindici anni*

c. I am twelve. I am happy. *Ho dodici anni e sono felice*

d. My sister is called Emanuela. *Mia sorella si chiama Emanuela.*

e. My name is Gianfranco. I am joyful. *Mi chiamo Gianfranco e sono contento*

f. I have a brother and a sister. *Ho un fratello e una sorella*

g. My name is Filippo and I am fourteen. *Mi chiamo Filippo e ho quattor~~undici~~dici anni*

h. My name is Gianfranco and I am eleven. *Mi chiamo Gian e ho undici anni*

i. My name is Rossana. I am ten. I have a brother and a sister. *Mi chiamo Ros, ho dieci anni ho un fratello e una sorella*

j. My sister is called Alberta. She is twelve. *Mia sorella si chiama Alberto, ha dodici anni*

k. I do not have a brother. I am sad. *Non ho un fratello. Sono triste*

 THE LANGUAGE GYM

Unit 1b. Talking about my age: WRITING

1. Complete the words

a. M_i_ ch_iamo_ Roberto.

b. Ho_____ quattor_dici_ a_nni_ .

c. H_a_ un f_ratello_ o.

d. M_i_ f_ratell_ o si chi_ama_ Giulio.

e. Mi _chia_ mo Patrizio.

f. Mio _fra_ tello s_i_ _chia_ ma Marco.

g. _h_ o tr_edi_ ci anni.

h. Mia so_rella_ a si ch_iama_ Katia.

2. Write out the number in Italian

nine = n_ove_

seven = s_ette_

twelve = d_odici_

five = c_inque_

fourteen = q_uattordici_

sixteen = s_eidici_

thirteen = t_redici_

four = q_uattordici_

3. Spot and correct the mistakes

a. Mi ciamo Paolo. _Chiamo_

b. Ho tredici anno. _anni_

c. Mio fratelo ha cinqe anni. _fratello / cinque_

d. Mio fratello se chiama Maria. _Si_

e. Me chiamo Patrizio. _Mi_

f. Mi sorela si chiama Alessandra. _sorella / mia_

4. Complete with a suitable word

a. Mia sorella si _chiama_ Laura.

b. _Mio_ fratello ha quindici anni.

c. Mi _chiamo_ Mario.

d. Ho un _fratello_ che si chiama Filippo.

e. Ho una _sorella_ che si chiama Annamaria.

f. Mio fratello _ha_ quattordici anni.

5. Guided writing – write 4 short paragraphs in the first person singular ['I'] each describing the people below

	Age	Feeling	Reason	Brother's name and age	Sister's name and age
Johann	12	well	joyful	Franz 9	Martha 8
Flutura	15	very well	excited	Bledar 13	Luljeta 5
Michael	11	bad	sad	Thomas 7	Gerda 12
Kyoko	10	very bad	angry	Ken 6	Rena 1

6. Describe this person in the third person:

Name: Giovanni

Age: 12

Brother: Marco, 13 years old

Sister: Serena, 15 years old

UNIT 2
Saying when my birthday is, where I am from and what languages I speak.

In this unit you will learn to say:

- When your birthday is
- Numbers from 15 to 31
- Months
- I am, he/she is
- Names of Italian speaking locations
- Where you live
- What is your nationality
- What languages you speak

UNIT 2
Saying when my birthday is
'Quando é il tuo compleanno?'
[When is your birthday?]

Mi chiamo Leonardo [My name is Leonardo]	**ho x anni** [I am x years]	**e il mio compleanno è il/*l'** [and my birthday is the]	1 - **uno/primo** 2 - **due** 3 - **tre** 4 - **quattro** 5 - **cinque** 6 - **sei** 7 - **sette** 8 - **otto** 9 - **nove** 10 - **dieci** 11 - **undici** 12 - **dodici** 13 - **tredici** 14 - **quattordici**	**gennaio** [January] **febbraio** [February] **marzo** [March] **aprile** [April] **maggio** [May]
La mia amica si chiama Caterina [My friend is called Caterina] **Il mio amico si chiama Francesco** [My friend is called Francesco]	**ha x anni** [he/she is x years]	**e il suo compleanno è il/*l'** [and his/her birthday is the]	15 - **quindici** 16 - **sedici** 17 - **diciassette** 18 - **diciotto** 19 - **diciannove** 20 - **venti** 21 - **ventuno** 22 - **ventidue** 23 - **ventitré** 24 - **ventiquattro** 25 - **venticinque** 26 - **ventisei** 27 - **ventisette** 28 - **ventotto** 29 - **ventinove** 30 - **trenta** 31 - **trentuno**	**giugno** [June] **luglio** [July] **agosto** [August] **settembre** [September] **ottobre** [October] **novembre** [November] **dicembre** [December]

Author's note: *il* and *l'* means 'the'. **Il tre aprile** translates 'the 3rd of April'. Beware that before **uno/otto/undici** you will need *l'* instead. Example: **l'otto marzo**. Can you guess why?

Unit 2a. Saying when my birthday is: VOCABULARY BUILDING

1. Complete with the missing word

a. Mi _Chiamo_ Gabriella [my name is Gabriella]

b. La mia _amica_ si chiama Eva [my friend is called Eva]

c. Il _mio_ amico si chiama Luca [my friend is called Luca]

d. Il mio _compleanno_ è il [my birthday is on the]

e. Il _cinque_ maggio [the 5th of May]

f. L' _otto_ novembre [the 8th of November]

g. Il quattro _luglio_ [the 4th of July]

h. Il ____ compleanno è il... [his/her birthday is on...]
suo

2. Match up

1.aprile	d	a.May	
2.novembre	e	b.my birthday	
3.dicembre	g	c.my friend (f)	
4.maggio	a	d.April	
5.gennaio	j	e.November	
6.febbraio	i	f.s/he is called	
7.il mio compleanno	b	g.December	
8.il mio amico	k	h.I am called	
9.la mia amica	c	i.February	
10.mi chiamo	h	j.January	
11.si chiama	f	k.my friend(m)	

3. Translate into English

a. Il quattordici gennaio = 14ᵗ Jan

b. L'otto maggio = 8ᵃ May

c. Il sette febbraio = 7ᵗ Feb

d. Il venti marzo = 20ᵃ marcu.

e. Il diciannove agosto = 19ᵃ August

f. Il venticinque luglio = 25ᵗ July

g. Il ventiquattro settembre = 24ᵃ Sept

h. Il quindici aprile = 15ᵗ April

4. Add the missing letter

a. com_p_leanno   c. ma_r_zo   e. a_p_rile   g. ge_n_naio   i. lu_g_lio   k. d_e_cembre

b. feb_b_raio   d. mag_g_io   f. giug_n_o   h. ag_o_sto   j. novem_b_re   l. se_t_tembre

5. Broken words

a. I_l_ t_re_ g_ennaio_ = [the 3rd of Jan]

b. I_l_ c_inque_ l_uglio_ = [the 5th of July]

c. I_l_ n_ove_ a_gosto_ = [the 9th of Aug]

d. I_l_ d_odici_ m_arzo_ = [the 12th of March]

e. I_l_ s_edici_ a_prile_ = [the 16th of April]

f. I_l_ d_iciannove_ d_ecembre_ = [the 19th of Dec]

g. I_l_ v_enti_ o_ttobre_ = [the 20th of Oct]

h. I_l_ v_entisette_ m_aggio_ = [the 27th of May]

i. I_l_ t_renta_ s_ettembre_ = [the 30th of Sept]

6. Complete with a suitable word

a. Mi _chiamo_ Simona.

b. Il mio _compleanno_ è il due marzo.

c. Ho nove _anni_ .

d. Il mio _fratello_ si chiama Gian.

e. Gian _ha_ dieci anni.

f. Il suo _compleanno_ è il tre giugno.

g. Il mio _compleanno_ è il primo aprile.

h. La mia amica _si_ chiama Claire.

i. Il _suo_ compleanno è il sei maggio.

j. Oggi è l' otto _ottobre_ .

k. _Mi_ chiamo Leonardo Rossi.

Mi chiamo Alberto. Ho dodici anni e il mio compleanno è il quindici settembre. La mia amica si chiama Gabriella e ha quattordici anni. Il suo compleanno è il ventotto maggio. Nel mio tempo libero sempre suono la chitarra con Gabriella! Il mio amico si chiama Carlo. Lui ha trentuno anni ed è professore. Il suo compleanno è il ventuno giugno. Carlo ha un fratello maggiore. Il suo compleanno è l'otto gennaio.

Mi chiamo Mohamed. Ho ventidue anni e il mio compleanno è il dieci settembre. La mia amica si chiama Fatima e ha quindici anni. Il suo compleanno è il ventotto maggio. Nel mio tempo libero guardo sempre la televisione.

Mi chiamo Martina. Ho sette anni e il mio compleanno è il cinque dicembre. Ho due fratelli, Giulio ed Enrico. Giulio ha undici anni ed è molto bravo. Il suo compleanno è il trenta settembre. Enrico invece è cattivo. Ha tredici anni e il suo compleanno è il sette agosto.

Mi chiamo Gianluca. Ho otto anni e il mio compleanno è il nove agosto. Mia sorella minore ha quattro anni. È molto simpatica. Il suo compleanno è il nove agosto. Stesso giorno! Il mio amico si chiama Renzo e ha diciassette anni. Il suo compleanno è il venticinque ottobre.

1. Find the Italian for the following items in Alberto's text

a. I am called: *Mi chiamo*

b. I am 12 years old: *ho dodici anni*

c. the eight of January: *il otto genaio*

d. my birthday is: *il mio compleanno è*

e. the 15th of: *è il quindici ...*

f. her birthday is on: *il suo compleanno è ..*

g. in my free time: *nel mio tempo libero*

h. my friend (m): *il mio amico*

i. is called: *si chiama*

j. he is 31: *lui ha trentuno anni*

k. the 21st of June: *il ventuno junio*

l. has an older brother: *ha un frattello mayore*

3. Answer the following questions about Martina's text

a. How old is she? *Quanti anni ha?*

b. When is her birthday? *Quando è il suo compleanno?*

c. How many brothers does she have? *Cuanti fratelli ha?*

d. Which brother is good? *Cual fratello è bravo?*

e. How old in Enrico?

f. When is his birthday? *Cuanto è il suo compleanno?*

Cuanti anni ha Enrico?

2. Complete with the missing words

Mi chiamo Anna. *Ho* tredici *anni*. *Ho* un gatto in casa. Il mio *compleanno* è il ventinove diciembre. Mio fratello *ha* nove *anni* e il suo compleanno è ___ dieci aprile.

4. Find Someone Who:

a. has a birthday in December

b. is 22 years old

c. shares a birthday with a sibling

d. likes to play the guitar with his friend

e. has a friend who is 31 years old

f. has a birthday in September

g. has a little sister

h. has one good and one bad sibling

Unit 2a. Saying when my birthday is: WRITING

1. Complete with the missing letters

a. Mi chiamo Giorgio.

b. Sono di Torino.

c. Il mio compleanno è il dieci giugno.

d. Ho quattordici anni.

e. La mia amica si chiama Carla.

f. Il mio amico Si chiama Gianfranco.

g. Il mio amico si chiama Michele.

h. Michele ha undici anni.

2. Spot and correct the mistakes

a. Il mia cumpleanno è il quattro gennaio. *mio o*

b. Mi ciamo Giovanni. *chiamo*

c. Mi chiama Simona. *chiamo*

d. La mia amiga si chiamo Caterina. *a*

e. Caterina ho undici anno. *ha anni*

f. Io ho cuattordici anni. *quattordici*

g. Il mio compleano è il primo de marzo.

h. Ho cuindici anni.

quindici

3. Answer the questions in Italian

a. *Come ti chiami? Mi chiamo ___Natalie___.

b. *Quanti anni hai? Ho ___venti quattro___ anni.

c. *Quando è il tuo compleanno? Il mio compleanno è il ___venturo maggio___.   *venti sette*

d. Quanti anni ha tuo fratello/sorella? Mio fratello ha ___anni.   *a sorella*

*Author's note: * Come means "what/how", *Quanti means "how many", *Quando means "when" ☺*

4. Write out the dates below in words as shown in the example

a. 15/05 = il quindici maggio

b. 10/06 =

c. 20/03 =

d. 19/02 =

e. 25/12 =

f. 01/01 =

g. 22/11 =

h. 14/10 =

5. Guided writing – write 4 short paragraphs in the 1st person singular ['I'] describing the people below

Name	Age	Birthday	Name of brother	Brother's birthday
Samuel	11	25/12	Nico	19/02
Francesca	14	21/07	Marco	21/04
Li	12	01/01	Wen	20/06
Andrea	16	02/11	Alfonso	12/10

6. Describe this person in the third person:

Name: Alessio

Age: 12

Birthday: 21/06

Brother: Leo, 16 years old

Birthday: 01/12

Unit 2a. Saying when my birthday is: TRANSLATION

1. Faulty translation: spot and correct (in the English) any translation mistakes you find below

a. Il mio compleanno è il ventotto aprile:
His birthday is on the 27th April

b. Mi chiamo Roberto: *His name is Roberto*

c. Ho ventitré anni: *I am 22 years old*

d. Il mio amico si chiama Paul:
My friend I am called Paul

e. Lui ha ventisei anni: *I have 26 years old*

f. Il suo compleanno è il quattro luglio:
My birthday and the 14th of July

2. From Italian to English

a. L'otto ottobre

b. Il mio compleanno è...

c. Il mio amico si chiama ...

d. Il suo compleanno è ...

e. L'undici gennaio

f. Il quattordici febbraio

g. Il venticinque dicembre

h. Il sette luglio

i. Il primo giugno

3. Phrase-level translation

a. my name is...

b. I am ten years old

c. my birthday is the...

d. the first of May

e. my friend is called Bella

f. she is twelve years old

g. her birthday is the...

h. the 23rd of August

i. the 29th April

Author's note: go back to e.
Did you make Bella a girl? "amica" Well done if you did! ☺

4. Sentence-level translation

a. My name is Luigi. I am 30 years old. My birthday is on the 11th March.

b. My brother is called Piero. He is 14 years old. His birthday is on the 18th August.

c. My friend is called Simone. He is 22 years old and his birthday is on the 14th January.

d. My friend is called Angela. She is 18 years old and her birthday is on the 25th July.

e. My friend is called William. He is 20 years old. His birthday is on the 24th September.

UNIT 2b
Saying what my nationality is and what languages I speak
'Di dove sono? - Quali lingue parlo?'
[Where am I from? - What languages do I speak?]

Sono [I am]	australiano/a [Australian]	Parlo [I speak]	un po' [a little]	australiano [Australian]	e [and]
	cinese [Chinese]		abbastanza bene [quite well]	cinese [Chinese]	anche [also]
	francese [French]		molto bene [very well]	francese [French]	
La mia amica Simona è [My friend Simona is]	italiano/a [Italian]	Parla [He/She speaks]	perfettamente [fluently]	italiano [Italian]	inoltre [moreover]
	inglese [English]			inglese [English]	invece [instead]
	polacco/a [Polish]			polacco [Polish]	però/ma [but]
	portoghese [Portuguese]			portoghese [Portoguese]	
Il mio amico Stefano è [My friend Stefano is]	rumeno/a [Romanian]			rumeno [Romanian]	
	scozzese [Scottish]			spagnolo [Spanish]	
	spagnolo/a [Spanish]			tedesco [German]	
	tedesco/a [German]				

Author's note: When making the negative form we simply add **non** before the verb.
i.e. **parlo** = I speak; **non parlo** = I don't speak; **mia sorella parla** = my sister speaks; **mia sorella non parla** = my sister doesn't speak. N.B. Nationalities and languages have no capital letter in Italian.

THE LANGUAGE GYM

Unit 2b. Saying what languages I speak: READING

Mi chiamo Giovanna. Ho dodici anni e vivo a Napoli. Sono italiana. Parlo perfettamente italiano e abbastanza bene polacco, peró non parlo bene inglese.
La mia amica Simona è francese e ha quindici anni. Parla molto bene italiano e tedesco. Parla perfettamente francese ma non parla cinese.

Mi chiamo Florin. Ho undici anni e sono rumeno. Parlo perfettamente rumeno. Parlo anche molto bene italiano e un po' bulgaro, ma non parlo tedesco. La mia amica Katrina parla perfettamente inglese perché sua mamma è inglese. Inoltre parla il francese, però non parla bene italiano.

Mi chiamo Mario. Ho nove anni e sono polacco. Parlo perfettamente polacco e molto bene italiano, peró non parlo bene inglese
Il mio amico Salvatore vive in Bulgaria peró é italiano. Ha dodici anni e parla perfettamente inglese e bulgaro, inoltre parla molto bene italiano, ma non parla francese.

1. Find the Italian for the following items in Mario's text

a. I am Polish

b. I speak Polish fluently

c. He speaks English fluently

d. He lives in Bulgaria

e. He speaks very well Italian

f. but I don't speak English well

2. Find Someone Who: answer the questions below about all 3 texts

a. Who speaks Italian fluently?

_____

b. Who speaks English fluently and why?

_____

c. Who would like to speak German?

_____

d. Who doesn't speak Italian well?

_____

e. Who speaks Romanian?

_____

f. Who doesn't speak English well?

WRITING

1. Broken words

a. Parlo perfettamente inglese e francese. Però non parlo cinese

[I speak English and French fluently. But I don't speak Chinese]

b. La mia amica parla bene polacco però non parla rumeno.

[My friend (girl) speaks well Polish, but she doesn't speak Romanian]

c. Sono italiano e parlo molto bene inglese ma non parlo portoghese.

[I am Italian and I speak very well English but I don't speak Portuguese]

d. Parlo perfettamente spanolo e portoghese ma non parlo molto bene italiano.

[I speak perfectly Spanish and Portuguese but I don't speak very well Italian]

e. Il mio amico Simone é tedesco e non parla italiano, però parla tedesco e inglese.

[My friend Simone is German and he doesn't speak Italian, but he speaks perfectly German and English]

Perfetta- mente

16

UNIT 2c
'Dove vivi? - Ti piace?'
[Where do you live? - Do you like it?]

Vivo a *[I live in]*	**Bari** **Bologna** **Milano** **Roma** **Siena** **Torino** **Venezia**	**Adoro** *[I love]* **Mi piace** *[I like]*	**la mia città** *[my city]*	**abbastanza** *[quite]* **molto** *[very]* **piuttosto** *[rather]*	**bella** *[pretty]* **brutta** *[ugly]* **grande** *[big]* **noiosa** *[boring]* **piccola** *[small]* **rumorosa** *[noisy]* **tranquilla** *[calm]* **turistica** *[touristic]*
Mia sorella vive a *[My sister lives in]*	**Casperia** **Garda** **Montalcino** **Jesolo** **Ostuni** **Senigallia** **Viareggio**	**Non mi piace** *[I don't like]* **Odio** *[I hate]*	**perché è** *[because it is]* **il mio paese** *[my town]*	**troppo** *[too much]* **un po'** *[a little]*	**bello** *[pretty]* **brutto** *[ugly]* **grande** *[big]* **noioso** *[boring]* **piccolo** *[small]* **rumoroso** *[noisy]* **tranquillo** *[calm]* **turistico** *[touristic]*

THE LANGUAGE GYM

Unit 2c. Where you live: Translating

Paragraph 1	Tick a box each time you spot the correct translation in the text			Translate the paragraph into English
Ciao, mi chiamo Roberto. Sono italiano e ho undici anni. Parlo bene inglese e perfettamente italiano. Vivo a Bologna. Mi piace la mia città perché è molto grande e turistica. Mia sorella ha ventuno anni e vive a Venezia.	I live in Bologna ✓ ①	I like my city ✓ ②	My sister	_____
	and she lives in Venezia ✓ 4	and touristic ✓ ③	and Italian fluently ✓	_____
	Hi, my name is Roberto ✓	because it is very big ✓	I speak English well ✓	_____
	I am Italian	and I am 11 ✓	is 21 ✓	_____

Paragraph 2				
Salve, mi chiamo Maria, sono polacca e ho dodici anni. Parlo bene italiano e perfettamente polacco. Vivo a Ostuni. Adoro il mio paese perché è bello e abbastanza piccolo. Mio fratello ha ventidue anni e vive a Roma.	Hello, my name is Maria	and he lives in Rome	I speak Italian well	_____
	and Polish fluently	because it is pretty	I live in Ostuni	_____
	and quite small	I love my town	I am Polish	_____
	and I am 12	My brother	is 22	_____

Paragraph 3				
Buonasera, mi chiamo Francisco. Sono spagnolo e ho quattordici anni. Parlo un po' italiano e molto bene spagnolo. Vivo a Roma. Non mi piace la mia città perché è troppo grande e rumorosa. Mio fratello vive a Catania e ha trenta anni.	I am Spanish	and I am 14	I live in Rome	_____
	Good evening, my name is Francisco	I speak Italian a little	and Spanish very well	_____
	I don't like my city	My brother	because it is too big	_____
	lives in Catania	and noisy	and he is 30	_____

UNIT 3
Describing hair and eyes

In this unit you will learn:

- To describe what a person's hair and eyes are like
- To describe details about their faces (e.g. beard and glasses)
- Colours
- I wear / s/he wears

You will also revisit:

- Common Italian names
- The verb "Avere" in the first and third person singular
- Numbers from 1 to 15

UNIT 3
Describing hair and eyes
'Di che colore sono i tuoi occhi e i tuoi capelli?'
[What colour are your eyes and hair?]

(Io) Mi chiamo *[I am called / I call myself...]* **(Lui/Lei) Si chiama** *[He/she is called]*	**Antonio** **Carlo** **Diego** **Emilia** **Francesca** **Gianfranco** **Giulia** **Isabella** **Marta** **Roberto**	**e** *[and]*	**ho** *[I have]* **ha** *[he/she has]*	**sei anni** *[6 years]* **sette anni** *[7 years]* **otto anni** *[8 years]* **nove anni** *[9 years]* **dieci anni** *[10 years]* **undici anni** *[11 years]* **dodicianni** *[12 years]* **tredicianni** *[13 years]* **quattordici anni** *[14 years]* **quindici anni** *[15 years]*
Ho *i capelli *[I have...hair]* **Ha i capelli** *[He/she has...hair]*	**biondi** *[blonde]* **castani** *[brown]* **colorati** *[coloured]* **neri** *[black]* **rossi** *[red]* **scuri** *[dark brown]*	**e**	**a spazzola** *[spiky]* **corti** *[short]* **di media lunghezza** *[medium length]* **lisci** *[straight]* **lunghi** *[long]* **ondulati** *[wavy]* **rasati** *[very short/crew-cut]* **ricci** *[curly]*	
Ho gli occhi *[I have... eyes]* **Ha gli occhi** *[He/she has... eyes]*	**azzurri** *[blue]* **marroni** *[brown]* **neri** *[black]* **verdi** *[green]*	**e**	**(non) porto** *[I don't] wear* **(non) porta** *[he/she doesn't] wear* **(non) ho** *[I don't] have* **(non) ha** *[he/she doesn't] have*	**gli occhiali** *[glasses]* **i baffi** *[a moustache]* **la barba** *[a beard]*

Author's note: *the word for 'hair'- **i capelli** in Italian is a masculine <u>plural</u> noun. When describing hair you should follow this order: colour/length/style: **Ho i capelli castani, lunghi e lisci** ☺*

Unit 3. Describing hair and eyes: VOCABULARY BUILDING

1. Complete with the missing word

a. Ho i capelli c_astani_ *[I have brown hair]*

b. Ho i capelli b_iondi_ *[I have blonde hair]*

c. Porto gli o_cchiali_ *[I wear glasses]*

d. Ho gli occhi a_zzurri_ *[I have blue eyes]*

e. Non porto gli o_cchiali_ *[I don't wear glasses]*

f. Ho i capelli di me_dia_ lunghe_zza_
[I have mid-length hair]

g. Ho i capelli n_eri_ *[I have black-coloured eyes]*

h. Ho i capelli r_ossi_ *[I have red hair]*

2. Match up

a	1. i capelli castani	a. brown hair
e	2. i capelli neri	b. black eyes
i	3. i capelli biondi	c. moustache
b	4. gli occhi neri	d. green eyes
j	5. gli occhiali	e. black hair
c	6. i baffi	f. short hair
k	7. gli occhi azzurri	g. long hair
D	8. gli occhi verdi	h. red hair
F	9. i capelli corti	i. blonde hair
G	10. i capelli lunghi	j. glasses
H	11. i capelli rossi	k. blue eyes

3. Translate into English

a. i capelli ricci = Curly hair

b. gli occhi azzurri = Blue eyes

c. porto gli occhiali = I wear glasses

d. i capelli biondi = Blonde hair

e. gli occhi verdi = Green eyes

f. i capelli rossi = Red hair

g. gli occhi neri = Black eyes

h. i capelli scuri = dark brown hair

4. Add the missing letter

a. Lu_n_ghi   c. ca_p_elli   e. azzur_r_i   g. ric_c_i   i. s_c_uri   k. o_c_chi

b. occ_h_iali   d. baf_f_i   f. v_e_rdi   h. _L_isci   j. di media lun_g_hezza   l. por_t_o

5. Broken words

a. H_o_ i c_apelli_ r_i_cc_i_ = *[I have curly hair]*

b. P_orto_ gl_i_ o_cchiali_ = *[I wear glasses]*

c. _H_o i c_apelli_ c_orto_ = *[I have short hair]*

d. N_on_ h_o_ i b_affi_ = *[I don't have a moustache]*

e. _H_o gli o_cchi_ m_arroni_ = *[I have brown eyes]*

f. _H_o _L_a b_arba_ = *[I have a beard]*

g. H_o_ o_tto_ a_nn_i = *[I am eight years old]*

h. M_i_ c_hiamo_ M_aria_ = *[My name is Maria]*

i. _H_o n_ove_ a_nn_i = *[I am nine years old]*

6. Complete with a suitable word

a. Ho dieci _anni_ .

b. _Ho_ la barba.

c. Mi _chiamo_ Antonio Bianchi.

d. Porto gli _occhiali_ .

e. Ho i _capelli_ lisci e corti.

f. Ho _i_ baffi.

g. Ho _gli_ occhi marroni.

h. Ho _i_ capelli neri.

i. Non _ho_ i baffi.

j. _Ho_ i capelli lunghi e ondulati.

k. _Mi_ chiamo Luca Ferrari.

l. Ho _dodici_ anni.

Unit 3. Describing hair and eyes: READING

Mi chiamo Marta. Ho dodici anni e vivo a Napoli, il capoluogo della Campania. Ho i capelli neri, lisci e corti e gli occhi azzurri. Porto gli occhiali. Il mio compleanno è il dieci settembre. Mia sorella ha i capelli lisci. Lei ha dieci anni e parla un po' tedesco.

Mi chiamo Alice. Ho quindici anni e vivo a Bellinzona, in Svizzera. Parlo italiano e francese. Ho i capelli rossi, ondulati e lunghi e gli occhi azzurri. Non porto gli occhiali. Il mio compleanno è il sedici dicembre.

Mi chiamo Naima. Ho nove anni e sono indiana. Vivo a Torino, il capoluogo del Piemonte. Ho i capelli castani, ondulati e di media lunghezza e gli occhi marroni. Non porto gli occhiali. Il mio compleanno è il cinque dicembre. Mio fratello si chiama Yamir. Ha quindici anni. Ha i capelli scuri, lunghi e lisci e gli occhi neri. Lui porta gli occhiali. Il suo compleanno è il tredici novembre. È molto muscoloso.

Mi chiamo Federico. Ho otto anni e vivo a Perugia, il capoluogo dell'Umbria. Ho i capelli castani, corti e ricci e gli occhi verdi. Porto gli occhiali. Il mio compleanno è il nove maggio. A casa ho tre animali: un cavallo, un cane e un gatto. Mio fratello si chiama Sergio. Ha quattordici anni. Ha i capelli biondi, lunghi e lisci e gli occhi verdi come me. Porta anche gli occhiali come mio padre. Il suo compleanno è il due giugno. È molto intelligente e parla cinese.

Mi chiamo Giuseppe. Ho dieci anni e vivo a Bari, il capoluogo della Puglia. Ho i capelli biondi, lisci e corti e gli occhi verdi. Porto gli occhiali. Il mio compleanno è l'otto aprile. Parlo molto bene spagnolo ma non parlo inglese.

1. Find the Italian for the following items in Marta's text

a. I am called: Mi chiamo

b. in Naples: a Napoli

c. I wear glasses: Porto gli occhiali

d. My birthday is: il mio compleanno è

e. the tenth of: il dieci

f. I have: Ho

g. straight: lisci

h. speaks German: parla tedesco

i. the eyes: gli occhi

2. Answer the following questions about Alice's text

a. How old is she?
15

b. Where is Bellinzona?
_____

c. What colour is her hair?
Red

d. What is her hair like?
Curly + long

e. What languages does she speak?
Italian + french

f. What colour are her eyes?
Blue

g. When is her birthday?
16th December

3. Complete with the missing words

Mi chiamo Roxana. Ho dieci anni e sono rumena. Vivo a Palermo, il capoluogo di Sicilia. Ho i capelli biondi, lisci e scalati e gli occhi verdi. Porto gli occhiali. Il mio compleanno è il ventisette di maggio.

4. Find someone who: answer the questions below about all 5 texts

a. Who has a brother called Sergio?
Federico

b. Who is eight years old?
Federico

c. Who celebrates their birthday on 9 May?
Federico

d. How many people wear glasses?
4

e. Who has dark brown hair and black-coloured eyes?
_____

f. Who can speak a bit of Chinese?
Sergio

g. Whose birthday is in April?
Giuseppe

h. Who has brown, wavy hair and brown eyes?
_____

Unit 3. Describing hair and eyes: TRANSLATION

1. Faulty translation: spot and correct (in the English) any translation mistakes you find below

a. Ho i capelli biondi: *I have black eyes*
blonde hair

b. Ho gli occhi azzurri: *He has brown eyes*
I have blue eyes

c. Ho la barba: *He has a beard*
I have a beard

d. Si chiama Pedro: *I am called Pedro*
He is called Pedro

e. Ha i capelli a spazzola: *I have long hair*
He/She has spiky hair

f. Ho i capelli rasati: *I have coloured hair*
I have crew-cut hair

g. Vivo a Roma: *He is from Rome*
I live in Rome

3. Phrase-level translation

a. 'The' blonde hair _i capelli biondi_

b. I am called _Mi chiamo_

c. I have _Ho_

d. 'The' blue eyes _gli occhi azzurri_

e. 'The' straight hair _i capelli lisci_

f. He has _Ha_

g. Ten years _dieci anni_

h. I have black eyes _Ho gli occhi neri_

i. I have nine years _Ho nove anni_

j. 'The' brown eyes _i capelli marroni castani_

k. 'The' black hair _i capelli neri_

2. From Italian to English

a. Ho i capelli biondi.
I have blonde hair

b. Ho gli occhi azzurri.
I have blue eyes

c. Ho i capelli lisci.
I have straight hair

d. Porta gli occhiali.
He wears glasses

e. Ho i baffi e la barba.
I have a moustache + a beard.

f. Porto gli occhiali da sole.

g. Non ho la barba.
I don't have a beard

h. Ho i capelli a spazzola.
I have spikey hair

i. Ho i capelli ondulati.
I have curly hair

4. Sentence-level translation

a. My name is Mark. I am ten years old. I have black and curly hair and blue eyes. *Mi chiamo Mark, ho dieci anni. Ho i capelli neri e ricci e gli occhi azzurri*

b. I am twelve years old. I have green eyes and blonde, straight hair.

c. I am called Jessica. I live in Milan. I have long blonde hair and brown eyes.

d. My name is Pietro. I live in Rome. I have black hair, short and spiky.

e. I am fifteen-years-old. I have black, curly long hair and green eyes.

f. I am thirteen years old. I have red, straight long hair and brown eyes.

in book ✓

 **THE LANGUAGE GYM**

Unit 3. Describing hair and eyes: WRITING

1. Split sentences

Ho i capelli	occhi verdi
Ho la	barba
Ho gli	biondi
Ho i	e ricci
Ho i capelli biondi	capelli neri
Mi chiamo	anni
Ho dieci	Marta

2. Rewrite the sentences in the correct order

a. capelli i ho ricci

b. ho la non barba

c. chiamo mi Riccardo

d. capelli ho rossi i

e. si fratello chiama Paolo mio

f. verdi occhi ho gli

3. Spot and correct the grammar and spelling errors

a. Ho i capelli nero

b. Mio fratello mi chiamo Antonio

c. Ho capeli ricci

d. Si chiamo Nadia

e. o cuatordici anni

f. Ho il capello lisci

g. Ho l'occhi verde

h. o la barba

i. Porto li ochiali

j. Ho no baffi

4. Anagrams

a. pellica = capelli

b. rbaba=

c. ohicc=

d. nina=

e. zuzarri=

f. dinbio=

g. rine=

h. cicri=

i. siros=

5. Guided writing – write 3 short paragraphs in the first person singular ['I'] describing the people below

Name	Age	Hair	Eyes	Glasses	Beard	Moustache
Peter	12	brown curly long	green	wears	does not have	has
Carla	11	blond straight short	blue	does not wear	does not have	does not have
Igor	10	red wavy medium length	black	wears	has	does not have

6. Describe this person in the third person:

Name: Cristian

Age: 15

Hair: black, curly, very short

Eyes: brown

Glasses: no

Beard: yes

UNIT 4
Saying where I live and am from

In this unit you will learn to talk about:

- Where you live and are from
- If you live in an apartment or a house
- What your accommodation looks like
- Where it is located
- The names of cities and countries where Italian is spoken
- Describe the weather
- The verb 'I am'

You will also revisit:

- Introducing yourself
- Telling age and birthday

UNIT 4
Saying where I live and I am from
'Dove vivi?'

[Where do you live?]

Mi chiamo Paolo e... [My name is Paolo and...]	vivo in [I live in]	un appartamento [a flat] un palazzo/ un edificio [a building]	antico [old] bello [pretty] brutto [ugly] confortevole [comfortable] grande [big] piccolo [small] moderno [modern]	in centro [in the centre] in campagna [in the countryside] in montagna [in the mountains]
		una casa [a house] una villa [a villa]	antica [old] bella [pretty] brutta [ugly] confortevole [comfortable] grande [big] piccola [small] moderna [modern]	in periferia [on the outskirts] sulla costa [on the coast]
	sono di [I am from]	Bari Bologna Cagliari Cosenza Firenze Genova Lugano Milano Palermo Torino Venezia	una città [a city]	in Calabria in Liguria in Lombardia in Piemonte in Puglia in Toscana in Sardegna in Sicilia in Sardegna in Svizzera in Veneto	nel nord dell'Italia [in the north of Italy] nel centro dell'Italia [in the centre of Italy] nel sud dell'Italia [in the south of Italy]

Author's note: *Italy surrounds two independent states: the Republic of San Marino and the Vatican City. In both states the official language is Italian. The language is also spoken in Croatia, Slovenia and Malta.* ☺

Unit 4. Saying where I live and am from: VOCABULARY BUILDING

1. Complete with the missing word

a. Vivo in _____ casa bella [I live in a pretty house]

b. Mi piace il mio _____ [I like my flat]

c. Sono ___ Firenze [I am from Florence]

d. _____ in una villa [I live in a villa]

e. Un appartamento in un _____ moderno

[a flat in a modern building]

f. Sono di Roma, la_____ dell'Italia

[I'm from Rome, the capital of Italy]

g. Vivo in una casa molto _____ in campagna

[I live in a very old house in the countryside]

h. Vivo in _____ [I live on the outskirts]

2. Match up

1. il centro	a. big
2. bello	b. small
3. grande	c. old
4. palazzo	d. pretty
5. antico	e. the centre
6. la periferia	f. the coast
7. la costa	g. I am from
8. Italia	h. the outskirts
9. sono di	i. ugly
10. brutto	j. I live in
11. piccolo	k. comfortable
12. vivo in	l. building
13. confortevole	m. Italy

3. Translate into English

a. Sono di Venezia =

b. Vivo in una casa =

c. Il mio appartamento è piccolo =

d. Sono di Siena, in Toscana =

e. in un palazzo moderno =

f. Sono di Cosenza, nel sud dell'Italia =

g. Vivo in una villa a Positano sulla costa =

h. Sono di Torino, nel nord dell'Italia =

4. Add the missing letter

a. Rom_   c. Mil_no   e. Ital_a   g. Ven_zia   i. F_renze

b. Bar_   d. Sviz_era   f. Cos_nza   h. To_ino   j. Tosc_na

5. Broken words

a. S____ d__ L_____, i__ S _____
= [I am from Lugano, in Switzerland]

b. V___ i___ u____ c_____ v_____
= [I live in an old house]

c. S___ d___ R_____, l__ c_____ d____ I_____
= [I am from Rome, the capital of Italy]

d. V_____ i__ u___ c_____ s____ c_____ d__ Calabria
= [I live in a house on the coast of Calabria]

e. V____ i__ u___ v____ p_____ i__
c_____ = [I live in a small villa in the countryside]

6. Complete with a suitable word

a. Sono _____ Bologna.

b. Vivo _____ centro.

c. In un _____ antico.

d. Vivo in una casa in _____.

e. Roma è la capitale dell' _____.

f. Vivo in un appartamento _____.

g. Sono di _____.

h. Una _____sulla costa.

i. Città di San _____, in San Marino.

j. Vivo a Positano sulla _____.

Unit 4. "Geography test": Using your own knowledge (and a bit of help from Google/your teacher) match the numbers to the city or region

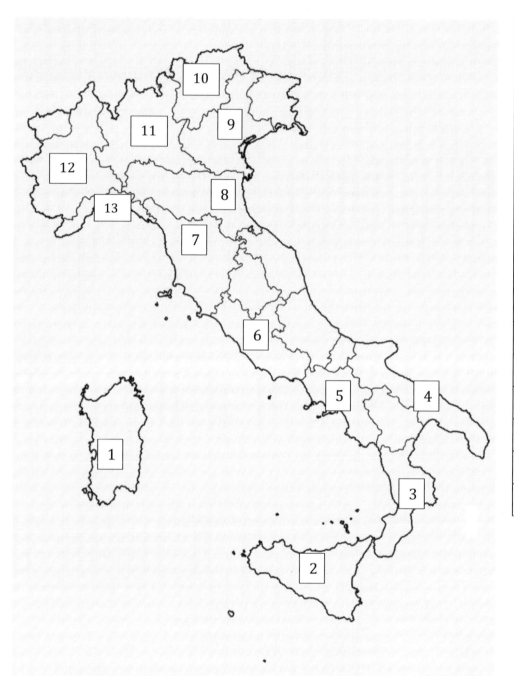

Italy	
Num	**City or Region**
	Bologna
	Bolzano
	Calabria
	Firenze
	Genova
	Milano
	Napoli
	Puglia
	Roma
	Sardegna
	Sicilia
	Torino
	Venezia

Unit 4. Saying where I live and am from: READING

Mi chiamo Gianluigi. Ho ventidue anni e il mio compleanno è il nove agosto. Vivo a Borgo Maggiore, <u>in</u> San Marino. Vivo in una casa piccola in centro città.

Ho due fratelli, Edoardo e Dario. Mi piace molto Edoardo ma Dario non mi piace perché è molto stupido.

Il mio amico Francesco vive a Siena, in Toscana. Lui vive in un appartamento in un palazzo abbastanza antico, in centro.

Mi chiamo Matilda. Ho quindici anni e vivo a Cagliari, in Sardegna. Nella mia famiglia siamo quattro persone: i miei genitori, mio fratello Giorgio ed io. Il mio compleanno è l'undici settembre, anche quello di Giorgio. Siamo gemelli! Mio zio vive a Malta.

Mi chiamo Stefania. Ho nove anni e vivo a Rimini, sulla costa adriatica in Italia. Vivo con la mia famiglia: i miei genitori, mia sorella maggiore Sara ed io. Il mio compleanno è il nove maggio e il compleanno di Sara è il trenta marzo. Lei ha undici anni. La mia casa è piuttosto grande e confortevole e si trova sulla costa. Mi piace troppo!

Mi chiamo Bella. Ho ventuno anni e vivo a Monte Carlo con la mia amica Marina. Abitiamo in un appartamento piccolo e moderno in periferia. Il mio compleanno è il due giugno e il mio compleanno di Marina è il dodici giugno.

Ho un cane che si chiama Buck. È molto grande e buono. Il suo compleanno è il primo aprile. Buck ha tre anni. Ho **anche** *[also]* un ragno, buono **ma** *[but]* brutto, che si chiama Aracno. Anche il compleanno del mio ragno è il primo di aprile. **Quindi** *[therefore]* faccio una festa per i due animali lo stesso giorno. È **più** *[more]* pratico.

---

1. Find the Italian for the following in Bella's text

a. my name is

b. I am 21 years old

c. I live in...

d. a small flat

e. on the outskirts

f. the 2nd of June

g. I have a dog

h. he is very big

i. his birthday is on the 1st April

j. he is 3 years old

k. I also have a spider

2. Complete the statements below based on Gianluigi's text

a. I am _____ years old

b. My birthday is on the _____ of _____

c. I live in a _____ house in the _____ of the city

d. I have two _____

e. I like Edoardo but Dario is _____

f. My friend Francesco _____ in Siena

g. He lives in a _____ in a quite old _____

3. Answer the questions on the four texts above

a. How old is Matilda?

b. Why do Matilda and Giorgio have the same birthday? What do you think a '**gemelli**' means?

c. Who only likes one of his siblings?

d. Who has two pets that share a birthday?

e. Why is it convenient that they share a birthday?

f. Who has a friend that lives in a different city?

g. Who lives with their really good friend?

h. Who lives in Monte Carlo?

i. Whose birthday is on the 12th of July?

4. Correct any of the statements below [about Stefania's text] which are incorrect

a. Stefania vive a Napoli, nel sud Italia.

b. Nella famiglia di Stefania ci sono *[there are]* quattro persone.

c. Il suo compleanno è a marzo.

d. Il compleanno di Sara è il tre marzo.

e. Stefania vive in una casa piuttosto grande ma brutta sulla costa.

f. Le piace molto la sua casa.

Unit 4. Saying where I live and am from: TRANSLATION/WRITING

1. Translate into English

a. vivo in

b. una casa

c. un appartamento

d. confortevole

e. molto grande

f. in un palazzo

g. antico

h. moderno

i. in centro

j. in periferia

k. sulla costa

l. sono di

m. in Italia

n. in Svizzera

o. vivo a Glasgow

2. Gapped sentences

a. Vivo a Bari in una _____antica *[I live in Bari in an old villa]*

b. Una casa in _____ *[A house in the countryside]*

c. Vivo in un _____ piccolo *[I live in a small flat]*

d. Una _____ in _____ *[A house on the outskirts]*

e. _____ ___ Roma, la capitale dell' _____, ma vivo a Malta.
[I am from Rome, the capital of Italy, but I live in Malta]

3. Complete the sentences with a suitable word

a. Sono _____ Borgo Maggiore, nella Repubblica di San Marino.

b. _____ di Firenze,il capoluogo della Toscana.

c. Sono argentino, vivo nella _____ del Vaticano.

d. Vivo in un _____ grande in _____ .

e. Vivo a Bologna, in una casa nuova e _____ .

f. Vivo in un appartamento_____ in centro.

g. Vivo a Grisignana, in Croazia, in _____ casa moderna.

4. Phrase-level translation [En to It]

a. I live in _____

b. I am from _____

c. a house _____

d. a flat _____

e. ugly (m) _____

f. small (m) _____

g. in an old building

_____

h. in the centre _____

i. on the outskirts _____

j. on the coast _____

k. in Tuscany _____

5. Sentence-level translation [En to It]

a. I am from Pisa, in Tuscany in Italy. I live in a big and pretty house on the outskirts.

_____

_____

b. I am from Amalfi, in the south of Italy. I live in a small and comfortable apartment near the coast.

_____

_____

c. I am from Bellinzona, in Switzerland. I live in a big flat in a new building in the centre.

_____

_____

d. I am from Venice, in the north of Italy. I live in a flat in a building on the outskirts. I like my flat.

_____

_____

Unit 4. Saying where I live and am from: WRITING

1. Complete with the missing letters

a. Mi chia_ _ Angela

b. Vi_ _ in una ca_ _ m_d _ rn_

c. V_v_ in un ap_artam_nto grand_

d. _ _vo a Pisa, in una _ _sa i_ cent_ _

e. So_ _ di Mil_ no in Lom_ ard_a

f. Io _ono d_ Rom_, la cap_tale del_'Ital_a

g. V_ _ o in una v_l_a grand_ in per_ feri_

h. _ono di Firen_ e in T_ scan_

2. Spot and correct the mistakes

a. Sono de Cosenza en Calabria.

b. Sono en Bari a Puglia.

c. Vivo in una casa piccolo a Malta.

d. Vivo in una appartamento grando.

e. Vivo a un palazzo nuovo.

f. Vivo en Rome con la mia familia.

g. Sono de Siena en Tuscana.

h. Vivo in una vila in campana.

3. Answer the questions in Italian

a. Come ti chiami? M_____

b. Quanti anni hai? H_____

c. *Di dove sei? Sono di _____

d. *Dove vivi? Vivo a _____

d. Vivi in una casa o in un appartamento? Vivo in_____

*Author's note: * Di dove sei?= 'Where are you from?'*
Dove vivi?= 'Where do you live?'
Vivo a Edimburgo/Roma = *I live in Edinburgh/Rome*

4. Anagrams (regions of Italy and countries)

a. neVeto = *Veneto*

b. scanaTo =

c. gliaPu =

d. laCabria =

e. monPiete =

f. diaLombar =

g. noVacati =

h. razzeSvi =

i. noMariSan =

j. gnadeSar =

5. Guided writing – write 4 short paragraphs in the 1st person singular ['I'] describing the people below

Name	Age	Birthday	City	Country or region
Samuel	12	20/06	Roma	Lazio (Italia)
Alex	14	14/10	Lugano	Svizzera
Andrea	11	14/01	Monte Carlo	Monaco
Charles	13	17/01	Taormina	Sicilia (Italia)
Nina	15	19/10	Amalfi	Campania (Italia)

6. Describe this person in the third person:

Name: Alessio

Age: 16

Birthday: 15th May

Country of origin: Glasgow, Scotland *[Scozia]*

Country of residence: Lucca, Italy *[Italia]*

UNIT 4b
Describing the weather
'Che tempo fa in Italia?'
[What is the weather like in Italy?]

A volte *[Sometimes]* **Di solito** *[Usually]* **Mai** *[Never]* **Normalmente** *[Normally]* **Ogni tanto** *[Every now and then]* **Raramente** *[Rarely]* **Sempre** *[Always]* **Spesso** *[Often]* **Tutti i giorni** *[Every day]*	**in estate** *[in the summer]* **in autunno** *[in autumn]* **in inverno** *[in winter]* **in primavera** *[in spring]*	**in Italia** **in Puglia** **in Trentino** **in Veneto** **in Sardegna** **in Calabria** **in Toscana** **in Liguria** **in Lombardia** **in Sicilia** **in Piemonte** **in Veneto** **in montagna** *[in the mountains]* **al mare** *[at the seaside]*	**fa** *[it's]* ***c'è** *[it's]* **nevica** *[it snows]* **piove** *[it rains]* **pioviggina** *[it drizzles]*	**caldo***[warm]* **freddo***[cold]* **bel tempo** *[good weather]* **mal tempo** *[bad weather]* **fresco***[cool]* **sole***[sunny]* **nebbia***[foggy]* **vento** *[windy]* **tempesta***[stormy]*

Author's note: *** c'è** literally means "there is". *C'è sole- there is sun/c'è nebbia- there is fog*

Unit 4b. Saying where I live and the weather: *READING*

Mi chiamo Massimo. Vivo a Roma in una casa piccola in centro città.
In inverno spesso piove. Però in estate vado a Cecina, in Toscana con la mia famiglia. Ho una casa piuttosto grande e tutti i giorni fa bel tempo. Vado sempre al mare perché fa troppo caldo e mi piace.

Mi chiamo Mario. Ho diciotto anni e vivo a Milano con la mia amica Roberta. Abitiamo in un appartamento un po' moderno in periferia. Il mio compleanno è il tre aprile. In Lombardia, in inverno c'è nebbia. In primavera pioviggina tutti i giorni e non mi piace. In estate o vado in montagna con la mia famiglia o vado al mare con i miei amici. Preferisco la montagna perché fa fresco e in estate fa sempre bel tempo.

Mi chiamo Daniela. Ho tredici anni e vivo a Trento, in Trentino, con mia sorella, in una casa molto grande in montagna. L'inverno fa freddo e nevica sempre. Mi piace la primavera perché fa fresco e piove raramente.

1. Find the Italian for the following in Massimo's text

a. a small house

b. I live in

c. I go to

d. with my family

e. in city centre

f. it's good weather

g. every day

h. Always

i. it's too warm

j. at the seaside

2. Complete the statements below based on Daniela's text

a. I am _____ years old

b. I live in _____, in _____ with my _____

c. My house is _____

d. In winter it's _____

e. I like _____ because it's _____

f. It rarely _____

h. My _____ __ Daniela

Mi chiamo Alessandro. Ho dieci anni e vivo a Catania in Sicilia. La mia casa è piccola ma confortevole e si trova sulla costa. Mi piace molto!

Tutti i giorni vado al mare perché fa sempre bel tempo e piove raramente. Non mi piace in estate perché fa troppo caldo.

3. Answer the questions about Mario

a. How old is Mario?

b. Who does he lives with?

c. Where does he live?

d. When is his birthday?

e. What's the weather like in Lombardia in spring?

f. Does he like the weather in Lombardia?

g. Where does he go with his family during the summer?

h. Where does he go with his friends during the summer?

i. Which one does he prefer and why?

4. Correct any of the statements below [about Alessandro's text] which are incorrect

a. Alessandro vive a Catania in una casa grande.

b. In Sicilia nevica sempre.

c. In estate ogni tanto va al mare.

d. A Catania in estate fa troppo caldo.

e. Ogni tanto va al mare.

f. Gli piace l'estate perché fa caldo.

g. In Sicilia fa sempre bel tempo.

h. In Sicilia fa mal tempo.

i. La sua casa si trova in centro.

THE LANGUAGE GYM

33

UNIT 5
Talking about my family and relationships.
Counting to 100

Revision quickie – Numbers 1-100 / Dates / Birthdays

**In this unit you will learn
to talk about:**
- How many people there are in your family and who they are
- If you get along with them
- Words for family members
- What their age is
- Numbers from 31 to 100

You will also revisit
- Numbers from 1 to 31
- Hair and eyes description

Talking about my family
Quante persone ci sono nella tua famiglia? - Vai d'accordo con...?
[How many people are there in your family? - Do you get on well with...?]

Ci sono quattro persone nella mia famiglia *[There are four people in my family...]*	**mio nonno Alfonso** *[my grandfather Alfonso]*		**un** *[1]*	**anno**
	mio padre Giuseppe *[my father Giuseppe]*		**due** *[2]*	**anni**
			tre *[3]*	
			quattro *[4]*	
	mio zio Luciano *[my uncle Luciano]*		**cinque** *[5]*	
			sei *[6]*	
Nella mia famiglia siamo in quattro *[We are a family of four...]*		**Lui ha**	**sette** *[7]*	
	mio fratello maggiore /minore *[my big/little brother]*		**otto** *[8]*	
			nove *[9]*	
			dieci *[10]*	
	mio cugino Marco *[my cousin, Marco]*		**venti** *[20]*	
			ventuno *[21]*	
			ventidue *[22]*	
Vado d'accordo con... *[I get on well with...]*			**ventitré** *[23]*	
	mia nonna *[my grandmother]*		**trenta** *[30]*	
			trentuno *[31]*	
			trentadue *[32]*	
	mia madre Lina *[my mother Lina]*		**trentatré** *[33]*	
			trentaquattro *[34]*	
Non vado d'accordo... *[I do not get on well with...]*			**trentacinque** *[35]*	
	mia zia Anna *[my aunt Anna]*		**trentasei** *[36]*	
		Lei ha	**trentasette** *[37]*	
			trentotto *[38]*	
	mia sorella maggiore /minore *[my big/little sister]*		**trentanove** *[39]*	
			quaranta *[40]*	
			cinquanta *[50]*	
	mia cugina Lara *[my girl cousin Lara]*		**sessanta** *[60]*	
			settanta *[70]*	
			ottanta *[80]*	
			novanta *[90]*	
			cento *[100]*	

Author's note: the number 1, **uno**, becomes shortened to 'un' before a noun. After 20 in Italian simply put numbers together, no space, no hyphen. i.e. 25 **venticinque**. The final vowel of the tens number disappears when you add **uno**(1) or **otto**(8); i.e. 41 **quarantuno**, 48 **quarantotto**. When you add the number **tre** (3) the final vowel becomes é: 53 **cinquantatré**

Unit 5. Talking about my family + Counting to 100: VOCAB BUILDING

1. Complete with the missing word

a. Nella mia f_____ c'è *[In my family there is]*

b. Ci sono _____ persone *[There are five people]*

c. Mio _____ Alfonso *[My grandfather Alfonso]*

d. Mio nonno _____ ottanta anni
[My grandfather is 80 years old]

e. Mia _____ Lina *[My mother Lina]*

f. Lei _____ cinquanta anni *[She is 50 years old]*

g. Vado d' _____ con mio fratello
[I get on well with my brother]

2. Match up

1. Sedici	*a. 66*
2. Sessantasei	*b. 48*
3. Ventuno	*c. 13*
4. Dieci	*d. 16*
5. Trentatré	*e. 10*
6. Tredici	*f. 21*
7. Quarantotto	*g. 15*
8. Cinquantadue	*h. 5*
9. Cinque	*i. 33*
10. Quindici	*l. 52*

3. Translate into English

a. Non vado d'accordo con =

b. Mia nonna Luigina =

c. Mio zio =

d. Ci sono quattro persone =

e. Nella mia famiglia=

f. Vado d'accordo con =

g. Mio padre =

h. Ha venti anni =

4. Add the missing letter

a. fami _lia   c. p _rsone   e.frat _llo   g. ma_re   i. vado _'accordo   k. tren_adue

b. z_o   d. n_nno   f. ma_giore   h. cugi _o   j. n_lla   l. nov_nta

5. Broken words

a. C__ s_____ s___ p_____ n____ m__ f_____
= *[there are 6 people in my family]*

b. M___ s_____ h__ d_____ a_____
= *[My sister is 12 years old]*

c. N____ m___ f_____ c'__ = *[In my family there is]*

d. M__ c_____ s__ c_____ = *[my male cousin is called]*

e. M__ p_____ h___ q_____ a_____
= *[My father is 46 years old]*

f. N___ v____ d' a_____ c___ m__ f_____
m_____ = *[I do not get on well with my older brother]*

g. V___ d'a_____ c___ = *[I get on well with]*

6. Complete with a suitable word

a. Nella mia _____

b. Ci_____ tre persone

c. Mia sorella _____

d. Ha quattordici _____

e. Mia _____ Gina ha
trentacinque anni

f. _____ d'accordo con mio padre

g. _____ mia famiglia ci sono ...

h. Non vado _____con mia zia

i. Mio zio _____ quarantasei anni

j. Mio _____ ha trentanove anni

k. Vado d'accordo _____ mio nonno

Unit 5. Talking about my family + Counting to 100: VOCABULARY DRILLS

1. Match up

Nella mia	there are
famiglia	in my
ci sono	with
sette	I get on well
persone	seven
vado d'accordo	family
con	people

2. Complete with the missing word

a. Ci_____ cinque persone [There are five people]

b. Mio _____ John ha sessanta anni [my uncle John is 60]

c. Vado _____con mia cugina [I get on well with my cousin]

d. ____ vado d'accordo ____ mia zia [I don't get on well with my aunt]

e. Mia zia Anna _____ quarantasette anni [My aunt Anna is 47]

f. Lui ha _____ anni [He is 18]

g. Lei _____ ventinove anni [She is 29]

h. Mia _____ Luigina ha ottanta anni [my granmother Luigina is 80]

3. Translate into English

a. Lui ha settantacinque anni.

b. Lei ha quaranta anni.

c. Mio padre ha cinquantatré anni.

d. Non vado d'accordo con mio nonno.

e. Vado d'accordo con mia sorella.

f. Mia sorella minore ha cinque anni.

g. Ci sono sei persone nella mia famiglia

h. Vai d'accordo con tua sorella?

4. Complete with the missing letters

a. Mio fratello m___giore [My older brother]

b. Nella mia fa_ _ _lia ci s_ _ _ tre persone
[In my family there are 3 people]

c. Mio cugino h_ dici_ _ nove anni [My cousin is 19]

d. Vado molto d' acc_ __do con mio fratello
[I get on very well with my brother]

e. Mio z_ _ ha quaranta_ _ _ anni
[My uncle is 46 years old]

f. _ _ _ _ molto d'accordo con mi _ cugin_
[I get on very well with my female cousin]

g. Mio cug_ _ _ ha q_ _ndici anni
[My male cousin is 15 years old]

h. Vado abbastanza d'accordo con _ _ _ sorella
[I get on ok with my sister]

5. Translate into Italian:

a. In my family:_____

b. There are: _____

c. My father: _____

d. is 40 years old:_____

e. I get on well with my brother:

_____

6. Spot and correct the errors.

a. Nella mi familia ci sono tre persona

b. Mia nona Carla

c. Mio fratello a nove ani

d. Vado dacordo con mio cugino

e. Mia cugino ha otto anni

f. Mia sorrela maggior Benedetta

Unit 5. Talking about my family + Counting to 100: TRANSLATION

1. Match up

1. Venti	a. 30
2. Cinquanta	b. 70
3. Settanta	c. 100
4. Trenta	d. 50
5. Sessanta	e. 20
6. Novanta	f. 80
7. Ottanta	g. 40
8. Quaranta	h. 60
9. Cento	i. 90

2. Write out in Italian

a. 35 = trentacinque

b. 63 = s_____

c. 89 = o_____

d. 74 = s_____

e. 98 = n_____

f. 100 = c_____

g. 82 = o_____

h. 24 = v_____

i. 17 = d_____

3. Write out with the missing number

a. Io ho t_____ anni *[I am 32]*

b. Mio padre ha c_____ anni
[My father is fifty-seven]

c. Mia madre ha q_____ anni
[My mother is forty-eight]

d. Mio nonno ha c_____ anni
[My grandfather is one-hundred years old]

e. Noi abbiamo t_____ anni *[We are thirteen]*

f. Loro hanno n_____ anni *[They are ninety]*

g. I miei cugini hanno q_____ anni
[My cousins are forty-four]

h. Lei ha s_____ anni? *[Is she seventy?]*

4. Correct the translation errors

a. My father is forty = mio padre ha quattordici anni

b. My mother is fifty = mia madre ha cinquantadue anni

c. We are forty-eight = noi abbiamo quarantadue anni

d. I am forty-two = ho quarantuno anni

e. They are thirty-four = loro hanno trentadue anni

5. Translate into Italian (please write out the numbers in letters)

a. In my family there are six people:_____

b. My mother is called Sara and she is 43:_____

c. My father is called Mohamed and he is 48:_____

d. My older sister is called Fatima and she is 31:_____

e. My younger sister is called Carmen and she is 18:_____

f. I am called Ariana and I am 27: _____

g. My grandfather is called Antonio and he is 87:_____

Unit 5. Talking about my family + Counting to 100: Writing

1. Spot and correct the spelling mistakes

a. querenta = *quaranta*

b. trentoono = _____

c. otantadue = _____

d. veintuno = _____

e. novente = _____

f. ciento = _____

g. septenta = _____

h. sedicci = _____

3. Rearrange the sentence below in the correct word order

a. mia Nella quattro famiglia persone sono ci
[In my family there are four people]

b. vado con mio d'accordo Non fratello
[I don't get on well with my brother]

c. padre, Mio si chiama che Piero anni cinquantadue ha
[My father, who is called Piero, is fifty-two]

d. padre mio ed io Nella famiglia mia madre, ci persone: sono tre mia
[In my family there are three people: my mother, my father and I]

e. si Mio che cugino, anni Ivan chiama ha trentasette
[My cousin, who is called Ivan, is thirty-seven]

f. nonno, anni Fernando che Mio si chiama ottantasette ha,
[My grandfather, who is called Fernando, is eighty-seven]

g. Vado con madre d'accordo mia. Lei anni cinquanta ha
[I get on well with my mother. She is 50]

2. Complete with the missing letters

a. Mia m__dre h__ quar__nta ann_

b. Mio pad__e h__ cin__uantuno a__ni

c. I miei nonni h__nno ott__nta an_i

d. M__a sore__la mino__e ha vent_ __nni

e. __ia no__na __a sett__ntasei a _ _ _ _

f. Mio fr__tel__o ma__g__ore ha ven__i an_i

4. Complete

a. in my family: n_____ m___ f_____

b. there are: c___ s_____

c. who is called: c_____ s___ c_____

d. my mother: m___ m_____

e. my father: m_____ p_____

f. he is fifty: l____ h____ c_____ a_____

g. I am sixty: i__ h___ s_____ a_____

h. she is forty: l____ h__ q_____ a_____

5. Write a relationship sentence for each person as shown in the example

e.g. Il mio migliore amico si chiama Paolo e ha quindici anni.

Name	Relationship to me	Age	How I get along with them
e.g. Paolo	*best friend*	*15*	*very well*
Giuseppe	father	57	well
Lina	mother	45	not well
Rosa	aunt	60	*quite* well
Andrew	uncle	67	not well
Alfonso	grandfather	75	*very* well

Author's note: *quite*=**abbastanza**/ *very*=**molto** ☺
*Vado abbastanza d'accordo con mio zio

Revision Quickie 1:
Numbers 1-100, dates and birthdays, hair and eyes, family

1. Match up

a. 11	1. quindici
b. 12	2. dodici
c. 18	3. sedici
d. 14	4. diciotto
e. 17	5. undici
f. 16	6. diciannove
g. 15	7. quattordici
h. 13	8. venti
i. 19	9. diciassette
j. 20	10. tredici

2. Translate the dates into English

a. il trenta giugno

b. il primo luglio

c. il quindici settembre

d. il ventidue marzo

e. il trentuno dicembre

f. il cinque gennaio

g. il sedici aprile

h. il ventinove febbraio

i. il diciotto maggio

3. Complete with the missing words

a. Il mio compleanno _____ il quindici aprile.

b. Ho quattordici _____.

c. Mio fratello _____ i capelli _____.

d. Di _____ sei?

e. Sono_____ Pisa.

e. Nella mia famiglia __ _____ quattro persone.

f. _____ madre ha gli _____ marroni.

h. Vivo ____Glasgow, in Scozia.

dove	é	di	ha	a
biondi	occhi	anni	ci sono	mia

4. Write out the solution in words as shown in the example

a. quaranta - trenta = *dieci*

b. trenta - dieci = _____

c. quaranta + trenta =_____

d. venti x due = _____

e. ottanta - venti = _____

f. novanta - cinquanta =_____

g. trenta x tre =_____

h. venti + cinquanta =_____

i. venti + trenta =_____

5. Complete the words

a. Mio no_ _ _ _ [my grandfather]

b. Mia cug_ _ _ _ [my female cousin]

c. G_ _ _ oc_ _ [the eyes]

d. Ver_ _ [green]

e. La ba_ _ _ [beard]

f. Gli o_ _ _ hi_ _ _ _ [glasses]

g. Mia sor_ _ _ _ _ [sister]

h. i_ h_ [I have]

6. Translate into English

a. Mia madre ha i capelli castani, corti e ricci

b. Ho gli occhi azzurri.

c. Mia zia ha quarantatré anni.

d. Mio nonno ha novantadue anni.

e. Mio padre porta gli occhiali.

f. Mio fratello ha i baffi e la barba.

g. Mio fratello minore ha i capelli rossi.

h. Mia sorella ha gli occhi blu e i capelli neri.

UNIT 6: (Part 1/2)
Describing myself and another family member (physical and personality)

In this unit you will learn:

- What your immediate family members are like
- Useful adjectives to describe them
- The third person of the verb 'Essere'(to be): 'è' (he/she is)
- All the persons of the verb 'Avere' in the present indicative

You will also revisit
- Numbers from 1 to 31
- Hair and eyes description

UNIT 6 (Part 1/2)
Intro to describing myself and another family member:
'Come sei fisicamente? – Che tipo di persona sei?'
[What do you look like? - What kind of person are you?]

		MASCULINE	FEMININE
Io *[I]*	**sono** *[am]*	**alto** *[tall]*	**alta** *[tall]*
		basso *[short]*	**bassa** *[short]*
		bello *[handsome]*	**bella** *[pretty]*
		brutto *[ugly]*	**brutta** *[ugly]*
Lui / Lei *[He/She]*	**è** *[is]*	**buono** *[good]*	**buona** *[good]*
		forte *[strong]*	**forte** *[strong]*
		grosso *[fat]*	**grossa** *[fat]*
		magro *[slim]*	**magra** *[slim]*
Io *[I]*	**sono** *[am]*	**antipatico** *[unfriendly]*	**antipatica** *[unfriendly]*
		cattivo *[bad]*	**cattiva** *[bad]*
		divertente *[fun]*	**divertente** *[fun]*
Mia sorella minore *[My younger sister]*		**generoso** *[generous]*	**generosa** *[generous]*
		gentile *[kind]*	**gentile** *[kind]*
Mio fratello maggiore *[My older brother]*	**è** *[is]*	**noioso** *[boring]*	**noiosa** *[boring]*
		simpatico *[nice/friendly]*	**simpatica** *[nice/friendly]*
Mia madre *[My mother]*		**socievole** *[sociable]*	**socievole** *[sociable]*
		sportivo *[sporty]*	**sportiva** *[sporty]*
Mio padre *[My father]*		**testardo** *[stubborn]*	**testarda** *[stubborn]*
		timido *[shy]*	**timida** *[shy]*

Unit 6. Vocabulary building

1. Match up

1. Sono simpatico	a. I am friendly
2. Sono antipatico	b. I am generous
3. Sono testardo	c. I am mean
4. Sono timida	d. I am short
5. Sono generoso	e. I am strong
6. Sono forte	f. I am shy
7. Sono cattiva	g. I am bad
8. Sono basso	h. I am tall
9. Sono alto	i. I am kind
10. Sono gentile	j. I am stubborn

(handwritten answers in left margin: a, g, j, f, b, e, c, d, h, i)

2. Complete

a. Mio fratello minore è s portivo
[My younger brother is sporty]

b. Mio padre è s oci<del>ovole</del> socievole
[My father is sociable]

c. Mia sorella maggiore è testardo
[My older sister is stubborn]

d. Mio fratello maggiore è d ivertente
[My older brother is fun]

42

3. Categories – sort the adjectives below in the categories provided

a. forte; b. sportivo; c. simpatico; d. testardo; e. bello;
f. intelligente; g. paziente; h. cattivo; i. generoso;
j. alto; k. grasso; l. noioso; m. brutto; n. divertente

Il fisico	La personalità

4. Complete the words

a. Sono noi_ _ _ (m)

b. Sono bel _ _ (m)

c. Sono spor_ _ _ _ _ (f)

d. Sono test _ _ _ _ _ (m)

e. Sono gener_ _ _ (f)

f. Sono al_ _ (f)

g. Sono sim_ _ _ _ _ _ _ (f)

h. Sono gro_ _ _ (m)

5. Translate into English

a. Mia sorella maggiore è generosa

b. Mio fratello minore è grosso

c. Mio cugino è noioso

d. Mia cugina è divertente

e. Sono alto e magro

f. Sono molto intelligente

g. Sono abbastanza sportiva

h. La mia amica Valentina è forte

6. Spot and correct the translation mistakes

a. **Sono forte**: He is strong ~~for~~ è ✓

b. **Lei è grossa**: He is slim grosso

c. **Sono molto bella**: I am very ugly brutta

d. **Mi madre è alta**: My mother is short bassa

e. **Mio fratello è basso**: My brother is tall alto

f. **Mia sorella è gentile**: My sister is boring noiosa

g. **Mio padre è buono**: My father is mean cattivo

7. Complete

a. M_a m_ _ _ e è g_ _ _ ile

b. M_o f_ _ t_ _ _ _ o è te_ _ _ _ _ do

c. Mi_ p_ _ re è br_ _ to ma simp_ _ ico

d. S_ _ o f_ _ _ e e b_ _ _ _ a

e. Lu_ è t_ _ _ a_ _ _ _

f. Le_ è ca_ _ _ _ v_ _

8. English to Italian translation

a. I am strong and funny (f)

b. My mother is very stubborn

c. My sister is short and slim

d. My brother is intelligent and sporty

e. I am friendly and generous (f)

f. My father is tall and fat

g. My brother is ugly but funny

h. I am strong and tall (m)

i. I am slim and sporty (f)

j. My mother is intelligent and friendly

k. My sister is generous but stubborn

l. I am not shy, I am sociable (f)

 **THE LANGUAGE GYM**

Grammar Time 1: ESSERE - To be (Part 1)

		Masculine (singular)
io	**sono** [I am]	**alto** **antipatico**
tu	**sei** [you are]	**basso** **chiacchierone** [chatty]
lui mio fratello mio padre	**è** [he is]	**forte** **grosso** **magro** **paziente** **simpatico**

		Masculine (plural)
noi mio padre ed io	**siamo** [we are]	**alti** **antipatici** **bassi** **chiacchieroni**
voi	**siete** [you all are]	**forti** **grossi**
loro, essi i miei fratelli i miei genitori	**sono** [they are]	**magri** **pazienti** **simpatici**

		Feminine (singular)
io	**sono** [I am]	**alta** **antipatica**
tu	**sei** [you are]	**bassa** **magra**
lei mia sorella mia madre	**è** [she is]	**forte** **grossa** **chiacchierona** **paziente** **simpatica**

		Feminine (plural)
noi mia madre ed io	**siamo** [we are]	**alte** **antipatiche** **basse** **chiacchierone**
voi	**siete** [you all are]	**forti** **grosse**
loro, esse le mie sorelle le mie zie	**sono** [they are]	**magre** **pazienti** **simpatiche**

Present indicative of *"Essere"* (to be) – Drills 1

1. Match up

1. Siamo	a. I am
2. Sono	b. You are
3. Sei	c. He is
4. È	d. They are
5. Siete	e. We are
6. Sono	f. You all are

2. Complete with the missing forms of *'Essere'*

a. (io) _____ molto chiacchierone [I am very talkative]

b. Mia madre _____ divertente [My mother is funny]

c. Le mie sorelle _____ pazienti [My sisters are patient]

d. Noi _____ molto pigri [We are very lazy]

e. I miei genitori _____ severi [My parents are strict]

f. Come _____ tu? [What are you like?]

g. Tu_____ generoso e timido [You are generous and shy]

h. Voi_____ molto forti! [You all are very strong!]

3. Translate into English

a. Mio padre è simpatico.

b. Mia madre è chiacchierona.

c. I miei fratelli sono timidi.

d. Mia sorella mimore non è molto alta.

e. Il mio migliore [best] amico è bello.

f. Mio nonno è molto gentile.

g. Mia sorella maggiore è molto buona.

h. Voi siete abbastanza sportivi.

4. Complete with the missing letters.

a. Noi siam_ molto simp_tici [We are very friendly]

b. Mia madre _ molto severa [My mother is very strict]

c. I miei genitori s_ _ _ molto pazient_
[My parents are very patient]

d. I miei cugini s_ _o un po' antipatici
[My cousins are a bit unfriendly]

e. Mia sorella ___ un po' grossa [My sister is a bit fat]

f. Voi s _ _ _ _ molto chiacchieroni!
[You are very talkative]

g. S_ _ _ un po' timido [I am a bit shy]

h. I miei amici s_ _ _ molto gentili
[My friends are very kind]

i. Come s_ _ tu? [What are you like?]

5. Translate into Italian

a. You are: (tu) _ _ _

b. He is: (lui) _

c. You guys are: (voi) _ _ _ _ _

d. They are: (loro) _ _ _ _

e. We are: (noi) _ _ _ _ _

f. She is: (lei) _

6. Spot and correct the errors.

a. Mi madre e molto simpatica

b. I miei genitori siamo molto pazienti e gentile

c. Mia sorella sei antipatico

d. Mia sorella ed io sono alta

e. Come siamo tu?

Present indicative of "Essere" (to be) – Drills 2

7. Complete with the missing letters

a. Sia____o alti [We are tall]

b. Se__ basso [You are short]

c. Mia madre __ magra [My mother is slim]

d. I miei professori so____ molto buoni
[My teachers are very good]

e. S__i molto bella [You are very pretty]

f. Non s__no timido [I am not shy]

g. Mio fratello ed io s____mo molto lavoratori
[My brother and I are very hard-working]

h. Lui ____ molto simpatico [He is very nice]

8. Complete with the missing forms of the verb ESSERE

a. Mia madre _____

b. I miei genitori _____

c. (io) _____

d. (loro) _____

e. Mia madre ed io _____

f. Mio nonno _____

g. Tu e le tue sorelle _____

h. Tu _____

i. Voi _____

9. Complete with the missing forms of ESSERE

a. (io) _____ di Londra.

b. Mia madre _____ molto alta e bella.

c. I miei amici_____ molto simpatico.

d. Mio fratello _____ abbastanza sportivo.

e. (io) _____ un po' grosso.

f. (loro) _____ basse.

g. Mio fratello ed io _____ forti.

h. Mio cugino Andrea ____ italiano.

10. Translate into Italian. Make sure the underlined words have a feminine ending in Italian ('a')

a. My mother is tall

b. My father is short

c. My brother is bad

d. My sister is generous

e. My grandfather is strict

f. My grandmother is patient

g. My mother is intelligent

11. English to Italian translation. Make sure that the words underlined end in the plural forms, as shown in the example below:

Ex. My mother and my sister are very **tall:** Mia madre e mia sorella sono molto alt**e**

a. My sisters are **patient** and **nice**: _____

b. My parents are very **friendly**: _____

c. I (f) am talkative and lazy:_____

d. My brother and I are very **tall**: _____

e. My mother and my sister are **beautiful**: _____

f. My girlfriend and her (sua) sister are very **short**: _____

Grammar Time 2: AVERE – to have (Part 1)
(Present indicative)

io	**ho** [I have]	**i capelli** [the hair]	**biondi** [blonde]
			castani [brown]
tu	**hai** [you have]		**colorati** [coloured]
lui **lei** **mia sorella** **mio fratello** **mia madre** **mio padre**	**ha** [he has]		**neri** [black] **rossi** [red] **scuri** [dark brown] **corti** [short] **di media lunghezza** [mid length] **lunghi** [long]
noi **mio padre ed io** **mia madre ed io**	**abbiamo** [we have]		**a spazzola** [spiky] **lisci** [straight] **ondulati/mossi** [wavy] **rasati** [very short/crew-cut] **ricci** [curly] **scalati** [layered]
voi	**avete** [you all have]		
loro **i miei fratelli** **i miei genitori**	**hanno** [they have]	**gli occhi** [the eyes]	**azzurri/blu** [blue] **marroni** [brown] **neri** [black] **verdi** [green] **grandi** [big] **piccoli** [small]

Verb drills

1. Translate into English	**2. Spot and correct the mistakes**
a. Abbiamo i capelli neri.	a. Mia madre ha il capello biondo.
b. Lui ha i capelli biondi e ondulati.	b. I miei fratelli hanno i cappeli neri.
c. Tu hai i capelli a spazzola.	c. (Io) ha i capelli castani e lunghi.
d. Voi avete i capelli rossi e di media lunghezza.	d. Lui hanno i capelli cortis è lisci.
e. Loro hanno gli occhi verdi e grandi.	e. (Noi) abbiamo capelli rossi e rici.
f. Lei ha gli occhi azzurri e piccoli.	f. Tu avete i capelli biondi è scalati.
g. Noi abbiamo i capelli castani e gli occhi neri.	

3. Complete with the missing verb ending

a. (io) h____ i capelli biondi.

b. Mia madre h__ gli occhi azzurri

c. Le mie sorelle han___ i capelli rossi

d. Mio padre h___ i capelli grigi

e. (Noi) abbi_____ i capelli neri

f. Mio nonno h___ i capelli bianchi

g. Tu h_____ gli occhi marroni

h. Mio cugino ed io abbia___ i capelli rossi

i. (Voi) Av_____ i capelli lunghi?

j. Mio fratello ed io abb_____ i capelli corti.

k. La mia amica Alberta h__ gli occhi scuri.

l. Voi av_____ i capelli mossi e corti.

m. Io h___ i capelli castani e mossi

n. (tu) H___ i capelli neri come tua madre?

4. Complete with: *ha, abbiamo* or *hanno*

a. Mia madre _____ i capelli biondi e mossi

b. I miei genitori _____ gli occhi marroni

c. Mia sorella ed io _____ i capelli rossi

d. I miei nonni _____ i capelli bianchi

e. I miei genitori _____ gli occhi verdi

f. Noi _____ i capelli castani e lunghi

g. Mia sorella minore ed io _____ i capelli neri ed ondulati.

h. Mio cugino _____ i capelli di media lunghezza.

i. Le mie tre sorelle _____ i capelli lisci.

5. Translate into Italian

a. We have black hair

b. You have long hair

c. You guys have blue eyes

d. She has green eyes

e. My father has brown curly hair

f. My sister has blonde straight hair

g. My uncle has grey short hair

h. My grandfather has no hair

i. My father and I have blonde hair

j. My uncle Paolo has green eyes

6. Guided writing – Write a text in <u>the first person singular (*Io*)</u> including the details below:

➢ You are 10 years old

➢ You have a brother and a sister

➢ Your brother is 15

➢ He has brown, straight, short hair and green eyes

➢ He is tall and handsome

➢ You have a sister

➢ She is 12

➢ She has black, curly, long hair and brown eyes

➢ Your parents are short, have dark hair and brown eyes

7. Write an 80 to 100 words text in Italian in which you describe four people you know very well, relatives, or friends. You must include their:

a. Name

b. Age

c. Hair (colour, length and type)

d. Eye colour

e. If they wear glasses or not

f. Their physical description

g. Their personality description

UNIT 6 (Part 2/2)
Describing my family and saying why I like/dislike them:
'Ti piace tuo/tua...? Perché?'
[Do you like your...? Why?]

Ci sono <u>**quattro**</u> **persone nella mia famiglia** *[There are <u>four</u> people in my family...]* **La mia famiglia è composta da...** *[My family consists of...]* **Nella mia famiglia** *siamo* **in quattro** *[We are a family of four...]* **Vado d'accordo con...** *[I get on well with...]* **Non vado d'accordo...** *[I do not get on well with]*	**mio nonno Alfonso** *[my grandfather Alfonso]* **mio padre Giuseppe** *[my father Giuseppe]* **mio zio Luciano** *[my uncle Luciano]* **mio fratello maggiore/minore Davide** *[my big/little brother Davide]* **mio cugino Marco** *[my cousin Marco]*	**Mi piace mio _____ perché è** *[I like my _____ because he is]* **Mio padre è molto/abbastanza** *[My dad is very/quite]* **Mio padre è anche un po'** *[My dad is also a bit]*	**antipatico** *[unfriendly]* **bello** *[handsome]* **bravo** *[good]* **cattivo** *[bad]* **divertente** *[fun]* **educato** *[polite]* **forte** *[strong]* **generoso** *[generous]* **gentile** *[kind]* **noioso** *[boring]* **severo** *[strict]* **simpatico** *[nice/friendly]* **sportivo** *[sporty]*
	mia nonna Luigina *[my grandmother Luigina]* **mia madre Lina** *[my mother Lina]* **mi zia, Anna** *[my aunt Anna]* **mia sorella maggiore /minore Emanuela** *[my big/little sister Emanuela]* **mia cugina Lara** *[my girl cousin Lara]*	**Mi piace mia _____ perché è** *[I like my _____ because she is]* **Mia madre è molto/abbastanza** *[My mum is very/quite]* **Mia madre è anche un po'** *[My mum is also a bit]*	**antipatica** *[unfriendly]* **bella** *[pretty]* **brava** *[good]* **cattiva** *[bad]* **divertente** *[fun]* **educata** *[polite]* **forte** *[strong]* **generosa** *[generous]* **gentile** *[kind]* **noiosa** *[boring]* **severa** *[strict]* **simpatica** *[nice/friendly]* **sportiva** *[sporty]*

THE LANGUAGE GYM

Unit 6. Describing my family: VOCABULARY BUILDING

1. Complete with the missing word

a. Nella mia famiglia _____ in...[We are... in my family]

b. Ci sono_____ persone [There are five people]

c. Mia _____ Giulia __... [My mother Giulia is...]

d. Vado d' _____con mio... [I get on well with my...]

e. Non _____d'accordo con mio nonno
[I don't get on well with my grandfather]

f. Mio zio___ molto educato [My uncle is very polite]

g. Mia _____ è molto simpatica [My aunt is very nice]

2. Match up

1. forte	a. intelligent
2. simpatica	b. kind
3. intelligente	c. good
4. bravo	d. fun
5. chiacchierone	e. boring
6. divertente	f. generous
7. generoso	g. friendly
8. gentile	h. polite
9. educato	i. talkative
10. noioso	j. pretty
11. bella	k. strong

3. Translate into English

a. Mi piace mio zio =

b. ...perché è generoso =

c. È molto sportivo =

d. Vado d'accordo con... =

e. Non mi piace mia zia...=

f. ...perché è cattiva e severa =

g. Sono gentile =

h. Mio nonno è chiacchierone =

4. Add the missing letter

a. gent_le   c. _impatico   e. _ugino   g. d'ac_ordo   i. ci s_ono   k. mi pi_ce

b. pers_ne   d. n_ioso   f. di_ertente   h. ant_patico   j. m_lto   l. per_hé

5. Broken words

a. N___ m__ fam_____c_ s____ = [In my family there are]

b. Q_____ p_____ = [Four people]

c. M___ m_____ è m_____s_____
= [My mother is very nice]

d. V_____ d'_____c____ = [I get on well with]

e. M___ z_____ è m_____ g_____
= [My uncle is very generous]

f. L_ m_____ f_____ è c_____ da...
= [My family consists of...]

g. M__ s_____ h__i c_____ l_____
= [My sister has long hair]

h. M___ p_____ è a_____i_____
= [My father is quite clever]

6. Complete with a suitable word

a. Ci sono quattro_____

b. _____ simpatica

c. _____ d'accordo

d. È molto _____

e. Ha i _____ biondi

f. _____ piace mia madre

g. Vado _____ con mia nonna

h. ...perché è _____ e buona

i. Ha gli _____blu e grandi

j. Mio cugino è _____ divertente

k. Mia _____ è intelligente

l. Mio nonno ha settanta _____

Unit 6. Describing my family: READING

Mi chiamo Alice. Ho nove anni e vivo a Glasgow, in Scozia. Siamo in cinque nelle mia famiglia: mio padre Mariusz, mia madre Giulia e le mie due sorelle, Olivia e Luna. Vado d'accordo con mia madre perché è paziente e gentile. **Invece** *[instead]* non vado d'accordo con Olivia perché è antipatica.

Mi chiamo Malika. Sono africana e vivo a Reggio Calabria, nel sud dell'Italia. Mi piace molto mio nonno perché è molto divertente . È intelligente ma timido.
Mio padre è abbastanza alto e grosso. Ha gli occhi marroni e i capelli rasati.

Mi chiamo Manolo. Ho quindici anni, sono argentino e vivo in Sicilia. Ho i capelli biondi a spazzola. Nella mia famiglia siamo in sei. Non vado d'accordo con mia sorella perché è testarda e antipatica. Vado d'accordo con i miei cugini perché sono molto simpatici.
Il mio cugino preferito si chiama Ian, è muscoloso e forte. È anche divertente ed educato. Ha i capelli scuri e corto e porta gli occhiali.

Sono Carlo Rossetti. Ho dieci anni e vivo a Milano, il capoluogo della Lombardia. Sono bello e intelligente. Nelle mia famiglia ci sono otto persone in totale. Mi piace mio zio Cesare e vado d'accordo **con lui** *[with him]* perché è simpatico e allegro. Invece, non mi piace mia zia perché è antipatica e severa!
Mia zia Maria ha i capelli biondi e ricci e gli occhi azzurri, **come me** *[like me]*. Il suo compleanno è il cinque maggio.

Mi chiamo Vasile. Ho dieci anni e vivo a Garda, in Italia. La mia famiglia è composta da cinque persone. Non vado d'accordo con mio padre perché è molto noioso e severo. Mi piace molto mia nonna perché è brava e generosa.

1. Find the Italian for the following items in Malika's text

a. I am called:

b. in the south:

c. my grandfather:

d. but:

e. very:

f. my father:

g. brown eyes:

h. very short hair:

2. Answer the following questions about Carlo's text

a. How old is he?

_____

b. Where is he from?

_____

c. Who does he get on well with? Why?

_____

d. Why does he like Cesare?

_____

e. Who does he not like?

_____

f. What does Maria look like?

_____

3. Complete with the missing words

Mi chiamo Francesca e ____otto anni. Sono indiana ma vivo ____ Verona. Nella mia familia ci _____sei persone. Vado d'accordo ____mio nonno perché ___ molto simpatico __ buono. Mio padre____ i capelli corti e ____ occhi verdi.

4. Find someone who? – answer the questions below about all 5 texts

a. Who has a granny who is very good?

_____

b. Who is 15 years old?

_____

c. Who celebrates their birthday on the 5th May?

_____

d. Who is African?

_____

e. Who gets on well with her mother?

_____

f. Who has brown eyes and very short hair?

_____

g. Who is muscular and strong?

_____

 THE LANGUAGE GYM

Unit 6. Describing my family: TRANSLATION

1. Faulty translation: spot and correct any translation mistakes (in the English) you find below

a. Nella mia famiglia siamo in quattro:
In my family I have fourteen people

b. Mia madre Lina e mia sorella Katia:
My mother Lina is my cousin Katia

c. Non vado d'accordo con mio padre:
I get on very well with my father

d. Mio zio ha la barba:
My uncle has a moustache

e. Ivan è molto simpatico e gentile:
Ivan is very unfriendly and fun

2. From Italian to English

a. Mi piace mio nonno.

b. Mia nonna è molto brava.

c. Mio cugino ha i capelli rasati.

d. Vado d'accordo con mio fratello maggiore.

e. Non vado d'accordo con mia cugina perché è noiosa e chiacchierona.

f. Mi piace mio zio perché è generoso.

g. Mio padre è simpatico e divertente.

h. Mio fratello minore è sportivo e gentile.

i. Non vado d'accordo con mio cugino Luca perché è stupido e cattivo.

3. Phrase-level translation

a. He is nice

b. She is generous

c. I get on well with...

d. I do not get along well with...

e. My uncle is fun

f. My little brother

g. I like my cousin Daniela

h. She has short and black hair

i. He has blue eyes

j. I don't like my granddad

k. He is very stubborn

l. ...because she is generous

4. Sentence-level translation

a. My name is Federico Bellini. I am nine years old. In my family there are four people.

b. My name is Carla. I have blue eyes. I get on well with my brother.

c. I do not like my brother because he is stubborn and silly.

d. My name is Peter. I live in Scotland. I like my uncle David because he is kind.

e. I do not get on well with my aunt because she is boring and talkative.

f. In my family we are five. I like my father because he is friendly and polite.

Unit 6. Describing my family: WRITING

1. Split sentences

Mio padre è	capelli neri
Mia madre è	d'accordo con
Ha gli	mio zio
Ha i	simpatico
Non mi piace	occhi neri
Mi piace molto	zia
Vado	generosa

2. Rewrite the sentences in the correct order

a. nella sei famiglia sono ci mia persone

_____

b. vado con fratello d'accordo mio

_____

c. è alto zio mio e magro

_____

d. mia occhi gli madre ha azzurri

_____

e. mia simpatica e zia è chiacchierona

_____

3. Spot and correct the grammar and spelling errors

a. Nella mia familia ce

b. Vado dacordo con...

c. No mi piace mi zia...

d. Mia sorella e bello

e. Non andare d'accordo con...

f. Mio padre e generosa

g. Ho i occhi azurri

h. Mio fratella sono gentile

i. Ha il capello corti e ricci

j. Io essere simpatica

4. Anagrams

a. fagliami =

b. patiantica =

c. ducateo =

d. blela =

e. inligtelente =

f. mispatica =

g. votispor =

h. vertendite =

5. Guided writing – write 3 short paragraphs describing the people below in the first person:

Name	Age	Family	Description	Likes	Dislikes
Piero	12	4 people	mother: brown eyes, long blonde hair	older brother because fun	cousin Gemma because unfriendly
Leo	11	5 people	father: green eyes, short black hair	grandma: because very generous	uncle Emilio: because stubborn
Mike	10	3 people	grandpa: blue eyes, very short grey hair	younger sister: because polite and kind	aunt Carolina: very strong but talkative

6. Describe this person in the third person (*lui/*he):

Name: Uncle Antonio

Hair: blonde, crew-cut

Eyes: blue

Opinion: get on well

Physical: tall and strong

Personality: nice, fun, generous.

UNIT 7
Talking about pets

Grammar Time: AVERE (pets and description)
Questions skills: Age / Descriptions / Pets

In this unit will learn how to say in Italian

- what pets you have at home
- what pet you would like to have
- what their name is
- some more adjectives to describe appearance and personality
- key question words

You will also learn how to ask questions about
- Name / age / appearance / quantity

You will revisit the following
- Introducing oneself
- Family members
- Describing people
- The verb *'Avere'* (to have) in the present indicative

UNIT 7
Talking about pets
'Che animale hai in casa?'
[What pet do you have at home?]

In casa ho *[At home I have]* **Non ho** *[I don't have]* **Il mio amico Fabio ha...** *[My friend Fabio has...]* **Mi piacerebbe** *[I would like to have]*	**un cane** *[a dog]* **un cavallo** *[a horse]* **un coniglio** *[a rabbit]* **un criceto** *[a hamster]* **un gatto** *[a cat]* **un pappagallo** *[a parrot]* **un pesce** *[a fish]* **un porcellino d'India** *[a guinea pig]* **un serpente** *[a snake]* **un topo** *[a mouse]* **un uccello** *[a bird]*	**che si chiama Alfredo** *[that is called Alfredo]* **è** *[he/it is]*	**piccolo** *[small]* **grande** *[big]* **arancione** *[orange]* **bianco** *[white]* **giallo** *[yellow]* **marrone** *[brown]* **rosso** *[red]* **verde** *[green]* **buffo** *[funny]* **carino** *[cute]* **divertente** *[fun]* **intelligente** *[clever]* **noioso** *[boring]*
Non mi piacerebbe *[I wouldn't like to have]*	**una gallina** *[a chicken]* **una giraffa** *[a giraffe]* **una scimmia** *[a monkey]* **una tartaruga** *[a turtle]*	**che si chiama Mya** *[that is called Mya]* **è** *[she/it is]*	**piccola** *[small]* **grande** *[big]* **arancione** *[orange]* **bianca** *[white]* **gialla** *[yellow]* **marrone** *[brown]* **nera** *[black]* **rossa** *[red]* **verde** *[green]* **buffa** *[funny]* **carina** *[cute]* **divertente** *[fun]* **intelligente** *[clever]* **noiosa** *[boring]*

THE LANGUAGE GYM

Unit 7. Talking about pets: VOCABULARY BUILDING

1. Complete with the missing word

a. In casa ho un u_____ *[I have a bird at home]*

b. Non ho un c_____ *[I don't have a rabbit]*

c. Mi piacerebbe avere un c_____ *[I'd like to have a dog]*

d. Non mi piacerebbe avere una t_____in casa
[I wouldn't like to have a turtle at home]

e. Abbiamo un g_____ *[We have a cat]*

f. Non ho un s_____ *[I don't have a snake]*

g. H_____ un ragno in casa *[I have a spider at home]*

h. Mi p_____ avere un criceto
[I'd like to have a hamster]

2. Match up

1.un gatto	a.a rat
2.un cane	b.a hamster
3.un cavallo	c.two fish
4.un uccello	d.a cat
5.un pesce	e.a turtle
6.una tartaruga	f.a fish
7.un criceto	g.a guinea pig
8.un pappagallo	h.a dog
9.due pesci	i.a parrot
10.un topo	j.a bird
11.un porcellino d'India	k.a horse

3. Translate into English

a. Ho un cane.

b. La mia amica Giovina ha un pappagallo.

c. Io ho due pesci.

d. Non ho un animale in casa.

e. Ho tre cani.

f. Mi piacerebbe avere un criceto.

g. In giardino abbiamo una tartaruga.

h. Il mio gatto ha cinque anni.

4. Add the missing letter

a. Il mio ca_e

b. Una tartar_ga

c. Un pap_agallo

d. Due pe_ci

e. Un pes_e

f. Un ga _to

g. Un cric_to

h. Un uccel_o

5. Anagrams

a. anec = cane

b. attgo =

c. tagarutar =

d. scepe =

e. penteser =

f. poto =

g. gnora =

h. nicoglio =

6. Broken words

a. I_ c_____ h___ u_ c_____ = *[At home I have a dog]*

b. Il mio a_____ h___ u___ p_____ = *[My friend has a fish]*

c. M__ f_____ h___ u___ t_____
= *[My brother has a turtle]*

d. N____ h___ u___ c_____ = *[I don't have a rabbit]*

e. H___ u_____ g_____ = *[I have a chicken]*

f. Alex h__ u_ p_____ d'_____ = *[Alex has a guinea pig]*

g. H____ u__ p_____ a_____ = *[I have a blue fish]*

7. Complete with a suitable word

a. Ho diei _____ in casa.

b. Il mio pesce si _____ Rex.

c. Mio nonno _____ un cane.

d. Mio fratello ha _____ criceto.

e. In _____ ho due animali.

f. Ho _____ gallina e una _____
in giardino.

g. Non ho un _____ in casa.

h. In casa ho due _____.

56

Unit 7. Talking about pets: READING

Mi chiamo Elisa. Ho otto anni e vivo a Edimburgo. Nella mia famiglia siamo in quattro: i miei genitori, mio fratello minore che si chiama Leo ed io. Leo è molto antipatico e fastidioso. Abbiamo due animali: un cane che si chiama Artù e un gatto che si chiama Zeus. Artù è molto veloce. Zeus è antipatico, proprio **come** [like] mio fratello!

Mi chiamo Robert e sono inglese. Ho nove anni e vivo a Verona. Ci sono quattro persone nella mia famiglia. Mio fratello maggiore si chiama Jack. Lui ha dodici anni ed è un simpaticone. Abbiamo due animali: un pappagallo che si chiama Rico e un gatto che si chiama Max. Rico è molto buffo. Max è un simpaticone, come mio fratello!

Mi chiamo Kumar e sono un bambino dello Sri Lanka. Ho nove anni e abito a Milano. La mia famiglia è composta da cinque persone: i miei genitori, due fratelli che si chiamano Arjuna e Hashan, ed io. Arjuna è molto chiacchierone. Hashan è molto serio e lavoratore. In casa abbiamo due animali: il criceto Sam e la tartaruga Bella. Il criceto è buffo e vivace. Bella è molto seria, come mio fratello Hashan.

Mi c_____ Gianni. Ho undici a_____ , sono italiano e v_____ a Roma. Nella mia famiglia s_____ in sei: i miei g_____ , due sorelle che si c_____ Ale e Marta. Ale __ molto chiacchierona e gentile. Marta è u__ po' pigra _____ antipatica. Ho due a_____ in casa: un pesce c_____ si chiama Maya e un gatto che s___ chiama Swift. Swift___ divertente e vivace. Maya è m_____ pigra, c_____ m__ s_____ Marta!

Mi chiamo Li Xiang e vivo a Prato, vicino Firenze. Ho dieci anni. Nella mia familia ci sono cinque persone: i miei genitori, le mie sorelle che si chiamano Shan e Mei ed io. Shan è molto generosa e gentile. Mei è un po' testarda e noiosa. Abbiamo due animali: un coniglio che si chiama Busy e un criceto che si chiama Lazy. Busy è molto tranquillo e carino. Lazy è rumorosa e **vivace** [lively].

1.c Find the Italian for the following in Elisa's text

a. two pets

b. which is called

c. a cat

d. very fast

e. like my brother

f. my parents

g. my name is

h. is unfriendly

i. we are four

2. Find someone who? – answer the questions below about Elisa, Robert, Li Xiang and Kumar

a. Who has a cat?

b. Who has a parrot?

c. Who has a hamster?

d. Who has a guinea pig?

e. Who has a rabbit?

f. Who has a dog?

3. Answer the following questions about Kumar's text

a. Where does Kumar live?

b. What is his brother Hashan like?

c. Who is fun and lively?

d. Who is like Hashan?

e. Who is Arjuna?

f. Who is Bella?

g. Who is Sam?

4. Fill in the table below

Name	Gianni	Robert
Age		
City/Nationality		
Pets		
Description of pets		

THE LANGUAGE GYM

Unit 7. Talking about pets: TRANSLATION

1. Faulty translation: spot and correct any translation mistakes you find below

a. Nella mia famiglia ci sono quattro persone e due animali: *In my family there are four people and three pets.*

b. Abbiamo due animali in casa, un cane e una scimmia: *At home we have two pets: a dog and a rabbit*

c. Il mio amico Paco ha una tartaruga che si chiama Speedy. Speedy è molto buffa: *My friend Paco has a duck called Speedy. Speedy is very boring.*

d. Mio fratello ha un cavallo che si chiama Dylan: *My sister has a parrot called Dylan*

e. Mia madre ha una gallina che si chiama Lella: *My father has a frog called Lella*

f. Ho un gatto che si chiama Sleepy. Sleepy è molto vivace: *I have a dog called Sleepy. Sleepy is very beautiful*

2. Translate into English

a. Un gatto simpaticone =

b. Un cane buffo e veloce =

c. Una gallina rumorosa =

d. Una tartaruga pigra =

e. Un cavallo intelligente =

f. Una scimmia vivace =

g. Un criceto curioso =

h. Ho due animali =

i. Non abbiamo animali in casa =

j. Mi piacerebbe avere un cane =

k. Non mi piacerebbe avere un pesce =

l. Ho un porcellino d'India ma mi piacerebbe avere un serpente =

3. Phrase-level translation [En to It]

a. a boring dog=

b. a lively parrot =

c. at home =

d. we have =

e. a beautiful horse =

f. a curious cat =

g. a funny monkey=

h. I have =

i. I don't have =

j. I would like to have =

4. Sentence-level translation [En to It]

a. My brother has a horse who is called Rayo.

b. My sister has a big turtle who is called Nicole.

c. I have a fat hamster called Pancione.

d. At home we have three pets: a fish, a rabbit and a parrot.

e. I have a rat called Stuart.

f. At home we have two pets: a dog and a hamster

g. I have two fish which are called Nemo and Dory

Unit 7. Talking about pets: WRITING

1. Split sentences

Ho un cane che	bianca
In casa abbiamo	avere un cavallo
Ho una gallina	si chiama Speedy
Ho un gatto	una scimmia
Mi piacerebbe	due animali
Mio fratello ha	casa
Non ho animali in	nero

2. Rewrite the sentences in the correct order

a. animali abbiamo In tre casa

b. una piacerebbe avere Mi topo

c. un Ho gatto un cane e

d. criceto amico nero Il mio ha Luigi un

e. Kiki verde un che Abbiamo si uccello chiama

f. due Abbiamo azzurri pesci

g. ha chiama sorella un che si Mia pappagallo Mango

3. Spot the mistake and rewrite the correct sentence[note: in several cases a word is missing]

a. In casa un cane e un gatto

b. Ho criceto nera

c. Piacerebbe avere un serpente

d. Mi avere una scimmia simpatica

e. Il amico Piero a due pesci

f. Il mio cavallo chiama Graham

g. Ho una cavallo bianco

h. In casa abiamo tre cane

4. Anagrams

a. neca =

b. miascim =

c. valloca =

d. llagina =

e. glioconi =

f. tocrice =

g. cellocu =

6. Describe this person in the third person:

Name: Massimo

Hair: blonde, short

Eyes: green

Personality: very nice

Physical: tall, muscular

Pets: a dog, a cat and two fish and would like to have a spider

5. Guided writing – write 3 short paragraphs (in 1st person)describing the pets below using the details in the box

Name	Animal	Age	Colour	Character or appearance
Davide	dog	4	white	affectionate
Gianfranco	monkey	6	black	funny
Dylan	horse	1	brown	beautiful

Grammar Time 3: AVERE (Part 2)
(Pets and description)

1. Translate

a. I have: io h __

b. You have: tu h __ __

c. She has: lei h__

d. We have: noi a__ __ __ __ __ __

e. You all have: voi a__ __ __ __

f. They have: loro h__ __ __ __

2. Translate into English

a. Ho un cavallo molto bello e veloce.

b. Mio fratello ha un gatto abbastanza brutto.

c. Mia madre ha un cane molto simpatico.

d. I miei genitori hanno un serpente nero.

e. In giardino abbiamo una gallina molto rumorosa.

f. In casa Cristina ha una tartaruga pigra.

3. Complete

a. I have a guinea pig: *Ho un p_____ d'India.*

b. It is two years old: *H_____ due anni.*

c. We have a turtle. It is 4 years old: *A_____ una tartaruga. H__ quattro anni.*

d. My sister has a dog: *Mia sorella ha u__ cane*

e. My uncles have two cats: *I miei zii h_____ due gatti*

f. They are three years old: *Loro h_____ tre anni*

g. My brother and I have a snake: *Mio fratello ed io a_____ un serpente*

h. Do you have pets?: *Voi a_____animali?*

i. What animals do you all have?: *Che animali a_____?*

4. Translate into Italian

a. I have a guinea pig. It is three years old.

b. We don't have pets at home.

c. My dog is three years old. It is very big.

d. I have three brothers. They are nice and funny.

e. My cousins have a horse and a chicken.

f. My auntie has blonde, curly and long hair. She is very pretty.

g. My brother and I have black hair and green eyes. We have a rabbit.

Question Skills 1: Age / Descriptions / Pets

1. Match question and answer

1. Quanti anni hai?	a. Sono di Palermo
2. Perché non vai d'accordo con tua madre?	b. Sto bene, grazie
3. Come sono i tuoi capelli?	c. Ho quindici anni
4. Di dove sei?	d. Il verde
5. Di che colore sono i tuoi occhi?	e. Perché è severa
6. Qual è il tuo colore preferito?	f. Il cane
7. Come stai?	g. Sono simpatico e chiacchierone
8. Hai animali in casa?	h. Si, perché è paziente
9. Qual é il tuo animale preferito?	i. Il venti giugno
10. Dove vivi?	j. Sono rossi
11. Come sei di carattere?	k. Sono azzurri
12. Come sei fisicamente?	l. Si, due. Un gatto e un pappagallo.
13. Vai d'accordo con tuo padre?	m. Vivo a Londra, in Inghilterra.
14. Quando è il tuo compleanno?	n. Sono basso e un po magro.

2. Complete with the missing words

a. Di _____ sei?
[Where are you from?]

b. _____ è Maria (di carattere)?
[What is Maria like (personality-wise)?]

c. _____ anni ha tuo padre?
[How old is your father?]

d. _____ stai? Sto _____, grazie.
[How are you? I am well, thank you]

e. _____ è il tuo compleanno?
[When is your birthday?]

f. _____ è il tuo cane?
[What is your dog like?]

g. _____ animali hai?
[How many pets do you have?]

3. Translate the following question words into English

a. Quale?

b. Quando?

c. Dove?

d. Come?

e. Di dove?

f. Chi?

g. Quanti?

h. Cosa?

i. Perché?

5. Translate into Italian

a. What is your name?

b. How old are you?

c. What is your hair like?

d. What is your favourite animal?

e. Do you get on with your father?

f. Why don't you get on with your sister?

g. How many pets do you have?

h. Where are you from?

4. Complete

a. Q_____ a_____ hai?

b. D_ d_____ sei?

c. D_____ v_____?

d. Q_____ è i__ t___ c_____?

e. H_____ u_ a_____ in casa?

f. C_____ s_____?

g. V__ d'_____ c___ t__ p_____?

THE LANGUAGE GYM

UNIT 8
Saying what jobs people do, why they like/dislike them and where they work

Grammar Time:- ARE verbs like lavorare + ESSERE

In this unit will learn how to say:

- What jobs people do
- Why they like/dislike those jobs
- Where they work
- Adjectives to describe jobs
- Words for common jobs
- Words for types of buildings
- The full conjugation of the verb 'Lavorare' (to work) in the present indicative

You will revisit the following:

- Family members
- The full conjugation of the verb 'Essere' (to be)
- Description of people and pets

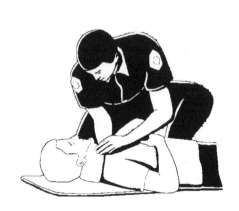

UNIT 8
Saying what jobs people do, why they like/dislike them and where they work
'Che lavora fa tuo/tua...?'
[What job does your...do?]

					Lavora in... *[He/she works in...]*
Mio padre *[My father]*	**è** *[he is]*	**attore** *[actor]* **avvocato** *[lawyer]* **casalingo** *[house-husband]* **contabile** *[accountant]* **contadino** *[farmer]*	**gli/le piace** *[he/she likes it]*	**ben pagato** *[well-paid]* **difficile** *[difficult]*	
Mio fratello *[My brother]*		**cuoco** *[chef]* **infermiere** *[nurse]* **impiegato** *[office-worker]* **uomo di affari** *[business man]*	**non gli/le piace** *[he/she doesn't like it]*	**dinamico** *[dynamic]* **divertente** *[funny]*	**un' azienda** *[a company]* **una fabbrica** *[a factory]* **campagna** *[the countryside]*
	lavora come *[works as]*			**facile** *[easy]*	**città** *[the city]*
Mio zio *[My uncle]*		**ingegnere** *[engineer]* **meccanico** *[mechanic]* **dottore** *[doctor]* **parrucchiere** *[hairdresser]* **professore** *[teacher]*	**perché è...** *[because it is...]*		**un garage** *[a garage]* **una fattoria** *[a farm]*
				gratificante *[rewarding]* **interessante** *[interesting]*	**un hotel** *[a hotel]*
Mia madre *[My mother]*	**è** *[she is]*	**attrice** *[actress]* **avvocatessa** *[lawyer]* **casalinga** *[house-wife]* **contabile** *[accountant]* **contadina** *[farmer]*	**(lui/ lei) ama il suo lavoro** *[he/she loves his/her job]*	**mal pagato** *[low-paid]* **noioso** *[boring]*	**un ristorante** *[a restaurant]* **una scuola** *[a school]*
Mia sorella maggiore *[My older sister]*		**cuoca***[chef]* **infermiera** *[nurse]* **impiegata** *[office-worker]* **ingegnere** *[engineer]* **donna di affari** *[business woman]*		**stimolante** *[exciting]*	**un teatro** *[a theatre]*
	lavora come *[works as]*		**(lui/ lei) odia il suo lavoro** *[he/she hates his/her job]*	**stressante** *[stressful]*	**un ufficio** *[an office]*
Mia zia *[My aunt]*		**meccanica** *[mechanic]* **dottoressa** *[doctor]* **parrucchiera** *[hairdresser]* **professoressa** *[teacher]*			**Lavora da casa** *[He/she works from home]*

Unit 8. Saying what jobs people do: VOCABULARY BUILDING

1. Complete with the missing word

a. Mio padre è _____ [My father is a lawyer]

b. Mia zia è _____ [My aunt is a teacher]

c. Mio fratello lavora come _____
[My brother works as a mechanic]

d. Mia madre è _____ [My mother is a doctor]

e. Mia sorella _____ lavora come _____
[My older sister works as an engineer]

f. Mia zia è _____ [My aunt is an accountant]

g. Mio _____ è _____ [My uncle is a nurse]

2. Match up

1.è noioso	a.it's stressful
2.è dinamico	b.it's fun
3.è difficile	c.it's hard
4.è divertente	d.it's active
5.è stimolante	e.it's rewarding
6.è stressante	f.it's boring
7.è facile	g.it's interesting
8.è gratificante	h.it's easy
9.è interessante	i.it's exciting

3. Translate into English

a. Mia madre è meccanica

b. Le piace molto il suo lavoro

c. Lavora in un garage

d. Mio fratello è contabile

e. Non gli piace il suo lavoro

f. Mio cugino è contadino

g. Lui ama il suo lavoro

h. Perché è divertente

4. Add the missing letter

a. È f_cile   e. È s_ressante

b. Gli _iace   f. L_vora come

c. Ing_gnere   g. È in_ermiere

d. _ottoressa   h. Pr_fessore

5. Anagrams

a. aDonndiafrifa =   e. triceAt =

b. cavvoAto =   f. Cobintale =

c. toreDot =   g. uoCco =

d. totreA =   h. pieImgato=

6. Broken words

a. M__ p_____ è c_____
= [My dad is a house husband]

b. L__ g_____ s___ t_____ = [He likes his job]

c. M__ f_____ è c_____ = [My brother is a chef]

d. L_____ i__ c_____, è c_____
= [He works in the countryside, he is a farmer]

e. Lui a_____ i___ s___ l_____ = [He loves his job]

f. P_____ è d_____ = [Because it is dynamic]

g. ___ m_____ g_____ = [It is very rewarding]

7. Complete with a suitable word

a. Mia madre è _____

b. Lei_____ il suo lavoro

c. Gli piace perché è _____

d. Lavora in _____

e. Mio _____ è parrucchiere

f. Non _____ piace il suo lavoro

g. Perché è molto _____

h. _____ zia è dottoressa

i. _____ odia il suo _____

Unit 8. Saying what jobs people do: READING

Mi chiamo Filippo. Ho venti anni e vivo a Lecce, nel sud dell'Italia. Siamo in tre nella mia famiglia. Ho un cane molto divertente che si chiama Fluffy. Mio padre lavora come medico in ospedale. Lui ama il suo lavoro perché è gratificante. Mia madre Daniela è impiegata, lavora in un ufficio. A volte, è un lavoro noioso ma va d'accordo con i suoi colleghi.

Mi chiamo George. Vivo con la mia familia a Bergamo, nel nord dell'Italia. Che lavoro fa mio padre? Mio padre è avvocato. Gli piace il suo lavoro perché è interessante. Purtroppo, a volte è un po' stressante. Mia madre è infermiera e le piace abbastanza il suo lavoro perché è molto dinamico. Ho un cane che si chiama Dido. È affettuso e buffo. Non mi piacciono i gatti!

Mi chiamo Fabio. Sono di Viareggio, in Toscana. Vado molto d'accordo con mia madre. È timida ma molto simpatica. Mia madre è ingegnere ed è molto impegnata. Nel futuro mi piacerebbe essere ingegnere, come mia madre! Odio mio zio, è intelligente ma cattivo. Mio zio è un uomo di affari ma odia il suo lavoro perché è difficile e viaggia molto. Ho una tartaruga che si chiama Speed. È lenta ma molto buffa.

M__ chiamo Marina. Ho tredici a_____ e v_____ a Rieti, nel centro dell'Italia. Nella mia f_____ ci sono cinque persone. Mio cugino Cristian ha trenta anni ed è molto ch_____e. Cristian è pr_____ e lavora in una s_____ secondaria. Vive a Liverpool, in Inglaterra. Gli piace il suo l_____perché è int_____ e gra_____. In casa ho __ animale piccolo ma carino. È un ra_____: una tarantola!

Mi chiamo Camilla. La mia famiglia è composta da quattro persone. Mia madre si chiama Valeria ed è cuoca, lavora in un ristorante cinese in centro. Le piace il suo lavoro perché è dinamico. Mio padre è casalingo ma non gli piace molto, perché non è ben pagato e noioso! In casa non ho un animale ma mi piacerebbe avere un cavallo. Mio cugino fa il cuoco. Lui ha un cavallo che si chiama Apollo, è grande e veloce. **Che forte!***[Cool!]*

1. Find the Italian for the following in Filippo's text

a. I am 20

b. I have a dog

c. my dad works as…

e. in a hospital

f. he loves his work

g. it is rewarding

h. sometimes

i. a boring job

j. gets on well with colleagues

2. Answer the questions on ALL texts

a. Who is Apollo?

b. Whose mum is a nurse?

c. Why does Cristian love teaching in a school?

d. Whose father is a doctor?

e. Who has a turtle?

f. What is George's dog like?

3. Answer the following questions about Fabio's text

a. Where does Fabio live?

b. What is his mum like [personality]?

c. Why does he hate his uncle?

d. What job does his uncle do?

e. Who is Speed and what is she like?

f. What job does Fabio would like to do and why?

4. Fill in the table below

Name	Marina [Pets]	Cristian [Jobs]
Age		
City		
Pets/Job		
Description of pets/job		

Unit 8. Saying what jobs people do: TRANSLATION

1. Faulty translation: spot and correct [IN THE ENGLISH] any translation mistakes you find below

a. Mio padre lavora come attore e gli piace molto perché è emozionante. Lavora in un teatro: *My father works as a cook and he really likes his job because it is interesting. He works in a school.*

b. Mia zia lavora come donna di affari in un ufficio. Le piace ma è difficile: *My aunt works as a business woman in a hair salon. She hates it but it's hard.*

c. Il mio amico Nuccio è infermiere. Lavora in un ospedale e gli piace il suo lavoro: *My friend Nuccio works as a doctor. He lives in a hospital and hates his work.*

d. Mio zio Gianfranco è cuoco in un ristorante italiano e lo trova divertente: *My uncle Gianfranco is a lawyer in an Italian firm and he finds it fun.*

e. Mia madre Susan è commercialista e lavora da casa. Odia il suo lavoro perché è ripetitivo: *My mother Susan is an actress and works in an office. She loves her work because it is dynamic.*

3. Phrase-level translation [En to It]

a. my big brother =

b. works as =

c. a farmer =

d. he likes =

e. his job =

f. because it's dynamic =

g. and fun =

h. but it's tough =

2. Translate into English

a. Mio zio lavora come =

b. Mio padre è commercialista =

c. Sono casalingo =

d. Sono infermiere =

e. *Faccio la cuoca=

f. *Faccio l'avvocato =

g. Le piace il suo lavoro=

h. Lavora in una fabbrica =

i. Lavora in un teatro =

j. Lavora in un'azienda =

k. È gratificante =

l. È difficile ma stimolante =

Author's note: *Faccio means "I do". You can say you do a job, however the verb **fare** "to do" must be followed by a definite article: Faccio la cuoca*

4. Sentence-level translation [En to It]

a. My brother is a mechanic

b. My father is a business man

c. My uncle is a farmer and hates his job

d. My sister works from home

e. At home I have a snake called Sally

f. We have a friendly dog and a mean cat

g. My aunt is a nurse. She likes her job...

h. ...because it is rewarding

i. My mother works in a hospital

Unit 8. Saying what jobs people do: WRITING

1. Split sentences

1.Mio fratello	a.donna di affari
2.Mia zia lavora	b.è avvocato
3.Mia madre lavora come	c.il professore
4.Gli piace perché	d. ma gratificante
5.Lei odia	e.in un'azienda
6.Faccio	f.il suo lavoro
7.È difficile	g.è stimolante

2. Rewrite the sentences in the correct order

a. Le suo il lavoro piace molto

b. Lavora in un commercialista come ufficio

c. casa da Mia lavora madre

d. come zio contadino Mio lavora

e. lavora Mio fratello un teatro in

f. Mio odia suo nonno lavoro il

g. mia amica La lavora un ristorante in

3. Spot the mistake and rewrite the correct sentence [note: in several cases a word is missing]

a. Mia zia e casalinga

b. È un lavoro noiosa e dinamica

c. Mi sorella lavora avvocatessa

d. Lei odia il suo lavoro perche e dificile

e. Faccio il dottore un ospedale en città

f. Le piace molto suo lavoro perché è facile

g. Mio padre odio il sua lavoro

h. Gli piace perché lavoro in campagna con l'animali.

4. Anagrams

a. eaTotr =

b. Tigracafinte =

c. Ritipetivo =

d. eL iaPce =

e. dinotaCon =

f. ranteRisto =

g. Psorfesossare =

6. Describe this person in Italian in the 3rd person

Name: Magdalena

Hair: blonde + green eyes

Physical: tall and slim

Personality: hard-working, nice

Job: nurse

Opinion: likes her job a lot

Reason: stressful but rewarding

5. Guided writing – write 3 short paragraphs describing the people below using the details in the box [in 1st person]

Person	Relation	Job	Like/ Dislike	Reason
Giorgio	My dad	Mechanic	Loves	Active and interesting
Luciano	My brother	Lawyer	Hates	Boring and well-paid
Lucas	My aunt	Farmer	Likes	Tough but exciting

Grammar Time 4: The present indicative of "Lavor**are**" and other ARE verbs

io	**lavor<u>o</u>** [I work]		**casalingo/a** [house-husband]
tu	**lavor<u>i</u>** [you work]		**contadino/a** [farmer]
			cuoco/a [chef]
lui mio fratello mio padre	**lavor<u>a</u>** [he works]		**commercialista** [accountant] **donna di affari** [business woman] **infermiere/a** [nurse]
lei mia sorella mia madre	**lavor<u>a</u>** [she works]	come [as]	**impiegato/a** [office-worker] **ingegnere** [engineer] **meccanico/a** [mechanic]
noi mio padre ed io	**lavor<u>iamo</u>** [we work]		**parrucchiere/a** [hairdresser] **uomo di affari** [business man]
voi	**lavor<u>ate</u>** [you all work]		**avvoc<u>ato</u>/avvocat<u>essa</u>** [lawyer]
loro le mie sorelle i miei fratelli	**lavor<u>ano</u>** [they work]		**dott<u>ore</u>/dottor<u>essa</u>** [doctor] **profess<u>ore</u>/professor<u>essa</u>** [teacher] **att<u>ore</u>/att<u>rice</u>** [actor] **scritt<u>ore</u>/scritt<u>rice</u>** [writer]

Drills

1. Match up

lavora	*I work*
lavoro	*You work*
lavorano	*He/she works*
lavorate	*We work*
lavoriamo	*You guys work*
lavori	*They work*

2. Complete with the correct option

a. Mio fratello _____ come parrucchiere

b. I miei genitori non _____

c. Mia sorella ed io _____ come impiegat**e**

d. La mia amica _____ come dottoressa

e. Mia madre _____ come ingegnere

f. Voi _____ come impiegat**i**

g. Perché tu non _____?

h. Io non_____ . Sono disoccupato.

lavoriamo	lavora	lavorate	lavori
lavorano	lavoro	lavora	lavora

3. Cross out the wrong option

	A	B
I miei genitori	lavorano	lavorate
Mio fratello	lavora	lavoro
Mio padre	lavori	lavora
I miei zii	lavoriamo	lavorano
Le mie zie	lavorano	lavorare
Tu ed io	lavoro	lavoriamo
Noi	lavori	lavoriamo
Voi	lavorate	lavoro
I miei cugini	lavorano	lavora
Io e lei	lavorate	lavoriamo

4. Complete the verb *Lavorare*

a. Mio fratello ed io non lavor__ __ __ __

b. I miei genitori lavor__ __ __

c. Mio padre lavor__ come avvocato

d. A volte i miei fratelli non lavor__ __ __ __

e. Tu non lavor__ mai !

f. Mia madre lavor__ da casa

g. Voi lavor __ __ __ come professori

h. Io lavor__ in un negozio di moda

i. Ma voi, quando lavor __ __ __?

5. Complete with the correct form of *'lavorare'*

a. I miei genitor_i_ _____ come avvocat_i_ [My parents work as lawyer_s_]

b. Mia madre _____ come profesoressa [My mother works as a teacher]

c. Tu _____ come contabile [You work as an accountant]

d. Mio zio _____ come contadino [My father works as a farmer]

e. Mio fratello non _____ , è disoccupato [My brother doesn't work, he is unemployed]

f. Le mie sorelle non _____ nemmeno [My sisters don't work either]

g. Mio cugino _____ come pompiere [My uncle works as a fireman]

h. I miei amici ed io non _____ [My friends and I don't work]

i. (io) _____ in un ristorante [I work in a restaurant]

j. Mia zia _____ in un negozio di abbigliamento [My aunt works in a clothing store]

k. Dove_____ (tu)? [Where do you work?]

Verbs like LAVOR<u>ARE</u>

Amare: to love

Ascoltare: to listen to

Cenare: to have dinner

Giocare: to play (sport)

Mangiare: to eat

Parlare: to speak

Praticare: to practise

Studiare: to study

Viaggiare: to travel

6. Complete the sentences using the correct form of the verbs in the grey box on the left

a. Am__ i miei nonni [I love my grandparents]

b. Cen__ con la sua famiglia [He has dinner with is family]

c. Lei pratic__ lo sci [She practises skiing]

d. Tu parl__ spagnolo? [Do you speak Spanish?]

e. No, io parl__ italiano [No, I speak Italian]

f. Voi studi__ __ __ matematica? [Do you all study Mathematics?]

g. Io ascolt__ musica rock [I listen to rock music]

h. Noi mangi__ __ __ la pizza a cena [We eat pizza for dinner]

THE LANGUAGE GYM

Grammar Time 5: ESSERE (Part 2)
(Present indicative of "Essere" and jobs)

Present Indicative of 'Essere'		Jobs (nouns)	
		Singular	**Plural**
		MASCULINE	
io	**sono** *[I am]*	attore	attori
		avvocato	avvocati
tu	**sei** *[you are]*	contabile	contabili
lui		contadino	contadini
mio fratello	**è** *[he is]*	cuoco	cuochi
mio padre		dipendente	dipendenti
noi		dottore/medico	dottori/medici
mio padre ed io	**siamo** *[we are]*	infermiere	infermieri
		ingegnere	ingegneri
voi	**siete** *[you all are]*	meccanico	meccanici
		parrucchiere	parrucchieri
loro		professore	professori
i miei fratelli	**sono** *[they are]*	scienziato	scienziati
i miei genitori			
		FEMININE	
io	**sono** *[I am]*	attrice	attrici
		avvocatessa	avvocatesse
tu	**sei** *[you are]*	contabile	contabili
lei		contadina	contadine
mia sorella	**è** *[she is]*	cuoca	cuoche
mia madre		dipendente	dipendenti
noi		dottoressa	dottoresse
mia madre ed io	**siamo** *[we are]*	infermiera	infermiere
		ingegnere	ingegnere
voi	**siete** *[you all are]*	meccanica	meccaniche
		parrucchiera	parrucchiere
loro		professoressa	professoresse
le mie sorelle	**sono** *[they are]*	scienziata	scienziate
le mie zie			

Drills

1. Match

Sono	She/he is
Siamo	You are
Sono	We are
Sei	I am
È	They are
Siete	You all are

2. Complete with the missing forms of ESSERE

a. Mia madre ed io _____ dottoresse

b. I miei fratelli _____ operai

c. Mia sorella _____ infermiera

d. I miei genitori ed io _____ giardinieri [gardeners]

e. Tu_____ avvocato?

f. Io _____ pompiere

g. Loro non _____ poliziotti [policemen]

h. Voi ragazze_____ modelle? [models]

i. Voi ragazzi _____ attori, vero?

j. I miei zii _____ cuochi in un ristorante in centro

3. Translate into English

a. Siamo parrucchieri

b. Sono poliziotti

c. Sei pompiere o contadino?

d. Tracy lavora come modella

e. Sono operai in un cantiere [building site]

f. Io sono poliziotto

g. Voi siete infermiere

h. Noi siamo scienziate.

i. Mio padre ed io siamo attori

j. Voi non siete professori

k. Io non sono attrice, sono scrittrice

4. Translate into Italian (easier)

a. My father is a doctor

b. My parents are policemen

c. My uncle is a lawyer

d. I am a teacher

e. My cousins are mechanics

f. My aunt is a scientist

g. My friend Valentino is an actor

5. Translate into Italian (harder)

a. My brother is tall and handsome. He is an actor.

b. My older sister is very intelligent and hard-working. She is an engineer.

c. My younger brother is very sporty and active. He is a footballer.

d. My mother is very strong and hard-working. She is a scientist.

e. My father is very patient, calm and organized. He is an accountant.

UNIT 9
Comparing people's appearance and personality

In this unit will learn how to say in Italian:
- More/less ... than
- As ... as
- New adjectives to describe people

You will revisit the following:
- Family members
- Pets
- Describing animals' appearance and character

UNIT 9
Comparing people

Io	sono [am]		affettuoso/a [affectionate]			
			bello/a [good-looking]			
			chiacchierone/a [chatty]			Dylan
Lei			rumoroso/a [noisy]			Gianfranco
Lui		più.. [more]	diligente [hard-working]		di... [than]	Simona
Mia cugina			divertente [funny]			Stefano
Mio nonno			gentile [kind]			me [me]
La mia amica Sara			giovane [young]			te [you]
Il mio amico Ben	è [is]	meno... [less]	grosso/a [fat]		di... [than]	noi
Il mio cavallo			intelligente [intelligent]			voi
Il mio cane			noioso/a [boring]			loro
Il mio ragazzo [bf]			pigro/a [lazy]			mia madre
La mia ragazza [gf]			serio/a [serious]			mia sorella
Francesca			sportivo/a [sporty]			mio fratello
Mario			tonto/a [silly]			mio padre
		tanto... [as]	tranquillo/a [relaxed]		quanto... [as]	mia zia
			vecchio/a [old]			mio zio
I miei fratelli	sono [are]		affettuosi/e			
I miei genitori			gentili			
I miei zii			giovani			
Le mie sorelle			sportivi/e			
Le mie amiche			tranquilli/e			
Le mie zie						

Author's note: [1] The adjectives above ending in '**o**' change to '**a**' with feminine nouns. Ex. *Io sono bello/ Mia sorella è bella* [2] Feminine adjective ending in '**a**' change into '**e**' in the plural. *Ex. Le mie sorelle sono belle* [3] Adjectives ending in '**e**'do not change in the feminine. However, they change to '**i**' in the plural. *Ex: Mio fratello è intelligente / I miei fratelli sono intelligenti*

Unit 9. Comparing people : VOCABULARY BUILDING

1. Complete with the missing word

a. Mio padre è più alto _____ mio fratello maggiore [My father is taller than my older brother]

b. Mia madre è _____ chiacchierona di mia _____ [My mother is less chatty than my aunt]

c. Mio _____ è più basso di _____ padre [My grandfather is shorter than my father]

d. I miei cugini sono più _____ di _____ [My cousins are lazier than us]

e. Il mio cane _____ più _____ del mio _____ [My dog is more noisy than my cat]

f. Mia zia è _____ bella di _____ madre [My aunt is less pretty than my mother]

g. Mio _____ è più _____ di me [My brother is more hard-working than me]

h. Il mio maestro ___ più _____ del mio pesce [My teacher is more chatty than my fish]

i. Mio fratello minore è _____ alto _____ me [My brother is as tall as me]

2. Translate into English

a. i miei cugini sono

b. più affettuosi

c. meno simpatici

d. più diligente

e. di mia sorella

f. tanto forte quanto

g. è più bello

h. della mia migliore amica

i. sono meno alto

j. è più vecchio

k. siamo più intelligenti

l. quanto mio zio

3. Spot and correct any English translation mistakes

a. Lui è più alto di me = He is taller than you

b. Lui è tanto serio quanto me = He is as good-looking as me

c. Lei è meno tranquillo delle sorelle = He is less quiet than me

d. Io sono meno grosso di mio zio = I am stronger than my uncle

e. Siamo meno giovani di voi = We are shorter than us

f. Tu sei tanto vecchia quanto lei = She is as old as him

g. Lara è tanto sportiva quanto Mara = Lara is as sporty as Mara

4. Complete with a suitable word

a. Mia madre è _____ alta _____ me.

b. _____ padre _____ più giovane di mio zio.

c. I miei genitori sono _____ alti quanto i _____ cugini.

d. I _____fratelli _____ più sportivi delle mie sorelle.

e. Il mio _____ è meno affettuoso _____ mio cane.

f. I miei nonni _____ tanto tranquilli _____ il mio gatto.

g. La mia amica è _____ bella della _____ tartaruga.

h. Mio zio non _____ tanto forte _____ mia _____.

5. Match the opposites

1. bello	a. basso
2. diligente	b. noioso
3. giovane	c. brutto
4. alto	d. tonto
5. divertente	e. meno
6. simpatico	f. pigro
7. più	g. vecchio
8. intelligente	h. antipatico

Unit 9. Comparing people : READING

Mi chiamo Fausto. Ho ventitré anni e vivo in Svizzera. Nella mia famiglia siamo in cinque: mamma, papà, i miei fratelli Ale e Stefano ed io. Stefano è più alto, bello e forte di Ale, però Ale è più intelligente e diligente di Stefano. I miei genitori si chiamano Antonio e Nina. **Entrambi** [both] sono molto carini, ma mio padre è più severo di mia madre. Inoltre, mia madre è più paziente e meno testarda di mio padre. Io sono tanto testardo quanto mio padre! In casa abbiamo due animali: un'anatra e un gatto. Sono entrambi molto simpatici, ma la anatra è più chiassosa. Tanto chiassosa quanto me...

Mi chiamo Mauro Ferrari. Ho quindici anni e vivo a Montalcino, in Toscana. La mia famiglia è composta da cinque persone: mamma, papà, mio fratello Marco e mia sorella Barbara. Marco è più sportivo di Barbara, ma Barbara è più alta e forte.

I miei genitori si chiamano Fabio e Gabriella. Mi piace mio padre perché è meno severo di mia madre. Inoltre, mia madre è più antipatica di mio padre. In casa abbiamo due animali: un pappagallo e un criceto. Entrambi sono molto simpatici, ma il mio pappagallo è più chiacchierone. Tanto chiacchierone quanto me...

Mi chiamo Victoria. Ho venti anni e vivo a Siena con i miei genitori e le mie due sorelle Ava e Grace. Ava è più bella di Grace, ma Grace è più simpatica.

I miei genitori sono affettuosi e gentili, ma mia madre è più divertente di mio padre. Inoltre, mia mamma è più buffa del mio papà. Io sono tanto buffa quanto mio madre!

In casa abbiamo due animali: un cane e un coniglio. Entrambi sono molto grossi, ma il mio cane è più pigro. Tanto pigro quanto me...

1. Find the Italian for the following in Fausto's text

a. I live in:

b. Mum, dad:

c. Good-looking:

d. Hard-working:

e. Less stubborn:

f. More patient:

g. But:

h. My duck:

i. Two pets:

j. Very kind:

k. As stubborn as:

2. Complete the statements below based on Victoria's text

a. I am _____ years old

b. Ava is more _____ than Grace.

c. Grace is more _____

d. My parents are very _____ and _____.

e. My mum is _____ than my dad

f. I am as _____ as my mother

g. We have _____ pets

h. My dog is _____lazy

4. Answer the questions on the three texts above

a. Where does Mauro Ferrari live?

b. Who is stricter, his mother or his father?

c. Who is as talkative as their parrot?

d. Who is as noisy as their duck?

e. Who has a stubborn father?

f. Who has a rabbit?

g. Who has an hamster?

h. Which one of Mauro's siblings is sportier?

i. Who is as funny as their mum?

3. Correct any of the statements below [about Mauro Ferrari's text] which are incorrect

a. Mauro Ferrari ha tre animali

b. Marco è meno sportivo di Barbara

c. Marco è più alto di Barbara

d. Mauro è tanto chiacchierone quanto il criceto

e. Suo [his] padre è più severo di sua madre

THE LANGUAGE GYM

Unit 9. Comparing people: TRANSLATION/WRITING

1. Translate into English

a. È così pigro come...

b. È più giovane di....

c. Meno gentile di...

d. Tanto sportivo quanto...

e. Sono meno chiacchierone di...

2. Gapped sentences

a. Mia mamma è _____ alta _____ mia zia
[My mum is taller than my aunt]

b. _____ padre _____ meno _____ di mio fratello maggiore
[My father is stronger than my older brother]

c. I miei cugini _____ meno_____ di noi
[My cousins are less sporty than us]

d. _____ fratello è _____tonto del suo _____
[My brother is more stupid than his friend]

e. Mia nonna _____ _____ gentile _____ mio nonno
[My granmother is as kind as my grandfather]

f. Alberta è _____ diligente di _____
[Alberta is more hard-working than us]

g. Il mio gatto è meno _____ del_____ cane
[My cat is less friendly than my dog]

h. Andrew _____ _____ testardo _____ sua moglie
[Andrew is more stubborn than his wife]

3. Phrase-level translation [En to It]

a. My mother is...

b. Taller than...

c. As slim as...

d. Less stubborn than...

e. I am shorter than...

f. My parents are...

g. My cousins are...

h. As fat as...

i. They are as strong as...

j. My grandparents are...

k. I am as lazy as...

4. Sentence-level translation [En to It]

a. My older sister is taller than my younger sister

b. My father is as stubborn as my mother

c. My teacher is more hard-working than me

d. I am less intelligent than my brother

e. My best friend is stronger and sportier than me

f. My tortoise is less fast than my hamster

g. My cousins are as friendly as my friends

h. My duck is noisier than my dog

i. Pedro is younger than Leonardo

j. Ronaldo is faster than Giorgio

k. We are as kind as my parents

Revision Quickie 2 : Family, Pets and Jobs

1. Match

1. Dipendente	a. Doctor
2. Avvocato	b. Waiter
3. Infermiere	c. Journalist
4. Cameriere	d. Nurse
5. Giornalista	e. IT worker
6. Medico	f. Employee
7. Commesso	g. Teacher
8. Informatico	h. Lawyer
9. Professore	i. Shop-assistant

2. Sort the words listed below in the categories in the table

a. operaio; b. alto; c. commesso; d. simpatico; e. basso;
f. cugino; g. professoressa; h. infermiere; i. zio; j. padre;
k. occhi; l. capelli; m. coniglio; n. pompiere; o. mamma; p.
fratello; q. pesce; r. castani; s. anatra; t. gatto;
u. informatico

Descrizioni	Animali	Lavori	Famiglia

3. Complete with the missing adjectives

a. Mio padre è _____ *[fat]*

b. Mia madre è _____ *[tall]*

c. Mio fratello è _____ *[nice]*

d. La mia amica è _____ *[generous]*

e. Mio cugino è _____ *[mean]*

f. Il mio gatto è _____ *[boring]*

4. Complete with the missing nouns

a. Mio padre lavora come _____ *[accountant]*

b. Mia madre è _____ *[scientist]*

c. Il mio migliore amico è _____ *[footballer]*

d. Mia sorella è _____ *[air hostess]*

e. Mio cugino è _____ *[student]*

f. Io lavoro come _____ *[doctor]*

g. Marta è _____ *[shop assistant]*

h. Tu lavori come_____ *[singer]*

5. Match the opposites

1. alto	a. vivace
2. bella	b. tonto
3. grossa	c. basso
4. pigro	d. silenzioso
5. intelligente	e. brutta
6. rumoroso	f. impaziente
7. cattivo	g. magra
8. paziente	h. buono

7. Complete with the correct verb

a. Mia madre ____ alta *[My mother is tall]*

b. _____ i capelli neri *[I have black hair]*

c. _____ come cantante *[I work as a singer]*

d. Mio padre ____ quaranta anni *[My father is 40]*

e. Quante persone ci _____ nella tua famiglia?

[How many people are there in your family?]

f. I miei amici _____ alti *[My friends are tall]*

g. Mio zio non _____ *[My uncle doesn't work]*

h. Il mio cane ___ _____Joy *[My dog is called Joy]*

i. Mio zio e mia zia _____ irlandesi

[My aunt and my uncle are Irish]

6. Complete the numbers below

a. Quatto_ _ _ _ _ [14]

b. Quara_ _ _ [40]

c. Sessa_ _ _ [60]

d. Cinqu_ _ _ _ [50]

e. Settan_ _ [70]

f. Nov_ _ _ _ _ [90]

UNIT 10
Saying what's in my school bag / classroom/ describing colour

Grammar Time: Avere & Agreements

In this unit will learn how to say:

- What objects you have in your schoolbag/pencil case/classroom
- Words for classroom equipment
- What you have and don't have

You will revisit the following:
- Colours
- How adjectives agree in gender and number with nouns
- Introducing yourself (e.g. name, age, town, country)
- Pets

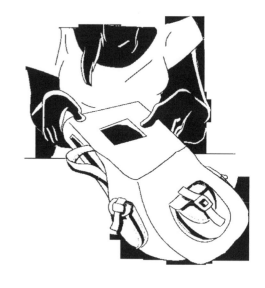

UNIT 10. Saying what's in my school bag/classroom:
'Cosa c'è nella tua aula/nel tuo zaino?'
[What is in your classroom/schoolbag?]

Nella mia aula *[In my classroom]*
Nel mio zaino *[In my schoolbag]*

C'è/Non c'è *[There is/There isn't]*	**un astuccio** *[a pencil case]*	**MASC**	azzurr**o**
	un banco *[a desk]*		bianc**o**
Ho/Non ho *[I have/I don't have]*	**un computer** *[a computer]*		giall**o**
	un diario *[a diary]*		grigi**o**
Ho bisogno/non ho bisogno di *[I need/ I do not need]*	**un dizionario** *[a dictionary]*		ner**o**
	un foglio *[a paper]*		ross**o**
	un libro *[a book]*		marrone
	un pennarello *[a felt-tip pen]*		verde
			arancione
Posso avere... *May I have...*	**un quaderno** *[an exercise book]*		blu
	un temperino *[a pencil sharpener]*		rosa
			viola
		MASC PLURAL	**per favore?**
	dei quaderni *[some exercise books]*		giall**i**
Ci sono/Non ci sono *[There are/There aren't]*	**dei pennarelli** *[some felt-tip pens]*		ross**i**
	una calcolatrice *[a calculator]*	**FEM**	azzurr**a**
	una colla *[a glue stick]*		bianc**a**
Il mio amico Paolo ha *[My friend Paolo has]*	**una gomma** *[a rubber]*		giall**a**
			grigi**a**
	una lavagna *[a whiteboard]*		ner**a**
	una matita *[a pencil]*		ross**a**
Il mio amico Paolo non ha *[My friend Paolo does not have]*	**una penna** *[a pen]*		marrone
	una riga *[a ruler]*		verde
			arancione
	una sedia *[a chair]*		blu
			rosa
		FEM PLURAL	viola
	delle forbici *[some scissors]*		gialle
	delle matite *[some pencils]*		ross**e**

Author's note: The words for colour **blu, rosa, viola** do not change in number or gender.
Ex. *La matita blu / le matite blu*

 **THE LANGUAGE GYM**

Unit 10. Saying what's in my school bag: VOCABULARY BUILDING

1. Complete with the missing words

a. Nel mio zaino ho un _____
[In my schoolbag I have an exercise book]

b. Ho bisogno di una _____ *[I need an eraser]*

c. Non ho _____ penna *[I don't have a pen]*

d. Il mio amico _____un foglio *[My friend has a paper]*

e. Ho una _____ *[I have a calculator]*

f. Posso _____ una_____ per favore?
[May I have a ruler please?]

g. _____ ho una _____ *[I don't have a chair]*

h. Il mio _____ non ha delle _____
[My friend doesn't have scissors]

2. Match up

1.una gomma	a.a pencil
2.una matita	b.a planner
3.un diario	c.I have a...
4.una sedia	d.a sharpener
5.ho un	e.a pen
6.ho bisogno di	f.I don't have a
7.non ho un	g.please
8.un temperino	h.an eraser
9.una penna	i.I need a
10.per favore	j.a chair

3. Translate into English

a. Ho una gomma e una riga

b. Mel mio zaino c'è un libro

c. Posso avere un diario per favore?

d. Nel mio astuccio c'è una penna

e. Ci sono tre matite rosse

f. Ho bisogno di un dizionario per favore

g. C'è un computer sul *[on the]* banco

h. Ho due quaderni verdi

4. Add the missing letter

a. Un tempe_ino

b. Una g_mma

c. Ho biso_no

d. Nel mio as_uccio

e. Una _iario

f. Uno zai__o

g. Delle fo_bici

h. Una lava_na

5. Anagrams

a. tiMate = Matite

b. uccioAst =

c. raneAncio =

d. Bicano =

e. orFbici =

f. inoZa =

g. llaCo =

h. rdVee =

6. Broken words

a. N____ m___ z_____ h_____ u__ a_____
= *[In my bag I have a pencil case]*

b. N___ m___ a_____ c___ s_____ d_____m_____
= *[In my pencil case there are some pencils]*

c. N____ h____ u____ g_____ = *[I don't have an eraser]*

d. H_ b_____ d___ u___ r_____ = *[I need a ruler]*

e. C'____ u_____ l_____ = *[There is a whiteboard]*

f. H__ d_____ p_____ b_____ = *[I have some blue pens]*

g. H___ b_____ d_ u__ p_____
= *[I need a felt tip pen]*

7. Complete with a suitable word

a. Ho un _____

b. Nel mio _____ c'è una riga

c. Mi piace il colore _____

d. Posso avere un_____ per _____

e. Un quaderno _____

f. Una _____ rossa

g. La mia _____ha un diario

h. Ho _____ di una colla

i. La mia maestra ha un _____

j. Ci sono dei _____ gialli

Unit 10. Saying what's in my school bag: READING

Mi chiamo Eloïse. Ho dodici anni e vivo a Parigi, in Francia. Siamo in quattro nella mia famiglia. Ho un gatto bianco. Nel mio zaino ci sono molte cose: una matita rossa, una penna gialla, una riga blu e una gomma bianca. La mia amica Claudia ha solo una matita nel suo astuccio. Però è **fortunata** [lucky] perché ha un cavallo grigio!

Mi chiamo Andrea. Ho quindici anni e vivo a Perugia, nel centro dell'Italia. Siamo in tre nella mia famiglia. Ho un criceto molto buffo. Nella mia classe c'è una lavagna, un computer e trenta banchi. La mia classe è molto grande. Io ho due matite grigie, una gomma, un temperino e una riga nuova. Il mio amico ha matite di tanti colori.

Mi chiamo Lucas. Ho diciotto anni e vivo a Mallorca, in Spagna. Mi piace la mia scuola. Nella mia aula ci sono venti banchi e venti sedie. La mia è una bella classe perché i miei amici sono simpatici ed il mio professore è molto divertente. Però, non ho una penna, né una matita, né una riga, né una gomma. Non ho niente. Praticamente, ho bisogno di tutto. A casa ho una gatta bianca molto carina.

Mi c_____ Leo. Ho otto a_____ e v_____ a Positano, in Italia. Nella mia a_____ ci sono ____ computer, una l_____ e tanti b_____. Nel _____ zaino ho un l_____, due penne, tre q_____ e una m_____. La mia **compagna** [classmate] Ariella ha molte p_____ colorate ma non ha un d_____. Mi piace molto il mio maestro perché ____ molto sim_____. A casa ____ un serpente verde!

Mi chiamo Emiliano. Ho undici anni e vivo a Buenos Aires, in Argentina. Parlo spagnolo. Nella mia famiglia ci sono quattro persone. Vado d'accordo con mia madre ma di meno con mio padre. Lui è un po' antipatico e fa l'avvocato. Nella mia classe non ci sono molte cose. C'é una lavagna ma non c'é un computer! Ci sono ventotto banchi, ma solo ventisette sedie. È un problema! Io ho una matita, una calcolatrice e un diario.

1. Find the Italian for the following in Eloïse's text

a. I am 12

b. I live in Paris

c. We are 4 people

d. a white cat

e. a red pencil

f. a yellow pen

g. there are many things

h. only has one

i. she is lucky

j. a grey horse

2. Find Someone Who – which person...

a. ...has a blue ruler?

b. ...has most tables in their class?

c. ...has a class with one student always standing?

d. ...has no school equipment?

e. ...has a green snake?

f. ...doesn't like their dad?

3. Answer the following questions about Lucas' text

a. Where does Lucas live?

b. Does he like his school?

c. How many tables and chairs are there in his class?

d. How does he describe his class and teacher?

e. What school equipment does he have?

f. What do you think is the meaning of the word 'né'?

g. What does he say about his pet?

4. Fill in the table below

Name	Leo	Andrea
Age		
City/town		
Items in bag/pencil case		

Unit 10. Saying what's in my school bag: TRANSLATION

1. Faulty translation: spot and correct [in the English] any translation mistakes you find below

a. Nella mia aula ci sono due lavagne e un computer. Non mi piace il mio professore = *In my class there is a whiteboard and a computer. I like my teacher.*

b. Non ho molte cose nel mio astuccio. Ho una matita rosa ma non ho una riga = *I have many things in my pencil case. I have a red pencil but I don't have an eraser.*

c. La famiglia del mio amico Emilio è composta da cinque persone. Lui ha bisogno di una matita nera e un diario = *My friend Emilio has five people in his family. He needs a black pen and a diary.*

d. Professoressa, posso avere un temperino e una gomma per favore?= *Mrs..., can I have a pencil sharpener and a ruler please?*

e. Nella mia classe ci sono trenta sedie e trenta banchi. Però non abbiamo dizionari! Prof, mi presta un dizionario? = *In my class there are thirty computers and thirty chairs. But we do not have rulers! Mr...can you lend me a ruler?*

2. Translate into English

a. Posso avere una gomma, per favore?

b. Ho una matita nera

c. Non ho un temperino grigio

d. Il mio amico ha un libro

e. Mi piace il mio professore

f. Dei fogli bianchi

g. Delle penne rosse

h. Non ho un dizionario di italiano

i. Prof, mi presta una matita per favore?

3. Phrase-level translation [En to It]

a. a red book=

b. a black calculator =

c. I don't have =

d. I need a... =

e. I like =

f. There are... =

g. Please, may I have... =

h. My friend has... =

i. In my schoolbag there is... =

4. Sentence-level translation [En to It]

a. There are 20 tables

b. There is a whiteboard

c. My teacher is nice

d. I have some blue pens

e. I have some orange pencils

f. I need an eraser and a sharpener

g. May I have a book, please?

h. My class is very big and pretty

i. My father is a teacher

Unit 10. Saying what's in my school bag: WRITING

1. Split sentences

1. Ho una	a. ha una penna
2. Il mio professore	b. banchi
3. La mia aula	c. quaderno per favore
4. Ci sono trenta	d. calcolatrice
5. Il mio amico non	e. è grande
6. Posso avere un	f. c' è un astuccio
7. Nel mio zaino	g. è simpatico

2. Rewrite the sentences in the correct order

a. Ho una calcolatrice di bisogno

b. una rossa matita Ho e una nera penna

c. mia molto grande aula è La

d. Il amico ha mio un libro blu

e. Non diario ho un né gomma una

f. casa Nella mia tartaruga ho verde

g. Mio è medico padre e in un lavora ospedale

h. favore per Posso una gomma avere

3. Spot and correct the grammar and spelling [note: in several cases a word is missing]

a. Nella mia clase ci sono venti banco.

b. Io ho un matita gialla.

c. Nel mio astucio c' è sono due gomme.

d. La amica ha tre astucci colorati.

e. Ho bisogno de dizionario.

f. Il mio amico Fernando a due rosse penne.

g. Mia madre ingegnere e lavora in cittá.

h. Sono alto e forte. Ho il capello biondo e l'occhi azzurri.

4. Anagrams

a. ccioastu = astuccio

b. gnavala =

c. pucomret =

d. chiban =

e. peritemno =

f. zionadirio =

g. preforessossa =

6. Describe this person in Italian:

Name: Diego

Pet: A black horse

Hair: brown,short + blue eyes

School equipment: has pen, 2 pencils, ruler, eraser

Does not have: sharpener, paper, dictionary

Favourite colour: blue

5. Guided writing – write 4 short paragraphs describing the people below using the details in the box [I]

Person	Lives	Has	Hasn't	Needs
Natalia	Verona	Exercise book	Pen	Diary
Ivan	Pisa	Ruler	Pencil	A paper
Katia	Cosenza	Felt-tip	Sharpener	A glue stick

Grammar Time 6: AVERE (Part 3) + AGREEMENTS
Present indicative of "Avere" (to have) and agreement training

school items		dodici	**age**
un astuccio	una calcolatrice	tredici	
un computer	una matita	quattordici	
un dizionario	una penna	quindici	
un libro	una sedia	sedici **anni**	
un quaderno		diciassette	
un pennarello		diciotto	
		diciannove	
		venti	

avere	ho [I have]	due nonni, due nonne	**family**
	hai [you have]	un fratello, una sorella	
	ha [he/she has]	due fratelli, due sorelle	
(non)	abbiamo [we have]	un figlio, una figlia	
	avete [you all have]	un cugino, una cugina	
	hanno [they have]	un fratellastro, una sorellastra	
		uno zio, una zia	

school	arte alle otto	un cane	**pets**
	scienze alle nove	un cavallo	
	spagnolo alle dieci	un coniglio	
lezione di	italiano alle undici	un criceto	
	geografia alle dodici	un gatto	
	storia all'una	un pappagallo	
	matematica alle due	un pesce	
	educazione fisica alle tre	una gallina	
		una tartaruga	
dei professori molto bravi		un uccello	
dei professori molto antipatici			

Present indicative of *"Avere"* + Agreements: Verb drills (1)

1. Match up

1. Io ho	a. we have
2. Tu hai	b. I have
3. Lui/lei ha	c. they have
4. Noi abbiamo	d. you have
5. Voi avete	e. he/she has
6. Loro hanno	f. you all have

2. Complete with the missing word (pets/family members)

a. Non _____ animali [I don't have pets]

b. _____ un gatto grigio [We have a grey cat]

c. _____ due tartarughe [They have two turtles]

d. _____ fratelli? [Do you have siblings?]

e. _____ animali? [Do you guys have pets?]

f. Matteo ____ un porcellino d'India [Matteo has a guinea pig]

g. Mio cugino non _____animali [My cousin doesn't have pets]

h. I miei cugini _____ tre cani [My cousins have three dogs]

3. Complete with the present indicative form of "avere"

io _____

tu _____

lui, lei _____

noi _____

voi _____

loro _____

4. Add in the correct ending

a. Mio cugino non h____ animali

b. I miei zii non ha_____ due gatti

c. Oggi (io) h____ lezione di storia

d. Alle dodici (noi) abb_____ geografia

e. Mio fratello h____ dieci anni

f. I miei genitori h_____ quaranta anni

g. Mio padre h____ i capelli bianchi

h. Le mie amiche han_____ i capelli rossi

i. Giulio e Stefano, (voi) av_____ una matita rossa?

5. Complete with the missing form of "avere"

a. Mio nonno _____ settantadue anni.

b. Mia madre _____ i capelli lunghi e neri.

c. Tu _____ gli occhi azzurri, invece io _____ gli occhi verdi.

d. Mio zio Mario non _____ capelli, è calvo!

e. Tu_____ fratelli o sorelle?

f. Voi _____ una matita e una gomma.

g. Io non _____ animali, ma mio fratello _____ un criceto.

6. Translate into Italian

a. My father has blue eyes

b. I don't have pets

c. I don't have a pen

d. In my pencil case I have a ruler

e. Do you have any felt-tip pens?

f. I have a dog at home

g. My mother has a black cat

h. My younger sister has a red schoolbag

i. Do you guys have history today?

j. No, we have Italian at ten.

Present indicative of "Avere" + Agreements
Verb drills (2)

7. Translate the pronoun and verb into Italian as shown in the example

I have: **(Io) ho**

You have: (   )

She has: (   )

He has: (   )

We have: (   )

You all have: (   )

They have: (   )

They do not have: (   )

8. Translate into Italian. Topic: Pets and colours

a. We have a blue parrot

b. I have two green turtles

c. My brother has a white guinea pig

d. My uncles have a black horse

e. My sister has a red and black spider

f. We don't have pets at home

g. Do you have pets at home?

9. Translate into Italian. Topic: family members

a. I don't have brothers

b. We have two grandparents

c. My mother has no sisters

d. Do you have any brothers or sisters?

e. Do you guys have cousins?

f. I don't have any brothers

g. You have one brother and one sister

10. Translate into Italian. Topic: School bag

a. They have five pencils

b. You have a rubber and a pen

c. I have a green exercise book

d. She does not have a pencil sharpner

e. Do you have a dictionary?

f. My teacher has some blu felt-tip pens

g. We do not have a glue stick

11. Translate into Italian. Topic: Hair and eyes

a. I have black hair

b. We have blue eyes

c. She has curly hair

d. My mother has blonde hair

e. Do you have grey eyes ?

f. They have green eyes

g. My brother has brown eyes

h. We do not have a beard

i. You all have beautiful eyes

j. My parents have red hair

k. You have no hair

l. My sister has very long hair

Grammar Time 7: Agreements (Part 1)

1. Complete the table

English	Italiano
Yellow	
	Rosa
	Grigio
Green	
Red	
	Viola
	Arancione
Black	
	Bianco
Blue	

2. Translate into English

a. Una matita gialla: _____

b. Un astuccio nero: _____

c. Due quaderni rosa: _____

d. Tre pennarelli verdi:_____

e. Una penna blu: _____

f. Due gomme azzurre: _____

g. Dei temperini arancione: _____

h. Dei fogli bianchi: _____

i. Uno zaino rosso: _____

j. Delle forbici bianche e nere:_____

3. Provide the feminine version of each adjective in the table

Maschile	Femminile
Giallo	
Verde	
Azzurro	
Rosso	
Bianco	
Nero	
Arancione	
Rosa	

4. Complete with the missing adjective

a. Io ho uno zaino _____ *[I have a red schoolbag]*

b. Non ho una penna _____ *[I don't have a black pen]*

c. Ho un astuccio _____ *[I have an orange pencil case]*

d. Ho una riga _____ *[I have a yellow ruler]*

e. Hai un foglio _____ *[You have a white sheet of paper]*

f. Abbiamo due forbici _____ *[We have two red scissors]*

g. Ho una calcolatrice _____ *[I have a pink calculator]*

h. Tu hai un libro _____ *[You have a green book]*

i. Posso avere una matita _____? *[May I please have a purple pencil?]*

5. Translate into Italian

a. a red chair

b. a black desk

c. a green schoolbag

d. a yellow pencil case

e. two green rulers

f. two blue scissors

6. Translate into Italian

a. I have a red pen and a blue diary

b. Felipe has a green schoolbag

c. Do you have a white pencil case?

d. Do you guys have any red markers?

e. I have a pink sheet of paper

f. We have a yellow schoolbag

g. My teacher has a black and white ruler

 **THE LANGUAGE GYM**

UNIT 11 (Part 1)
Talking about food:
Likes / Dislikes / Reasons

Grammar Time: Mangiare /Bere

In this unit will learn how to say:

- What food you like/dislike and to what extent
- Why you like/dislike it (old and new expressions)
- New adjectives
- The full conjugation of 'mangiare' *[to eat]* and 'bere' *[to drink]*

You will revisit the following
- Time markers
- Providing a justification

UNIT 11: Talking about food
Likes / Dislikes / Reasons [Part 1]
'Cosa ti piace mangiare/bere?'
[What do youlike to eat/drink?]

Singular			
Amo/Adoro *[I love]* **Mi piace molto** *[I like a lot]* **Mi piace** *[I like]* **Mi piace un po'** *[I like a bit]* **Non mi piace** *[I don't like]* **Odio** *[I hate]* **Preferisco** *[I prefer]*	**il caffè** *[coffee]* **il formaggio** *[cheese]* **il latte** *[milk]* **il miele** *[honey]* **il pane** *[bread]* **il pesce** *[fish]* **il pollo arrosto** *[roast chicken]* **il riso** *[rice]* **il succo di frutta** *[fruit juice]* **l'acqua** *[water]* **la carne** *[meat]* **la cioccolata** *[chocolate]* **la frutta** *[fruit]*	**perché è** *[because it is]*	**caldo/a** *[hot]* **delizioso/a** *[delicious]* **disgustoso/a** *[disgusting]* **dolce** *[sweet]* **grasso/a** *[oily, greasy]* **insipido/a** *[bland]* **malsano/a** *[unhealthy]* **piccante** *[spicy]* **ricco/a di vitamine** *[rich in vitamin]* **rinfrescante** *[refreshing]* **sano/a** *[healthy]* **saporito/a** *[tasty]*
Plural			
Amo/adoro *[I love]* **Mi piacciono molto** *[I like a lot]* **Mi piacciono** *[I like]* **Mi piacciono un po'** *[I like a bit]* **Non mi piacciono** *[I don't like]* **Odio** *[I hate]* **Preferisco** *[I prefer]*	**i gamberi** *[prawns]* **i pomodori** *[tomatoes]* **le arance** *[oranges]* **le banane** *[bananas]* **le cioccolate** *[chocolates]* **le mele** *[apples]* **le uova** *[eggs]* **le verdure** *[vegetables]* **gli hamburger** *[burgers]*	**perché sono** *[because they are]*	**caldi/e** *[hot]* **deliziosi/e** *[delicious]* **disgustosi/e** *[disgusting]* **dolci** *[sweet]* **grassi/e** *[oily, greasy]* **insipidi/e** *[bland]* **malsani/e** *[unhealthy]* **piccanti** *[spicy]* **ricchi/ricche di proteine** *[rich in protein]* **rinfrescanti** *[refreshing]* **sani/e** *[healthy]*

Author's notes:
[1] The adjectives above ending in 'o' change to 'a' with feminine nouns.
Ex. *Mi piace l**a** frutta perché è delizios**a***
[2] Adjectives ending in 'e' do not change in the feminine. However, they change to 'i' in the plural.
*Ex: La cioccolata è dolc**e** / Le cioccolate sono dolc**i**.*
[3] When used in the plural, the adjectives in 'o' change to 'i' and the adjective in 'a' change to 'e'.
Ex.: *Mi piacciono **i** gamberi perché sono saporit**i** /Mi piacciono l**e** verdur**e** perché sono san**e***

 **THE LANGUAGE GYM**

Unit 11. Talking about food (Part 1): VOCABULARY BUILDING (Part 1)

1. Match up

1. Le banane	a. Eggs
2. Le fragole	b. Apples
3. La carne	c. Prawns
4. Il pollo	d. Milk
5. L'acqua	e. Fruit
6. Il latte	f. Water
7. Le uova	g. Burgers
8. I gamberi	h. Chicken
9. Gli hamburger	i. Meat
10. La frutta	j. Bananas
11. Le mele	k. Strawberries

2. Complete

a. Mi piace molto il _____ [I like chicken a lot]

b. Adoro i _____ [I love prawns]

c. Mi piacciono le _____ [I like strawberries]

d. Amo il _____ [I love milk]

e. Adoro le _____ [I love bananas]

f. Preferisco l'_____ minerale [I prefer mineral water]

g. Non mi piacciono i _____ [I don't like tomatoes]

h. Odio il _____ [I hate fish]

i. Amo la _____ [I love fruit]

j. Non mi piacciono le _____ [I don't like eggs]

3. Translate into English

a. Mi piace la frutta

b. Odio le uova

c. Amo il pollo arrosto

d. Mi piacciono le mele

e. Odio la carne

f. Preferisco l'insalata verde

g. Non mi piacciono i pomodori

h. Odio il latte

4. Complete the words

a. Le uo_____

b. Le ban_____

c. La fr_____

d. Le verd_____

e. Gli hamb_____

f. I gam_____

g. I pom_____

h. L'ac_____

5. Fill the gaps with either *'mi piace'* or *'mi piacciono'* as appropriate

a. Non _____ le uova

b. _____ l'acqua

c. _____ il pollo

d. _____ gli hamburger

e. _____ le verdure

f. _____ la carne

g. _____ la frutta

h. _____ i gamberi

i. _____ la pasta

6. Translate into Italian

a. I like eggs

b. I love oranges

c. I hate tomatoes

d. I don't like prawns

e. I love fruit juice

f. I don't like vegetables

g. I really like milk

h. I like apples but I prefer grapes

i. I don't like cheese

Unit 11. Talking about food (Part 1): VOCABULARY BUILDING (Part 2)

1. Complete with the missing words. The initial letter of each word is given

a. Queste banane sono d_____
[These bananas are disgusting]

b. Queste mele sono d_____
[These apples are delicious]

c. Questo pollo è molto p_____
[This chicken is very spicy]

d. Non mi piace la c_____ [I don't like meat]

e. Questo caffè è molto d_____
[This coffee is very sweet]

f. Le salsicce sono m_____
[Sausages are unhealthy]

g. Le verdure sono s_____
[Vegetables are healthy]

h. Amo il _____ [I love milk]

2. Complete the table

Italiano	English
Il latte	
	Roast chicken
Il pesce	
Le uova	
	Water
	Bread
I cereali	
Il pane tostato	
	Vegetables

3. Complete with 'mi piace' or 'mi piacciono' as appropriate

a. _____ le mele

b. _____ il latte

c. Non _____ i cereali

d. _____ il pane tostato

e. _____ il succo di frutta

f. Non _____ la pasta

g. _____ il riso

h. Non _____ il caffè

4. Broken words

a. N___ m___ p_____ l____ u_____

[I don't like eggs]

b. A_____ l_____ m_____ [I love apples]

c. O_____ g____ h_____ [I hate burgers]

d. M___ p_____ m_____ l___ c_____

[I really like chocolates]

e. I__ m____c_____ è c_____ [my coffee is hot]

f. I__ p_____ è s_____ [fish is healthy]

g. I__ curry indiano è p_____ [Indian curry is spicy]

5. Complete each sentence in a way which is logical and grammatically correct

a. Le _____ non sono sane

b. Le banane sono _____

c. Non mi _____ il latte

d. Mi _____ il pollo arrosto

e. _____ il pesce perché è saporito

f. _____ la carne rossa p perché è malsana

g. _____ le verdure perché sono ricche di vitamine

THE LANGUAGE GYM

91

Ciao, mi chiamo Manuela. Cosa preferisco mangiare? Amo i frutti di mare, quindi mi piacciono molto i gamberi ed i calamari perché sono deliziosi. Mi piace molto il pesce perché è saporito e ricco di proteine. Soprattutto mangio il salmone, prodotto tipico scozzese, dove vivo. Mi piace abbastanza il pollo arrosto. Inoltre, amo la frutta specialmente uva e fragole. Non mi piacciono molto le verdure perché non sono saporite, ma fanno bene alla salute!

Salve, mi chiamo Alessandro. Cosa preferisco mangiare? Amo le verdure. Le mangio tutti i giorni. Le mie verdure preferite sono gli spinaci, le carote e le melanzane perché ricche di vitamine e minerali. Mi piace anche la frutta perché è sana, rinfrescante e deliziosa. Sono vegetariano. Odio la carne e il pesce. Anche se sono ricchi di proteine non sono saporiti.

Ciao, mi chiamo Violetta. Cosa preferisco mangiare? Adoro la carne, soprattutto la carne di agnello, perché molto saporita. Mi piace molto il pollo arrosto piccante, lo trovo saporito ed è ricco di proteine. Mi piacciono abbastanza le uova. Sono sane e ricche di vitamine e proteine. Mi piace abbastanza la frutta, soprattutto le ciliegie. Sono molto deliziose. Però non mi piacciono per niente le mele.

Ciao, mi chiamo James. Cosa mi piace mangiare? Preferisco la carne. La adoro perché è saporita, soprattutto mi piacciono molto gli hamburger. Mi piace anche la frutta perché è dolce. Non mi piacciono le verdure. Odio i pomodori e le carote. Non mi piacciono le uova. Sono ricche di vitamine e proteine ma sono disgustose. Non mi piacciono le patate fritte perché sono malsane.

Salve, mi chiamo Fernando. Cosa mi piace mangiare? Amo la carne rossa perché è saporita e ricca di proteine. Non mangio molto pesce perché è disgustoso. Mi piacciono abbastanza i calamari fritti, però non fanno bene alla salute. Mi piace moltissimo la frutta, soprattutto le banane, perché sono deliziose, ricche di vitamine e non sono care. Non mi piacciono le mele e odio le arance. Non mangio verdure.

1. Find the Italian for the following in Manuela's text

a. I love seafood

b. I really like prawns

c. Are delicious

d. because it is tasty

e. I eat salmon

f. I quite like

g. Moreover

h. Above all

i. They are not tasty

2. Fernando or Manuela? Write *F* or *M* next to each statement below

a. I love seafood - *M*

b. I hate oranges

c. I like fruit a lot

d. I don't like vegetables

e. I prefer salmon

f. I quite like squid

g. I prefer bananas

h. I don't eat much fish

i. I love red meat

3. Complete the following sentences based on Alessandro's text

a. Alessandro loves_____

b. He eats them _____

c. His favourite vegetables are _____,
_____ and _____

d. He also likes _____ because it is
_____ and _____

e. He hates _____ and _____

4. Fill in the table below about James

Loves	Likes a lot	Hates	Doesn't like

Unit 11. Talking about food (Part 1): Translation 1

1. Faulty translation: spot and correct [IN THE ENGLISH] any translation mistakes you find below

a. Adoro i gamberi: *I hate prawns*

b. Odio il pollo e la zuppa: *I like meat and soup*

c. Mi piace il miele: *I don't like honey*

d. Amo le arance e l'uva: *I love apples and grapes*

e. Le uova sono disgustose: *Eggs are tasty*

f. Le banana sono ricche di vitamine: *Bananas are rich in protein*

g. Il pesce fa bene alla salute: *Fish is unhealthy*

h. Preferisco la cioccolata calda: *I prefer hot water*

i. Le cioccolate fanno male alla salute: *Chocolates are healthy*

j. Mi piace il riso perché non ha glutine: *I hate rice because it is gluten-free*

k. Il pane è salato: *Fried squid is salty*

l. Il curry indiano è piccante: *Indian curry is sweet*

2. Translate into English

a. I gamberi sono saporiti e sani

b. Il pesce è delizioso e ricco di vitamine

c. Il pollo è ricco di proteine

d. Amo il riso perché non ha glutine.

e. La carne rossa è poco salutare

f. La frutta è rinfrescante e dolce

g. Le uova sono saporite e ricche di proteine

h. Preferisco l'acqua minerale.

i. La zuppa è buona e salutare.

3. Phrase-level translation [En to It]

a. Spicy chicken:

b. This coffee:

c. I quite like:

d. Very sweet:

e. A disgusting apple:

f. Some delicious oranges:

g. I don't like:

h. I love pizza because:

i. It is refreshing:

j. Mineral water:

k. It is bland:

4. Sentence-level translation [En to It]

a. I like spicy chicken a lot

b. I like oranges because they are healthy

c. Meat is tasty but unhealthy

d. This coffee is hot

e. Eggs are disgusting but healthy

f. I love oranges. They are delicious and rich in vitamins

g. I love fish. It is tasty and rich in protein

h. Vegetables are disgusting

i. I prefer fruit because is refreshing

j. This tea is sweet

Unit 11. Talking about food (Part 1): Translation 2

Paragraph 1	Tick a box each time you spot the correct translation in the text				Translate the paragraph into English
Ciao, mi chiamo Albert e sono australiano. Faccio colazione alle sette. Mi piace mangiare la frutta perché è sana. A pranzo mangio un panino al formaggio o una zuppa di verdure. Di solito bevo acqua o una limonata. La sera ceno a casa. Amo le salsicce perché sono saporite.	For lunch I eat	I have breakfast	or a vegetable soup	In the evening	_____ _____
	because it is healthy	at seven	and Italian fluently	I love sausages	_____ _____
	Hi, my name is Albert	a cheese sandwich	because they are tasty	I usually drink	_____ _____
	and I am Australian	water or lemonade	I like eating fruit	I have dinner at home	_____ _____
Paragraph 2					
Salve, io sono Gloria. Normalmente a colazione mangio cereali e bevo un caffè in cucina. Di solito pranzo verso l'una, mangio un'insalata o una pizza. Mi piace moltissimo. Non mangio mai patate fritte perché penso che sono malsane. Odio il pesce perché è insipido.	Hello, I am Gloria	I never eat	I really like it	and I drink	_____ _____
	I usually have lunch	because I think that	Normally for breakfast	they are unhealthy	_____ _____
	chips	in the kitchen	it is bland	I eat cereals	_____ _____
	a coffee	a salad or a pizza	I hate fish because	around 1pm, I eat	_____ _____
Paragraph 3					
Buonasera, mi chiamo Yan. Sono cinese ma parlo italiano. Di solito non faccio colazione perché non ho tempo. A pranzo mangio sempre riso con verdure e pollo e bevo un té. Mi piacciono le cioccolate anche se preferisco le banane o le mele. La sera con la mia famiglia ceniamo verso le sette.	I am Chinese	and I am 14	I like chocolates	and I drink tea	_____ _____
	Good evening, my name is Yan	For lunch	and Spanish very well	I usually don't have breakfast	_____ _____
	vegetables and chicken	we have dinner around 7	because it is big	I eat rice with	_____ _____
	bananas and apples	because I do not have time	even if I prefer	In the evening with my family	_____ _____

Unit 11. Talking about food (Part 1): WRITING

1. Split sentences

Amo il pollo [1]	minerale
Odio le verdure perché	arrosto [1]
Preferisco la	è dolce
Questo caffè	sono disgustose
Mi piacciono	saporiti ma malsani
I calamari fritti sono	le mele
Adoro l'acqua	pizza

2. Rewrite the sentences in the correct order

a. il Amo arrosto pollo = *Amo il pollo arrosto*

b. le verdure Odio

c. caffè Questo amaro è

d. frutta bene fa La alla salute

e. minerale l' Preferisco acqua

f. rinfrescanti sono arance Le

g. Mi sono le piacciono uova perché deliziose

h. piace carne rossa è non Mi salutare la ma sana

i. pesce il Adoro arrostito

j. La è ricca frutta vitamine di

k. cibo Mi piccante il piace

3. Spot the mistake and rewrite the correct sentence (there may be missing words)

a. Mi piace le patate fritte e le gamberi =

b. Non piacciono le verdure =

c. Il pollo e saporito è picante =

d. Adoro il cafe caldo =

e. Preferisco la insalada verde =

f. Odio a carne e il pescie =

4. Anagrams

a. tteLa

b. berimGa

c. rneCa = Carne

d. saInlata

e. canPicte

f. Dilesozio

g. mineViat

5. Guided writing – write 4 short paragraphs describing the people below using the details in the box [I]

Person	Loves	Quite likes	Doesn't like	Hates
Loretta	Pizza because tasty	Milk because healthy	Red meat	Eggs because disgusting
Eddie	Chicken because healthy	Oranges because sweet	Fish	Meat because unhealthy
Angela	Honey because sweet	Fish because tasty	Fruit	Vegetables because bland

6. Write a paragraph on Sara in Italian [using the third person singular]

Name: Sara

Age: 18

Description: tall, good-looking, sporty, friendly

Occupation: student

Food she loves: chicken

Food she likes: vegetables

Food she doesn't like: red meat

Food she hates: fish

THE LANGUAGE GYM

Grammar Time 8: MANGIARE/BERE
Present Tense
Talking about food [Part 1]

Bere [to drink]		
(Io) bev<u>o</u> [I drink]	**acqua** [water] **aranciata** [orangeade] **caffè** [coffee] **cioccolata calda** [hot chocolate] **latte** [milk] **limonata** [lemonade] **succo di mela** [apple juice]	**a volte** [sometimes]
(Tu) bev<u>i</u> [you drink]		
(Lui/lei) bev<u>e</u> [he/she drinks]		**mai** [never]
(Noi) bev<u>iamo</u> [we drink]	**tè** [tea] **vino** [wine]	
(Voi) bev<u>ete</u> [you all drink]		**ogni tanto** [from time to time]
(Loro) bev<u>ono</u> [they drink]		
Mangiare [to eat]		**raramente** [rarely]
(Io) mangi<u>o</u> [I eat]	**carne** [meat] **cioccolata** [chocolate] **insalata verde** [green salad] **formaggio** [cheese] **frutta** [fruit] **pane** [bread] **pesce** [fish] **pollo arrosto** [roast chicken] **riso** [rice] **cioccolate** [chocolates] **gamberi** [prawns] **hamburger** [burgers] **uova** [eggs] **mele** [apples] **arance** [oranges] **banane** [bananas] **pomodori** [tomatoes] **verdure** [vegetables]	**spesso** [often]
(Tu) mang<u>i</u> [you eat]		
(Lui/lei) mangi<u>a</u> [he/she eats]		**tutti i giorni** [every day]
(Noi) mangi<u>amo</u> [we eat]		
(Voi) mangi<u>ate</u> [you all eat]		**tutte le sere** [every evening]
(Loro) mangi<u>ano</u> [they eat]		

1. Match

a. Mangio	1. *They eat*
b. Mangi	2. *She eats*
c. Mangia	3. *We eat*
d. Mangiamo	4. *You guys eat*
e. Mangiate	5. *You eat*
f. Mangiano	6. *I eat*

2. Translate into English

a. A volte mangio pasta

b. Lui beve un succo di mela

c. Ogni tanto bevo del vino

d. Noi mangiamo pesce

e. Beviamo sempre acqua

f. Mai mangiamo insalata

g. Spesso tu mangi del riso

h. Voi bevete caffè?

i. Cosa mangiate?

j. Non bevo mai latte

3. Spot and correct the mistakes

a. Mio padre mangio pasta al pomodoro

b. Mio fratello ed io non mangiare verdure

c. Mia madre mai bevi ciocolata calda

d. I miei fratelli bevete molto succo frutta

e. (io) Mai bere café

f. Mia sorella mangi carne tutti giorni

g. (voi) Mangiano carne di cavallo?

h. Cosa bevo tu?

4. Complete with the verb *"bere"* or *"mangiare"*

a. Mio padre _____ molta frutta

b. (io) mai _____ succo di kiwi

c. (Tu) _____ pollo?

d. Mia madre ed io _____ molta pasta

e. I miei genitori _____ molta acqua

f. Mia sorella _____ molta cioccolata calda

g. Noi non _____ mai vino

h. (voi) Cosa _____ a colazione?

5. Translate into Italian

a. I eat pasta

b. We drink orange juice

c. What do you eat?

d. What do you guys drink?

e. We eat a lot of meat

f. They don't eat a lot of fish

g. She never eats vegetables

h. We drink lots of mineral water

6. Translate into Italian

a. I never eat red meat. I don't like it because it is unhealthy.

b. I rarely eat sausages. I don't like them because they are fatty.

c. I drink fruit juice often. I love it because it is delicious and healthy.

d. I eat cheese every day. I love it because it is very tasty.

e. I rarely eat vegetables. They are tasty but I don't like them because they are disgusting.

f. I never drink tea or coffee because I don't like them.

THE LANGUAGE GYM

UNIT 12 (Part 2)
Talking about food:
Likes/ Dislikes / Reasons

Grammar Time: Agreement (food)

In this unit you will consolidate all that you learnt in the previous unit and learn how to say:

- What meals you eat every day
- What you eat at each meal
- The full present indicative conjugation of *'mangiare', 'pranzare', 'cenare'*
- 'The', 'This' and 'these' in Italian

You will revisit the following:

- The full present indicative conjugation of regular ARE verbs
- Noun-to-adjective agreement

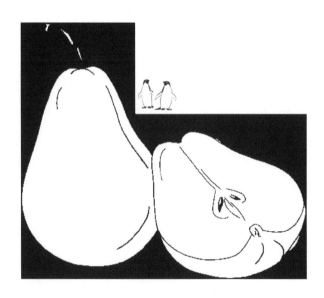

Unit 12 [Part 2]
Talking about food: Likes/ Dislikes/ Reasons
'Cosa ti piace mangiare? Perché?'
[What do you like to eat? Why?]

Meals		un cornetto SING [croissant]		amaro/a [bitter]
				aspro/a [acidic , sour]
A colazione [For breakfast]		un panino al prosciutto/ al formaggio [ham/cheese sandwich]		delizioso/a [delicious]
				disgustoso/a [disgusting]
A pranzo [For lunch]	mangio [I eat]	un'insalata mista [a mixed salad]	perché è [because it is]	dolce [sweet]
				insipido/a [bland]
		una mela/pera [an apple/a pear]		malsano/a [unhealthy]
A merenda [For snack]				nutritivo/a [nutritious]
		una pizza [a pizza]		piccante [spicy]
		una zuppa [a soup]		rinfrescante [refreshing]
A cena [For dinner]		acqua [water]		ricco/a di vitamine [rich in vitamins]
	bevo [I drink]	un caffè [a coffee]		saporito/a [tasty]
		latte [milk]		sano/a [healthy]
		un succo di arancia [an orange juice]		succoso/a [juicy]
Like/dislike		**PLU**		
Mi piace/Mi piacciono [I like]		i biscotti [biscuits]		amari/e [bitter]
		i calamari [squid]		aspri/e [acidic, sour]
	moltissimo [very much]	i dolci [cakes]		deliziosi/e [delicious]
Non mi piace/ Non mi piacciono [I don't like]		i gamberi [prawns]		disgustosi/e [disgusting]
	molto [a lot]	i panini al formaggio [cheese sandwiches]	perché sono [because they are]	dolci [sweet]
	un po' [a bit]	i pomodori [tomatoes]		insipidi/e [bland]
Amo/Adoro [I love]		le arance [oranges]		piccanti [spicy]
	per niente [at all]	le mele [apples]		saporiti/e [tasty]
Preferisco [I prefer]		le pesche [peaches]		sani/e [healthy]
		le salsicce [sausages]		
Odio [I hate]		le verdure [vegetables]		

THE LANGUAGE GYM

Unit 12. Talking about food – Likes/Dislikes (Part 2): VOCABULARY

1. Match

1. L'acqua	a. sandwich
2. Il pesce	b. water
3. Il riso	c. roast chicken
4. Il panino	d. fish
5. Il pollo arrosto	e. cheese
6. La carne	f. icecream
7. I calamari	g. prawns
8. I gamberi	h. strawberries
9. Il gelato	i. sausages
10. Il formaggio	j. rice
11. Le salsicce	k. squid
12. Le fragole	l. vegetables
13. Le verdure	m. meat

2. Complete with the missing words

a. Adoro l' _____ = [I love salad]

b. Mi piacciono molto le_____= [I like vegetables a lot]

c. Mi piacciono i f _____ d__m_____ = [I like seafood]

d. A colazione mangio una _____
= [For breakfast I eat an apple]

e. Questo _____è delizioso = [This chicken is delicious]

f. Questa _____ è molto succosa =[This meat is very juicy]

g. Preferisco le _____ = [I prefer sausages]

h. Mi piace _____ il miele = [I like honey very much]

i. Mi _____ i dolci = [I like cakes]

3. Complete with the missing letters

a. L' a_ _ _ _ = water

b. La _ _ _ ne = meat

c. Il to_ _ _ = tuna

d. S _ _ _ = healthy

e. Il _ _ _ _ _ggio= cheese

f. Il pa _ _ _ _ = sandwich

g. Gli sp _ _ _ _ _ = spinach

h. La fr_ _ _ _ _= strawberry

i. Suc _ _ _ _= juicy

j. Col_ _ _ _ _ _ = breakfast

k. Ce_ _ _ = dinner

l. Il r _ _ _ = rice

m. Il gel _ _ _ = ice cream

n. Disg_ _ _ _ _= disgusting

o. Molti_ _ _ _ _ = very much

p. Bu_ _ _ = good

q. Il p_ _ _ = bread

r. Pi _ _ _ _ _ e = spicy

4. Match

1. Nutritivo	a. Good
2. Fritto	b. Delicious
3. Succoso	c. Juicy
4. Saporito	d. Healthy
5. Salutare	e. Nutritious
6. Buono	f. Disgusting
7. Delizioso	g. Fried
8. Grasso	h. Sweet
9. Disgustoso	i. Fatty
10. Dolce	j. Tasty
11. Amaro	k. Bitter

5. Sort the items below into the appropriate category

a. delizioso	e. buono	i. mela	m. agnello	q. salmone	u. latte
b. dolce	f. gamberi	j. fragola	n. bistecca	r. pollo	v. pesca
c. saporito	g. yogurt	k. gelato	o. insipido	s. nutritivo	w. carota
d. banana	h. malsano	l. succoso	p. sano	t. spinaci	x. formaggio

frutta	verdura	aggettivi	pesce o carne	latticini [dairy products]

Unit 12. Talking about food – Likes/Dislikes (Part 2): READING

Mi chiamo Robert, vivo in Inghilterra. Cosa mangio? Spesso mangio poco a colazione. Solo una mela o una banana e un cappuccino. A pranzo, mangio un panino al prosciutto e delle patate fritte. Bevo acqua o una coca cola. Le patate fritte non sono sane, ma le adoro perché sono saporite.

Nel pomeriggio mangio un gelato a merenda o della frutta. Adoro le pesche perché sono succose.

A cena di solito mangio del pesce con le verdure, mi piacciono i frutti di mare. A volte mangio un'insalata. Mi piacerebbe mangiare del formaggio ma mia madre dice che non è sano. Lei odia il formaggio.

Mi chiamo Stefano. Cosa mangio? Normalmente a colazione non mangio molto. Solo un uovo e una tazza di tè. Il tè mi piace dolce, con molto zucchero. A volte bevo succo di pera. A pranzo mangio pollo arrosto con verdure e bevo acqua minerale. Mangio molte verdure perché sono nutritive e fanno bene alla salute. Mi piacerebbe mangiare più spesso i gamberi perché mi piacciono moltissimo. Dopo la scuola, a merenda, mangio il pane tostato col miele e un succo di arancia. Amo il miele perché è delizioso e ricco di vitamine. A cena mangio molto. Di solito mangio il riso, bistecca con patate e frutta. A volte mangio un piatto di pasta perché è ricca di carboidrati ed è veloce da cucinare.

1. Find the Italian for the words below in Stefano's text.

a. for breakfast : a c_____

b. a cup of tea: u___t_____d_ t___

d. sugar: z_____

e. pear juice: s_____d__m_____

f. for lunch: a p_____

g. they are good for you: f_____
    b_____a_____s_____

h. after school: d_____s_____

i. toast : p_____t_____

j. rich in vitamins: r_____ d____
    v_____

k. for dinner: a c_____

l. a plate of pasta: u__p_____ d_p_____

m. it is fast: è v_____

o. to cook: d__ c_____

2. Complete the following sentences based on Stefano's text

a. Normally, at breakfast I do not eat _____. Only an _____ and a cup of _____

b. I like my tea _____ with a lot of _____

c. For _____ I eat _____ _____ with _____ and I drink _____ _____

d. I eat a lot of vegetables because they are _____ and good for _____

e. As a snack I eat_____ with _____ and drink an _____ _____

f. Usually I eat _____, _____ with potatoes or _____

g. Sometimes I eat a_____ of pasta because it is rich in _____

3. Find the Italian for the following in Robert's text

a.I live in England.

b. I often have a small breakfast

b. ham sandwich

c. chips are not healthy

d. but I love them

e. I eat an ice cream

f. I like seafood

g. I would like to eat

h. my mother says

i. they are juicy

j. in the afternoon

k. I usually eat

l. it is not healthy

m. she hates cheese

4. Who says this, Robert or Stefano? Or both?

a. I would love to eat cheese – *Robert*

b. I love honey

c. I drink pear juice

d. I don't eat much for breakfast

e. I would like to eat prawns   more often

f. I have toasts with honey

g. I love peaches

h. Chips are not healthy

i. I usually eat rice

j. I drink mineral water

k. His mother hates cheese

l. I have a cappuccino at breakfast

Mi chiamo Luca, vivo a Melbourne, in Australia. Cosa mi piace mangiare? Normalmente al mattino mangio molto: una banana, due o tre uova, pane con prosciutto, una spremuta d'arancia e una tazza di caffè. Il caffè mi piace dolce. A pranzo, di solito, mangio solo del pollo con patate o verdure e bevo acqua minerale o succo di frutta. Adoro il pollo perché è salutare e ricco di proteine. A volte mangio asparagi. Mi piacciono perché sono amari ma contengono vitamine. Nel pomeriggio, dopo scuola, faccio merenda con pane, burro e marmellata e bevo una tazza di tè. A cena mangio molto di più. Di solito mangio pasta, carne con verdure e gelato o torta di mele come dolce. Mi piacerebbe mangiare della cioccolata, perché è deliziosa, però mia madre dice che fa male.

5. Answer the following questions on Luca's text

a. How much does he eat at breakfast?

b. What does he eat/drink? [4 things]

c. How does he like coffee?

d. What juice does he drink at lunch?

e. What does he have with chicken?

f. Why does he like asparagus?

g. What does he have for snack in the afternoon?

h. What desserts does Luca eat?

i. Why doesn't his mother allow him to eat chocolate?

6. Find in Luca's text the following:

a. a word for dessert, starting with G:

b. a vegetable starting with A:

c. a drink starting with S:

d. a type of cold meat starting with P:

e. a fruit starting with B:

f. a dairy product starting with B:

g. an adjective starting with D:

h. a container starting with T:

i. a verb starting with M:

j. a fruit starting with A:

k. an adjective starting with S:

l. a meal starting with C:

Unit 12. Talking about food – Likes/Dislikes (Part 2): WRITING

1. Split sentences

Sempre mangio pollo	con latte
Mangio cereali	con burro
Mangio il pane tostato	arrosto
Mi piace l'insalata	frutta favorita
La carne rossa è	piccante
Il curry è	o caffè
L'uva è la mia	verde
Bevo té	deliziosa ma malsana

2. Complete with the correct option

a. Amo i _____, soprattutto le cozze.

b. Normalmente __ _____ mangio una zuppa.

c. Sempre mangio _____ a colazione.

d. A volte preparo _____ arrosto con mia madre.

e. _____ alle sette con la mia famiglia.

f. Normalmente, mangio una frutta a _____.

g. Mi piace molto il _____ perché è dolce

h. Il caffè è _____, ma è buono.

i. Non mi _____ il latte, che schifo!

j. La frutta è nutritiva e _____.

ceno	pollo	a pranzo	merenda	amaro
miele	frutti di mare	cereali	piace	leggera

3. Spot and correct the grammar and spelling mistakes [note: in several cases a word is missing]

a. Normalmente a pranzo io mangiare un panino

b. Bevo aqua o succo fruta.

c. La carne rosa non è sana, pero mi piacce.

d. Adoro la spremuta darancia.

e. Nel pomeriggio a merenda magio pane marmellata.

f. Beviamo una taza de caffe con late.

g. Mi piace moltissimo il capacino perché è delizioso.

h. A cena mangio pasta o piza con prosutto.

i. Non mi piaciono per niente le verdure, anche se sono sano.

j. La mia frutta preferito è la mela. È deliciosa!

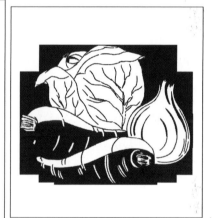

6. Sentence level translation EN - IT

a. I love fruit juice because it is sweet and refreshing.

b. I don't like salmon because it is disgusting.

c. At tea time I eat a cheese sandwich.

d. I always drink milk with honey. I like it because it's sweet.

e. I like fish, especially seafood.

5. Guided writing – write 3 short paragraphs in the first person [I] using the details below

Person	Lunch [usually]	Opinion	Sometimes	Meal
Matthew	chicken and rice	likes because it is tasty	cake or ice cream	dinner
Bridget	fish and chips	delicious but unhealthy	cereals and fruit	breakfast
Luciana	salad or soup	really healthy and light	toast and jam	snack

Grammar Time 9: ARE Verbs (Part 2)
PRANZARE, CENARE, MANGIARE

PRANZARE [to eat for lunch]	al ristorante [at the restaurant] a mensa [at the canteen] a casa [at home] a casa di mia madre [at my mum's house]	e [and] di solito [usually] sempre [always] spesso [often]	MANGIARE [to eat]	una mela un panino una pizza
Pranzo [I have lunch] Pranzi [you] Pranza [he/she] Pranziamo [we] Pranzate [you all] Pranzano [they]			Mangio [I eat] Mangi [you] Mangia [he/she] Mangiamo [we] Mangiate [you all] Mangiano [they]	lasagne pasta salsicce
CENARE [to eat for dinner]	a mezzogiorno [at midday] all'una [at one] alle due [at two]			spaghetti verdure
Ceno [I have dinner] Ceni [you] Cena [he/she] Ceniamo [we] Cenate [you all] Cenano [they]	alle sei [at six] alle sette [at seven] alle otto [at eight]			

Author's note: *Pranzare, cenare* and *mangiare* belong to the group of regular verbs ending in –*are*, in the infinitive form. What patterns do you notice in the Present Tense?

DRILLS

1. Complete with the missing letters

a. (io) Mangi__ o cereali a colazione

b. Mia madre pranz__ all'una

c. I miei genitori pranz__ __ __ alle due

d. Mio nonno mangi__ pollo arrosto

e. Noi mangi__ __ __ molta frutta

f. (Io) Cen__ sempre alle sei

g. Cosa mang__ tu?

h. Loro cen__ __ __ alle sette?

i. Noi pranzi__ __ __ in cucina.

j. A mezzogiorno voi pranz__ __ __ a scuola.

k. Mio fratello pranz__ alle tre in campagna

l. Tu cen__ alle otto con la tua famiglia.

2. Complete with the missing forms of *'Mangiare'*

a. (Io) Non _____ molto. Prendo solo un panino.

b. Mia madre _____ sempre la frutta.

c. I miei genitori _____ pesce a cena.

d. Mia sorella a colazione _____ cereali con latte.

e. E voi, cosa _____ a pranzo?

f. Ciao Marco, cosa _____ (tu) a merenda?

g. Noi non _____ mai il formaggio, è disgustoso!

3. Spot and correct the errors with the verbs *'Pranzare'* and *'Cenare'*

a. (Io) Non pranziamo a casa

b. Mia madre ceno alle sei

c. Mio fratello ed io ceni alle sette

d. Mio padre pranzate in ufficio

e. Voi pranzano a scuola

f. Loro cena sempre alle cinque

g. La mia amica tutti i giorni pranzo a mezzogiorno.

4. Translate into English

a. Mia madre è dottoressa, lei pranza in ospedale.

b. Mia sorella mangia la cioccolata tutti i giorni.

c. A volte io ceno alle sei a casa di mia madre.

d. Normalmente io pranzo a mensa verso l'una.

e. Che cosa mangiate? Mangiamo un'insalata mista.

f. Noi di solito ceniamo alle sette.

g. Voi sempre mangiate pane tostato a colazione.

h. Di solito loro cenano al ristorante.

5. Translate into Italian

a. I have dinner – C_____

b. We have lunch – P_____

c. She eats – M_____

d. They have lunch – P_____

e. He has dinner – C_____

f. They have dinner – C_____

g. I have lunch – P_____

h. You all eat – M_____

6. Translate into Italian

a. For breakfast I eat two eggs and one sausage. Also, I drink a coffee with milk.

b. My friend Paolo has lunch at school. Only a ham sandwich and an apple.

c. We have dinner at six. We eat a steak or fish with potatoes.

d. At noon I drink a cup of coffee with my friend.

e. My friend Carlo never eats red meat. He only eats fish or chicken.

f. My parents have lunch at home, but my brother has lunch in the garden.

g. I like fruit. I eat oranges every day. Sometimes I have dinner at the restaurant.

h. I always eat at the canteen.

THE LANGUAGE GYM

Grammar Time 10: AGREEMENTS (Part 2) (Food)

Il [the] **Lo** [the] **Questo** [this]	**caffè** **MASC** **cappuccino** **pane** **tè** **succo di frutta** **spaghetto** **zucchero**	**è** **[is]**	**amaro** **buono** **delizioso** **dolce** **fresco** **malsano** **saporito** **salato** **sano**
La [the] **Questa** [this]	**carne** **FEM** **frutta** **marmellata** **mela** **pasta** **pizza**		**amara** **buona** **deliziosa** ***dolce** **fresca** **malsana** **saporita** **salata** **sana**
I [the] **Gli** [the] **Questi** [these]	**MASC PLURAL** biscotti grissini panini spaghetti zuccheri	**sono** **[are]**	**amari** **buoni** **deliziosi** **dolci** **freschi** **malsani** **saporiti** **salati** **sani**
Le [the] **Queste** [these]	**FEM PLURAL** **carote** **fragole** [strawberries] **mele** **salsicce** **verdure**		**amare** **buone** **deliziose** **dolci** **fresche** **malsane** **saporite** **salate** **sane**

***Author's note:** adjectives ending in –e, like dolce [sweet], do not change in the feminine but they change into –i in the plural. Ex: 'il gelato è dolce'; 'i gelati sono dolci'. **La** becomes **l'** before a vowel: l'acqua, l'uva.*

1. Choose the correct option as shown in the example

	A	B
Questo pesce è	**sano**	sana
Questo pane è	delizioso	deliziosa
Questa carne è	grasso	grassa
Il latte è	fresco	fresca
La pizza è	salato	salata
Questa mela è	sano	sana
Questi panini sono	buone	buoni
Queste fragole sono	dolce	dolci

2. Write the opposite version of the adjectives below

Maschile	Femminile
	disgustosa
delizioso	
	amara
dolce	
fresco	
	sana
saporiti	
	salate

3. Translate into English

a. Questi gamberi sono salati

b. Questo agnello è buono

c. Questo pollo è molto saporito

d. Questa mela non è molto fresca

e. Questi biscotti sono dolci

f. Queste salsicce sono malsane

g. Questa pizza è un po' salata

4. Tick off the correct sentences and correct the incorrect ones

a. Questi gamberi sono buono

b. Questo agnello è saporito

c. Questo pollo sono molto salati

d. Questa mela è molto deliziosa

e. Gli spaghetti sono saporiti

f. Queste salsicce sono molto grasso

5. Complete

a. Il pesce è disgustos___

b. Le mele sono san___

c. La carne rossa è malsan___

d. I biscotti sono troppo dolc___

e. Gli spaghetto sono saporit___

f. Queste fragole sono delizios___

g. Queste banane sono fresch___

h. Questo caffè è amar___

6. Translate into Italian

a. This fish is disgusting

b. These prawns are delicious

c. This coffee is too sweet

d. These sausages are very fatty

e. These vegetables are very tasty

f. These oranges are very healthy

g. This pasta is very good

h. This fruit is refreshing

 **THE LANGUAGE GYM**

Question Skills 2: Jobs/School bag/Food

1. Translate into English

a. Dove pranzi a mezziogiorno?

b. Che lavoro fa tua madre?

c. Cosa c'è nel tuo zaino?

d. Qual è il tuo **cibo** *[food]*preferito?

e. Cosa ti piace bere?

f. A che ora ceni con la tua famiglia?

g. Ti piace il caffè?

h. Perché non mangi verdure?

i. Mangi spesso il gelato?

j. Di che colore è il tuo astuccio?

k. Perché mangi la frutta?

l. Di solito cosa mangi a colazione?

2. Match the answers below to the questions in activity 1

1. Si, mi piace molto.

2. Mi piace bere la spremuta d'arancia.

3. A colazione di solito mangio un cornetto alla marmellata.

4. Si, lo mangio spesso. È delizioso.

5. Perché non mi piacciono.

6. La pizza margherita.

7. Perché è fresca e dolce.

8. Io e la mia famiglia ceniamo alle sette.

9. Ci sono due libri, una matita e un tablet.

10. Mia madre è poliziotta.

11. A mezzogiorno pranzo a scuola.

12. Il mio astuccio è verde.

3. Provide the questions to the following answers

a. Non mangio carne.

b. Mangio sempre le verdure perché sono sane.

c. Lavoro come dentista.

d. Amo la frutta perché è deliziosa e sana.

e. Pranzo a scuola.

f. A volte mangio pesce a cena.

g. Vivo a Edimburgo.

h. Sono di Roma.

i. Non ho animali.

j. La mia bibita *[drink]* preferita è la limonata.

k. Mio padre è un avvocato.

l. Nel mio astuccio ci sono due penne e una gomma.

4. Complete

a. C_____ c'__ n___ t___ zaino?

b. C___ l_____fai? Faccio il cuoco.

c. A c___ o___ c_____ con la tua famiglia?

d. C_____ m_____ a colazione?

e. Q____ è l__ t__ bibita p_____?Il latte!

f. Q_____ è i__ t__ c_____ preferito? La pasta!

g. D__ d_____ sei? Sono di Leeds.

h. D_____ p_____ normalmente? A scuola!

UNIT 13
Talking about clothes and accessories I wear, how frequently and when

Grammar Time 11: -ARE Verbs (Part 2) Indossare + Agreements

Revision Quickie 3: Jobs, food, clothes and numbers 20-100

In this unit you will learn how to:

- Say what clothes you wear in various circumstances and places
- Describe various types of weather
- Give a wide range of words for clothing items and accessories
- Use a range of words for places in town
- Make the full present indicative conjugation of *'portare'* (to wear)

You will revisit:
- Time markers
- Frequency markers
- Colours
- Self-introduction phrases
- Present indicative of *'Avere'*
- Noun-to-adjective agreement

UNIT 13
Talking about clothes
'Che vestiti porti di solito?'
[What clothes do you usually wear?]

A volte *[Sometimes]* **Di solito** *[Usually]* **Mai** *[Never]* **Raramente** *[Rarely]* **Sempre** *[Always]*	**porto/ indosso** *[I wear]*	**una** *[a]*	**FEM** **borsa** *[bag]* **camicia** *[shirt]* **canottiera** *[tank top/ vest]* **cintura** *[belt]* **collana** *[necklace]* **cravatta** *[tie]* **giacca** *[jacket]* **gonna** *[skirt]* **maglietta** *[a T-shirt]* **sciarpa** *[scarf]* **tuta** *[tracksuit]* **uniforme** *[uniform]*	bian**ca** *[white]* gial**la** *[yellow]* ne**ra** *[black]* ros**sa** *[red]* ver**de** *[green]* *blu *[blue]* rosa *[pink]* viola *[purple]* ca**ra** *[expensive]* como**da** *[comfy]* firma**ta** *[designer]* sporti**va** *[sporty]*
Quando fa caldo *[When it is hot]* **Quando fa freddo** *[When it is cold]*		**un** *[a]*	**MASC** **berretto** *[baseball cap]* **cappotto** *[coat]* **costume** *[swimsuit]* **maglione** *[jumper]* **cappello** *[hat]* **completo** *[suit]* **vestito** *[dress]*	bian**co** giallo ca**ro** *[expensive]* firma**to** *[designer]* sporti**vo** *[sporty]*
In casa *[At home]* **In palestra** *[At the gym]* **In spiaggia** *[At the beach]* **A scuola** *[At school]* **In ufficio** *[In the office]*	**porta/ indossa** *[he/she wears]*		**PLURAL MASC** **calzini** *[socks]* **pantaloni** *[trousers]* **pantaloni corti** *[shorts]* **sandali** *[sandals]* **jeans** *[jeans]* **vestiti** *[clothes]* **occhiali da sole** *[sun glasses]* **stivali** *[boots]*	bian**chi** gial**li** ca**ri** *[expensive]* firma**ti** *[designer]* sporti**vi** *[sporty]*
			PLURAL FEM **scarpe** *[shoes]* **scarpe coi tacchi** *[high heel shoes]* **scarpe da ginnastica** *[sports shoes]*	azzur**re** bian**che** ca**re**

Author's note: *Bear in mind that the words for colour **blu, rosa, viola** do not change in number or gender. *Ex. Le scarpe rosa/ I pantaloni blu*

Unit 13. Talking about clothes: VOCABULARY BUILDING

1. Match up

1. stivali	a. a baseball cap
2. una maglietta	b. trainers
3. un vestito	c. some trousers
4. scarpe da ginnastica	d. a suit
5. dei pantaloni	e. a T-shirt
6. un completo	f. boots
7. un berretto da baseball	g. a dress

2. Translate into English

a. Indosso una maglietta nera.

b. Indosso un vestito grigio.

c. Non porto scarpe da ginnastica.

d. Mia madre porta un cappello blu.

e. Non porto un orologio.

f. Non indosso mai orecchini.

g. Indosso una tuta e una canottiera.

h. Non porto mai un completo.

i. Sempre indosso sandali.

j. Non porto mai un cappello

k. Mio fratello sempre indossa i jeans

l. Io porto sempre gli occhiali da sole.

3. Complete with the missing word

a. In casa _____ una _____
[At home I wear a T-shirt]

b. A scuola indosso un' _____ n_____
[At school I wear a black uniform]

c. In palestra _____ una tuta _____
[At the gym I wear a pink tracksuit]

d. In spiaggia _____ porto un _____
[At the beach I wear a swimsuit]

e. Porto sempre un _____ nero e _____
_____ bianche [I always wear a black dress and white high heels shoes]

f. Raramente _____ scarpe ___ _____
[I rarely wear sports shoes]

g. Non _____mai un completo
[I never wear a suit]

4. Anagrams [clothes and accessories]

a. un colleppa

b. un ologioro

c. una parscia

d. una gliematta

e. un pocapott

f. una nanga

g. un stucome

h. leso da liocchia

i. gliomane

j. stitove

k. persca

l. feunimor

5. Complete each sentence in a way which is logical and grammatically correct

1. Raramente porto una sciarpa _____.

2. Non porto un _____ verde.

3. Indosso sempre una _____ bianca.

4. A scuola, a volte indosso un'_____ grigia.

5. In palestra non porto mai una _____.

6. Di solito in spiaggia indosso _____ neri.

6. Complete with the missing letters

a. Porto sti_____ neri [I wear black boots]

b. In c_____ [at home]

c. Ho un_____ [I have a watch]

d. Porto una cr_____ rossa
[I wear a red tie]

e. Indosso un com_____ azzurro
[I wear a blue suit]

f. Lui porta un be_____ da baseball
[He wears wears a baseball hat]

g. Mia sorella sempre indossa vestiti n_____
[my sister always wears black dresses]

Unit 13. Talking about clothes: READING

Mi chiamo Leire. Sono spagnola. Sono di San Sebastian. Ho quindici anni. Sono molto sportiva e ho molti vestiti di colori e stili differenti. Preferisco i vestiti di buona qualitá ma non troppo cari. Di solito in casa indosso una tuta. Ho tre o quattro tute diverse. Quando vado a scuola, indosso qualcosa di comodo: un maglione, dei jeans **aderenti** *[skinny]* e delle scarpe da ginnastica.

Mi chiamo Claudia. Sono francese. Ho tredici anni, ho i capelli lunghi e castani. Amo comprare vestiti, soprattutto scarpe. Ho molte scarpe e firmate. Mi piacciono i vestiti italiani perché sono di buona qualitá. Quando fa freddo di solito porto un cappotto e dei pantaloni neri. A volte porto una giacca sportiva. Quando fa caldo, in spiaggia porto dei pantaloncini corti, una canottiera e dei sandali.

Mi chiamo Hilda. Sono tedesca. Ho dodici anni. Mi piace molto la moda italiana. Mi piacerebbe comprare una borsa Prada o Armani perché le borse firmate sono belle e di buona qualitá. Di solito però indosso vestiti sportivi: una tuta o un maglione, perché sono comodi. Ho **un armadio** *[a wardrobe]* grande. Mi piacerebbe comprare un paio di scarpe coi tacchi, quando sono grande!

Mi chiamo Giulia, sono italiana ma vivo in Scozia. Ho quattordici anni. In casa di solito indosso una maglietta e dei jeans. Ho molti maglioni e giacche. Quando vado a scuola, indosso un'uniforme: camicia bianca, gonna grigia, cravatta verde e scarpe nere. Sono molto sportiva. Quando vado in palestra indosso una tuta e delle scarpe da ginnastica. Quando fa freddo porto un cappotto rosso e una sciarpa blu.

1. Find the Italian for the following in Leire's text

a. I am from

b. very sporty

c. many clothes

d. good quality clothes

e. a tracksuit

f. when I go to school

g. something comfy

h. different styles

i. a jumper

j. trainers

2. Find the Italian for the following in Giulia's text

a. I live in Scotland

b. at home I usually wear

c. T-shirt and jeans

d. I have many jumpers

e. when I go

f. I wear a uniform

g. grey skirt

h. black shoes

i. I am sporty

j. when it is cold

3. Complete the following statements about Claudia's text

a. She is _____ and she is _____years old

b. She loves buying _____, especially _____

c. She has many branded _____and _____

d. When it's cold she wears a _____ and _____
_____

e. Sometimes he wears a_____ _____

4. Answer in Italian the questions below about Hilda

a. Come si chiama?

b. Di dov'è?

c. Quanti anni ha?

d. Cosa le piace molto?

e. Cosa indossa di solito?

5. Find someone who...

a. ...loves branded clothes

b. ...is from Germany

c. ...wears a sports jacket

d. ...would like to buy high heels when she is older

e. ...has many jackets and jumpers

f. ...has a lot of t-shirts and jeans at home

g. ...wears skinny jeans for school

Unit 13. Talking about clothes: WRITING

1. Split sentences

A casa porto	porto una maglietta
Quando fa	una tuta comoda
In palestra	porto scarpe con i tacchi
Quando fa caldo	freddo porto una sciarpa
Non indosso mai jeans	indosso dei pantaloncini
In ufficio	Levi's
Indosso pantaloni	nera
Lei porta una camicia	neri

2. Complete with the correct option

a. In _____ indosso vestiti belli ma comodi.

b. A scuola lei _____ un'uniforme verde.

c. In palestra porto delle _____ da tennis.

d. In spiaggia indosso un _____

e. Quando _____ caldo porto una _____

f. In casa mia madre porta _____ tuta.

g. Mia sorella indossa una _____ firmata

h. _____ fa freddo, indosso un _____

cappotto	borsa	una	porta	quando
scarpe	casa	fa	costume	maglietta

3. Spot and correct the grammar and spelling mistakes [note: in several cases a word is missing]

a. Quando freddo mia nonna indossa uno sciarpa.

b. In casa porto una tuta comodo.

c. Ho molte scarpe nera.

d. Mio fratello porta bereto bianco.

e. A scuola un' uniforme elegante.

f. Mi piacciono i vestito firmati.

g. Di solito indossare vestiti buona qualità.

h. Sempre porto una gona rosso.

5. Describe this person in Italian using the 3rd person

Name: Giacomo

Lives in: London

Age : 20

Pet: A black dog

Hair: blond + green eyes

Always wears: white shirt

Never wears: shorts

At the gym wears: an Adidas tracksuit

4. Guided writing – write 3 short paragraphs in the first person [I] using the details below

Person	Lives	Always wears	Never wears	Likes
Amparo	Madrid	coat	skirt	belt
Charlotte	Sydney	white t-shirt	coats	sunglasses
Flavia	Milan	black dress	shorts	designer bag

Grammar Time 11: ARE Verbs (Part 3)
PORTARE + AVERE + AGREEMENTS

PORTARE [to wear]			MASC	
(Io) porto [I wear]	**un** [a]	**berretto** [baseball cap]	bianco	
(Tu) porti [you wear]		**cappotto** [coat]	giallo	
(Lei/lui) porta [he/she wears]		**costume** [swimsuit]	nero	
(Noi) portiamo [we wear]		**cappello** [hat]	caro [expensive]	
(Voi) portate [you all wear]		**completo** [suit]	comodo [comfy]	
(Loro) portano [they wear]		**gilè** [waistcoat]	firmato [designer]	
		maglione [jumper]	sportivo [sporty]	
		vestito [dress]		
AVERE [to have]	**una** [a]	**borsa** [bag] FEM	bianca [white]	
(Io) ho [I have]		**camicia** [shirt]	gialla [yellow]	
(Tu) hai [you have]		**canottiera** [tank top/ vest]	rossa [red]	
(Lei/lui) ha [he/she has]		**cintura** [belt]	verde [green]	
(Noi) abbiamo [we have]		**collana** [necklace]	rosa [pink]	
(Voi) avete [you all have]		**cravatta** [tie]	viola [purple]	
(Loro) hanno [they have]		**giacca** [jacket]	cara [expensive]	
		gonna [skirt]	comoda [comfy]	
		maglietta [shirt]	firmata [designer]	
		sciarpa [scarf]	sportiva [sporty]	
		tuta [tracksuit]		
		uniforme [uniform]		

DRILLS

1. Complete with the missing verb endings

a. (io) Non port_ mai una tuta

b. Che vestiti port__ (tu) di solito?

c. Mio fratello h___ molte magliette

d. I miei genitori h_____ vestiti firmati

e. Il mio professore di arte indoss_ un gilè

f. Voi port_____ un'uniforme a scuola

g. In spiaggia (noi) port_____ un costume

h. (io) h___ molti jeans e pantaloni

i. Che scarpe av_____? (voi)

j. Mia madre ed io ab_____ molti vestiti cari

k. Lei port__ una borsa firmata

l. Quando fa freddo (tu) port_ una sciarpa

2. Complete with the missing verbs

a. Mia madre _____ molti vestiti di marca [My mother has a lot of branded clothes]

b. I miei fratelli sempre _____ magliette [My brothers always wear t-shirts]

c. La mia professoressa di solito _____ una gonna [My teacher usually wears a skirt]

d. I miei professori sempre _____ giacca e cravatta [My teachers always wear a blazer and tie]

e. La mia amica ____ molte borse e scarpe coi tacchi [My friend has many bags and high heels shoes]

f. Io e il mio amico Pablo _____ molte camicie nere. Nel mio armadio _____ molti jeans.
[My friend Pablo and I have many black shirts. In my wardwrobe there are many jeans]

g. I miei genitori _____ molti vestiti sportivi [My parents wear a lot of sporty clothes]

h. Voi non _____ scarpe da ginnastica blu [You all don't have blue trainers]

3. Complete with the correct form of 'Portare'

a. (io) port_ una maglietta.

b. Mia madre port_ un vestito elegante.

c. I miei fratelli non port_____ berretti.

d. Noi sempre port_____ jeans e legging.

e. Le mie amiche port_____ legging neri.

f. Che vestiti port__ tu?

g. (noi) Mai port_____ un cappello.

h. In palestra (io) port___ una tuta comoda.

4. Complete with the correct form of 'Avere'

a. (io) Non h___ una cintura marrone.

b. Noi non abb_____ vestiti firmati.

c. Mio fratello___ molte magliette bianche.

d. La mia amica Giovina_____ molte scarpe coi tacchi e borse.

e. Mio fratello _____ tante cravatte rosse.

f. Mia nonna non ____ vestiti eleganti.

g. Voi _____ un berretto da baseball nero.

5. Translate into English

a. Non indosso mai giacche sportive.

b. Lui indossa sempre pantaloni verdi.

c. Non abbiamo cappelli e borse.

d. Lei porta sempre dei legging neri.

e. Tu hai molte scarpe di marca.

f. Voi indossate scarpe da ginnastica Nike.

g. Che vestiti porti a scuola?

h. In palestra a volte porto pantaloncini.

i. In spiaggia non indosso mai calzini.

j. Portiamo un'uniforme per andare a scuola.

6. Translate into Italian

a. Do you have baseball caps?

b. We have many shoes.

c. I don't have an elegant dress.

d. My father has many suits and ties.

e. My mother never wears jeans.

f. I never wear trainers.

g. What clothes do you usually wear?

h. They never wear uniforms.

i. At the gym I wear a tracksuit.

j. Do you wear sports clothes often?

Revision Quickie 3: Jobs, food, clothes and numbers 20-100

1. Complete (numbers)

a. 100 = ce

b. 90 = no

c. 30 = tr

d. 50 = ci

e. 80 = ot

f. 60 = se

g. 40 = qu

2. Translate into English (food and clothes)

a. la sciarpa

b. la bibita

c. il cibo

d. la gonna

e. il panino

f. l'acqua

g. la carne

h. i frutti di mare

i. la colazione

j. il cappotto

k. le scarpe

l. le verdure

m. la spremuta d'arancia

n. la cena

3. Write in a word for each letter in the categories below as shown in the example

LETTERA	Vestiti e accessori	Cibo o bibita	Numeri	Lavori
S	sciarpa	salsicce	sessanta	soldato
C				
V				
T				
O				

4. Match

indosso	I like
ho	I drink
sono	for lunch I have
ci sono	I live
mangio	I work
bevo	I have
pranzo	for dinner I have
lavoro	there is
ceno	I am
vivo	there are
c'è	I wear
mi piace	I eat

5. Translate into English

a. Non indosso mai gonne lunghe.

b. Mangio sempre pane con marmellata a merenda.

c. Lavoro come assistente di volo.

d. Bevo spesso caffè con latte.

e. Mi piace una bibita fresca.

f. A volte pranzo all'una con mia sorella.

g. Di solito ceno **verso** [around] le sette.

h. Non ho vestiti cari, né firmati.

i. Nel mio armadio ci sono molte magliette e jeans.

UNIT 14
Saying what I and others do
in our free time

Grammar Time: Giocare, Fare, Andare

In this unit you will learn how to say:

- What activities you do using the verbs
  '**giocare**' (play), '**fare**' (do) and '**andare**' (go)
- Other free time activities

You will revisit:
- Time and frequency markers
- Weather
- Expressing likes/dislikes
- Adjectives
- Pets

UNIT 14
Saying what I (and others) do in our free time
'Che cosa fai nel tuo tempo libero?'
[What do you do in your free time?]

A volte *[Sometimes]* **Nel mio tempo libero** *[In my free time]* **Sempre** *[Always]* **Tutti i giorni** *[Every day]* **Venerdì** *[Friday]* **Sabato** *[Saturday]* **Domenica** *[Sunday]* **Quando fa bel tempo** *[When the weather is good]* **Quando fa maltempo** *[When the weather is bad]*	**gioco** *[I play]* **mi piace giocare** *[I like playing]*	**a**	**pallone/calcio** *[football]* **pallacanestro** *[basketball]* **pallavolo** *[volleyball]* **scacchi** *[chess]* **tennis** *[tennis]* **alla playstation** *[PlayStation]*
	faccio *[I do]*		**atletica** *[athletics]* **arrampicata** *[rock climbing]* **ciclismo** *[cycling]* **corsa** *[jogging]* **i compiti** *[homework]* **equitazione** *[horse riding]* **ginnastica** *[gymnastics]* **nuoto** *[swimming]* **sci** *[skiing]* **trekking** *[hiking]*
	vado *[I go]*		**a casa del mio amico** *[to my friend's house]* **al centro sportivo** *[to the sports centre]* **al cinema** *[to the cinema]* **al parco** *[to the park]* **in bicicletta** *[on a bike ride]* **in discoteca** *[clubbing]* **in montagna** *[to the mountains]* **in piscina** *[to the pool]* **in palestra** *[to the gym]* **in spiaggia** *[to the beach]*

Unit 14. Free time: VOCABULARY BUILDING – Part 1

1. Match up

1.Gioco a pallavolo	a.I do horse-riding
2.Gioco a golf	b.I play volleyball
3.Faccio equitazione	c.I play basketball
4.Gioco a carte	d.I play golf
5.Faccio ciclismo	e.I go swimming
6.Faccio nuoto	f.I play football
7.Gioco a calcio	g.I go cycling
8.Gioco a pallacanestro	h.I play cards

2. Complete with the missing word

a. Gioco a _____ [I play chess]

b. _____ equitazione [I go horse riding]

c. _____ a carte [I play cards]

d. Mi piace fare _____ [I like doing gymnastics]

e. Gioco a_____ [I play basketball]

f. Faccio _____ [I do athletics]

g. Mi piace fare _____ [I like going swimming]

h. Faccio _____ [I go rock climbing]

i. Faccio _____ [I do weights]

j. Non faccio i _____ [I don't do my homework]

gioco	pesi	atletica	arrampicata	faccio
compiti	ginnastica	scacchi	pallacanestro	nuoto

3. Translate into English

a. Nel mio tempo libero gioco a calcio.

b. Spesso gioco a pallacanestro

c. A volte faccio arrampicata.

d. Raramente faccio equitazione.

e. Quando fa bel tempo vado a pesca.

f. Tutti i giorni mi piace fare ciclismo.

g. Raramente vado in discoteca.

h. Domenica vado al cinema.

i. Quando fa bel tempo, vado in spiaggia

j. Faccio i compiti tutti i giorni.

k. A volte, vado a casa del mio amico.

4. Broken words

a. Faccio eq_____ [I go horse-riding]

b. Faccio n_____ [I go swimming]

c. Vado a p_____ [I go fishing]

d. Vado in b_____ [I go on a bike ride]

e. Gioco a s_____ [I play chess]

f. Vado in d_____ [I go clubbing]

g. Gioco a c_____ [I play cards]

h. Faccio a_____ [I do rock climbing]

5. 'Vado', 'Gioco' or 'Faccio'?

a. _____ a pallacanestro

b. _____ in bicicletta

d. _____ a carte

e. _____ nuoto

f. _____ in montagna

g. _____ a tennis

h. _____ pesi

i. _____ equitazione

6. Bad translation – spot any translation errors and fix them

a. Non vado mai in discoteca: *I often go clubbing*

b. Spesso gioco a carte: *I play chess often*

c. Raramente faccio trekking: *I go swimming rarely*

d. Quando fa bel tempo gioco a golf: *when the weather is nice I go hiking*

e. Vado in bici due volte a settimana: *I go biking every day*

f. Spesso gioco a scacchi: *I never play chess*

g. Sempre faccio arrampicata: *I never go hiking*

h. Spesso vado in piscina: *I go swimming from time to time*

Unit 14. Free time: READING

Mi chiamo Thomas Weidner. Sono tedesco. Nel mio tempo libero faccio molto sport. Il mio sport preferito è l'arrampicata. Faccio arrampicata tutti i giorni. Quando fa mal tempo **sto a casa** [I stay at home] e gioco a scacchi o a carte. Mi piace giocare ai videogiochi su playstation o Xbox. Sempre gioco alla playstation.

Mi chiamo Verónica. Sono spagnola, di Barbastro. Ho i capelli rossi. Sono molto simpatica e divertente, ma non sono molto sportiva. Preferisco leggere libri [reading books], giocare ai videogiochi o a scacchi e ascoltare musica. Quando fa bel tempo, tuttavia, corro nel parco del **mio quartiere** [my area] o gioco a tennis con mio fratello. Non mi piace andare in palestra, né in piscina. Odio il nuoto perché non mi piace l'acqua.

Mi chiamo Nicola. Sono inglese. Nel mio tempo libero mi piace molto leggere libri e giornali. Mi piace anche giocare a carte e a scacchi. Non sono molto sportiva ma a volte vado in palestra e faccio pesi. Inoltre, quando fa bel tempo faccio trekking in campagna con il mio cane. Il mio cane si chiama Doug ed è grande e bianco.

Mi chiamo Annie. Sono francese. Adoro andare in bicicletta. Vado in bici tutti i giorni con i miei amici. È il mio sport preferito. A volte faccio arrampicata, corsa o trekking. Non mi piace né il tennis né il calcio. Odio anche il nuoto. Mi piace giocare sul telefonino e **inviare** [to send] WhatsApp ai miei amici. Due volte alla settimana vado in discoteca col mio fidanzato. Amo ballare.

1. Find the Italian for the following in Thomas' text

a. I do a lot of sport

b. My favourite sport

c. Climbing

d. Every day

e. When the weather's bad

f. I play chess

g. Also

h. I play on the PlayStation

2. Find the Italian in Annie's text for

a. I love biking

b. with my friends

c. sometimes

d. I do swimming

e. I go clubbing

f. I go rock climbing

g. with my boyfriend

h. playing on the phone

3. Complete the following statements about Verónica

a. She is _____from_____

b. She is very _____and _____

c. She plays videogames or _____

d. When the weather is nice she _____

e. She also plays tennis with her_____

f. She doesn't enjoy the gym nor the _____

4. List 8 details about Nicola

1 _____

2_____

3_____

4_____

5_____

6_____

7_____

8_____

5. Find someone who...

a. ...enjoys reading newspapers

b. ...hates swimming

c. ...does a lot of sport

d. ...does weight lifting

e. ...goes clubbing twice a week

120

Unit 14. Free time: TRANSLATION

1. Gapped translation

a. Non vado mai in discoteca: *I _____ go clubbing*

b. Spesso gioco a pallacanestro: *I often play _____*

c. Gioco a tennis due volte alla settimana: *I play tennis* _____

d. Gioco a _____: *I play volleyball*

e. Tutti i giorni gioco a _____: *every day I play cards*

f. A volte, vado al parco: _____, *I go to the park*

g. Non faccio mai pesi: *I never do* _____

h. Quando____ bel tempo vado a _____: *When the weather is nice, I go fishing*

2. Translate to English

a. Due volte a settimana

b. A volte

c. Quando fa brutto tempo

d. A casa del mio amico

e. Al centro sportivo

f. Tutti i giorni

g. Faccio arrampicata

h. Vado in spiaggia

i. Vado a pesca

3. Translate into English

a. Non vado mai a pesca con mio padre

b. Gioco a carte con mio fratello

c. Faccio trekking con mia madre

d. Gioco a pallone con la mia migliore amica

e. Raramente gioco alla playstation con mio cugino

f. Spesso vado al cinema con la mia ragazza *[girlfriend]*

4. Translate into Italian

a. Bike: B_____

b. Rock climbing: A_____

c. Basketball: P_____

d. Fishing: P_____

e. Weights: P_____

f. Videogames: V_____

g. Chess: S_____

h. Cards: C_____

i. Hiking: T_____

j. Jogging: C_____

5. Translate into Italian

a. I 'do' jogging

b. I play chess

c. I 'do' rock climbing

d. I 'do' swimming

e. I 'do' horse riding

f. I do weights

g. I do my homework

h. I play videogames

i. I 'do' cycling

j. I 'do' gymnastics

THE LANGUAGE GYM

Unit 14. Free time: WRITING

1. Split sentences

Vado al centro	parco
Spesso gioco	volte a settimana
Vado a casa	sportivo tutti i giorni
Faccio corsa nel	a pallavolo
Gioco a	bicicletta
Faccio sport due	della mia amica
A volte vado in	in palestra
Faccio pesi	carte

2. Complete the sentences with a suitable word

a. Non faccio _____ ginnastica

b. A volte_____ a pallavolo

c. Raramente _____ arrampicata

d. Spesso_____ equitazione

e. Gioco a tennis _____ _____ giorni

f. Vado a _____ del mio amico John.

g. Nel mio_____ libero mi piace nuotare.

h. Mi _____ giocare a rugby

i. Gioco_____ golf una volta a settimana

3. Spot and correct mistakes
[note: in some cases a word is missing]

a. Facio ecquitazione:

b. Giooco a palavolo:

c. Vado a casa mio amico:

d. Tutti giorni vado bicicletta:

e. Faccio gli compiti:

f. Vado a piscina:

g. Gioco a calicio:

h. mi piace gioco a tennis:

4. Complete the words

a. Sca_____

b. Pallac_____

c. Ginn_____

d. Video_____

e. Equi_____

f. Atle_____

g. Pall_____

h. Pisc_____

5. Write a paragraph for each of the people below in the first person singular (I):

Name	Sport I do	How often	Who with	Where	Why I like it
Giovina	Hiking	every day	with my friend	in the countryside	it's fun
Dylan	Weight-lifting	often	with my friend James	at home	it's healthy
Simona	Jogging	when the weather is nice	alone	in the park	it's relaxing

Grammar Time 12: Giocare, Fare and Andare (Part 1)
Present tense

	Giocare *[to play]*	
A volte *[Sometimes]* **Due volte a settimana** *[Twice a week]* **Tutti i giorni** *[Every day]* **Raramente** *[Rarely]*	**(io) gioco** *[I play]* **(tu) giochi** *[you play]* **(lui/lei) gioca** *[he/she plays]* **(noi) giochiamo** *[we play]* **(voi) giocate** *[you all play]* **(loro) giocano** *[they play]*	**a carte** *[cards]* **a calcio/pallone** *[football]* **a hockey** *[hockey]* **a pallacanestro** *[basketball]* **a scacchi** *[chess]* **a tennis** *[tennis]*
	Fare *[to do]*	
Quando ho tempo *[When I have time]* **Quando fa maltempo** *[When the weather is bad]* **Quando fa bel tempo** *[When the weather is good]*	**(io) faccio** *[I do]* **(tu) fai** *[you do]* **(lui/lei) fa** *[he/she does]* **(noi) facciamo** *[we do]* **(voi) fate** *[you all do]* **(loro) fanno** *[they do]*	**arrampicata** *[rock climbing]* **ciclismo** *[cycling]* **i compiti** *[homework]* **corsa** *[jogging]* **equitazione** *[horse riding]* **nuoto** *[swimming]* **una passeggiata** *[a walk]*
	Andare *[to go]*	
Lunedì *[Monday]* **Martedì** *[Tuesday]* **Mercoledì** *[Wednesday]* **Giovedì** *[Thursday]* **Venerdì** *[Friday]* **Sabato** *[Saturday]* **Domenica** *[Sunday]*	**(io) vado** *[I go]* **(tu) vai** *[you go]* **(lui/lei) va** *[he/she goes]* **(noi) andiamo** *[we go]* **(voi) andate** *[you all go]* **(loro) vanno** *[they go]*	**a pesca** *[fishing]* **al centro sportivo** *[to the sports centre]* **al cinema** *[to the cinema]* **al mare** *[to the seaside]* **al parco** *[to the park]* **in bicicletta** *[on a bike ride]* **in discoteca** *[clubbing]* **in montagna** *[to the mountains]* **in palestra** *[to the gym]* **in piscina** *[to the pool]* **in spiaggia** *[to the beach]*

THE LANGUAGE GYM

1. Match

Faccio	He/she does
Fai	We do
Fa	You do
Facciamo	I do
Fate	They do
Fanno	You all do

2. Complete with the correct ending

a. (io) Non facci____ mai i compiti.

b. Mio padre gioc____ spesso a pallone con me.

c. Che sport fa___ tu?

d. (noi) lunedì gioch_____ a tennis.

e. (voi) Cosa fa_____ domenica?

f. I miei amici sempre gioc_____ alla Playstation.

g. (tu) Non gioc____ mai ai videogiochi.

h. Mio fratello maggiore f____ atletica tutti i giorni.

i. I miei cugini non f___ ginnastica, gioc_____ a golf.

j. Mia madre ed io, il sabato, facc_____ nuoto.

3. Write the correct form of GIOCARE (to play)

a. I play: _____

b. You play: _____

c. She plays: _____

d. We play: _____

e. You guys play: _____

f. They play: _____

g. My brothers play: _____

h. You and I play: _____

i. He and I play: _____

4. Complete with the first person of FARE, ANDARE and GIOCARE: *faccio, vado, gioco*

a. A volte_____ a pallavolo.

b. _____ sport tutti i giorni.

c. _____ a pallavolo.

d. Raramente_____ a carte.

e. Non _____mai ciclismo, _____ equitazione.

f. _____ alla playstation tutti i giorni.

g. Quando fa bel tempo_____ al mare.

h. _____ arrampicata quando ho tempo.

i. La domenica_____ allo stadio con mio padre.

j. Sempre _____ i compiti nel pomeriggio.

5. Spot and correct the translation errors

a. Vado a pesca *[You go fishing]*

b. Vai in chiesa *[We go to church]*

c. Andiamo al centro commerciale

[You guys go to the shopping mall]

d. Non vado mai a casa di Marta

[We never go to Marta's house]

e. Vanno al cinema una volta a

settimana

[She goes to the cinema once a week]

f. Lei va a sciare in inverno

[She goes skiing at the weekend]

6. Complete the forms of ANDARE below

a. V___ _ in palestra *[I go to the gym]*

b. V_ _ _ _ _ in chiesa *[They go to church]*

c. A_ _ _ _ _ _ in spiaggia *[We go to the beach]*

d. V_ _ _ _ in piscina *[They go to the swimming pool]*

e. Dove v_ _ _ ? V_ _ _ _ a casa

   [Where are you going? I am going home]

f. Tu v_ _ _ a teatro *[You go to the theatre]*

g. V_ _ _ andate allo stadio? *[Do you all go to the stadium?]*

7. Complete with *fa, gioca* or *va* as appropriate

a. Mia madre _____ molto sport.

b. Mio padre _____ in chiesa raramente.

c. Mio fratello _____ alla moschea tutti i venerdì.

d. Mio nonno mai _____ a carte con me.

e. Mio fratello maggiore _____ karate.

f. La mia amica Sara sempre _____ in bici.

g. Mio fratello minore _____ sempre ciclismo.

h. Mia zia ____ una **passeggiata** *[walk]* tutti i giorni.

8. Complete with *fanno, giocano* or *vanno* as appropriate

a. I miei amici _____ a pallacanestro

b. I miei fratelli non _____ sport

c. Le mie sorelle _____ a pallone

d. Mamma e papá _____ a carte

e. I miei cugini spesso _____ a golf

f. I miei professori_____ in piscina tutti i giorni.

g. I miei zii _____ in chiesa molto raramente

h. Loro _____ arrampicata una volta alla settimana.

i. Loro_____ ciclismo in estate?

j. I miei amici Luke e Paul _____ alla Xbox tutte le sere.

k. I miei nonni non _____ in piscina, loro _____ al parco a fare una passeggiata.

9. Translate into English

a. Non giochiamo mai a pallone. ✗

b. Luigi fa i compiti tutti i giorni. ✓

c. A volte vado in chiesa la domenica. ✓

d. Mio fratello va a scuola di calcio il sabato .

e. Quando fa bel tempo faccio una passeggiata.

f. Ogni martedì vado in palestra a fare pesi.

g. Quando fa mal tempo gioco con Xbox a casa.

10. Translate into Italian.

a. We never go to the swimming pool

b. They do sport rarely

c. She plays basketball every day

d. When the weather is nice, I do jogging

e. I rarely do cycling

f. I often do rock climbing

g. My father and I often play badminton

h. My sister plays tennis twice a week

i. I go to the swimming pool on Saturdays

j. When the weather is bad I go to the gym

k. They rarely do their homework

l. We never play football, we play volleyball.

UNIT 15
Talking about free time and giving opinions

GRAMMAR TIME: Giocare/ Fare/ Andare
Question skills: Clothes / Free time/ Opinions

In this unit you will learn how to say:
- What free-time activities you do and give your opinion
- Where you do them and who with
- Words for places in town

You will also learn how to ask and answer questions about:
- Clothes
- Free time

You will revisit:
- Sports and hobbies
- The verbs 'fare', 'andare' and 'giocare' in the present indicative
- Pets
- Places in town
- Clothes
- Family members
- Numbers from 1 to 100
- Weather

Unit 15
Talking about free time and giving opinions
Cosa fai nel tuo tempo libero?
[What do you do in your free time?]

Nel mio tempo libero *[In my free time]*	**gioco** *[I play]*	**a carte** *[cards]* **a pallone** *[football]* **a tennis** *[tennis]* **ai videogiochi** *[videogames]*	**perché è** *[because it is]* **anche se è** *[even if it is]*	**appassionante** *[thrilling]* **difficile** *[difficult]*
Durante le vacanze *[During my holidays]* **In estate** *[In the summer]*	**la mia amica Maria gioca** *[my friend Maria plays]*	**con i miei amici** *[with my friends]* **con i suoi amici** *[with his/her friend]*	**secondo me è** *[according to me it is]* **a mio parere è** *[in my opinion it is]*	**dinamico/a** *[dynamic]* **divertente** *[fun]*
In inverno *[In the winter]*	**faccio** *[I do]*	**arrampicata** *[rock climbing]* **ciclismo** *[cycling]*		**emozionante** *[exciting]*
Il fine settimana *[At the weekend]* **La domenica** *[On Sunday]*	**il mio amico Leo fa** *[my friend Leo does]*	**corsa** *[jogging]* **nuoto** *[swimming]* **sci** *[skiing]*	**penso che è** *[I think it is]* **mi piace perché è** *[I like it because]*	**facile** *[easy]* **fantastico/a** *[fantastic]* **faticoso/a** *[tiring]*
A volte *[Sometimes]*	**vado** *[I go]*	**al cinema** *[to the cinema]* **al parco** *[to the park]*		
Spesso *[Often]* **Sempre** *[Always]* **Tutti i giorni** *[Everyday]*	**il mio amico Andrew va** *[my friend Andrew goes]*	**allo stadio** *[to the stadium]* **in palestra** *[to the gym]* **in bici** *[on a bike ride]*	**non mi piace perché è** *[I do not like it because]*	**interessante** *[interesting]* **noioso/a** *[boring]* **pericoloso** *[dangerous]* **rilassante** *[relaxing]*
	ascolto musica *[I listen to music]* **leggo un libro** *[I read a book]* **guardo Netflix** *[I watch Netflix]* **prendo il sole** *[I sunbathe]* **suono il piano** *[I play the piano]*			

Unit 15. Talking about free time and opinions: VOCABULARY BUILDING 1

1. Match up

1. In estate	a. at the weekend
2. In inverno	b. during my holidays
3. Nel mio tempo libero	c. every day
4. Il fine settimana	d. sometimes
5. Durante le vacanze	e. in my free time
6. A volte	f. in summer
7. Tutti i giorni	g. in winter

2. Translate into English

a. Nel mio tempo libero

b. Il fine settimana

c. Sempre ascolto musica

d. A volte guardo la tele

e. In inverno faccio sci

f. Durante le vacanze

g. In estate faccio nuoto

h. Prendo il sole

i. Leggo un libro

3. Complete with the missing word

a. Il _____ settimana [At the weekend]

b. _____ le vacanze [During the holidays]

c. Vado in bici tutti i _____
[I go on the bike every day]

d. Nel mio tempo _____ faccio nuoto
[In my free time I do swimming]

e. In inverno vado in _____
[In the winter I go to the gym]

f. A _____ vado allo stadio con mio fratello
[Sometimes I go to the stadium with my brother]

g. La domenica mia madre _____ spesso al cinema
[On Sunday my mum often goes to the cinema]

h. La mia amica Sara _____ a pallone
[My friend Sara plays football]

4. Anagrams

a. emprs	g. rantedu
b. a tevol	h. le cavazen
c. sospes	i. uttit i nigior
d. vernoin in	j. li nefi tisetmana
e. ni testae	k. cogio
f. la menicado	l. ciofac

5. Bad translation- spot any translation errors and fix them

1. Il fine settimana vado al parco - *I go to the park every day*

2. La domenica il mio amico gioca a tennis- *On Sunday my friend plays the violin*

3. A volte guardo Netflix – *I often watch Netflix*

4. La mia amica Maria spesso va allo stadio - *My friend Maria never goes to the stadium*

5. In estate prendo il sole - *In summer I go skiing.*

6. Sempre suono il piano - *I play the piano in my free time*

6. Complete

a. Durante le _____
[during the holidays]

b. Il fine _____
[at the weekend]

c. _____ a tennis *[I play tennis]*

d. _____ un libro *[I read a book]*

e. Gioco con i miei _____
[I play with my friends]

f. _____ mio tempo libero
[In my free time]

g. _____ il violino
[I play the violin]

h. Spesso _____ musica
[I often listen to music]

Unit 15. Talking about free time and opinions: VOCABULARY BUILDING 2

1. Match up

1. faticoso	a. fun
2. emozionante	b. relaxing
3. divertente	c. in my opinion
4. io penso che	d. easy
5. a mio parere	e. tiring
6. rilassante	f. I think that
7. secondo me	g. exciting
8. facile	h. according to me

2. Complete with the missing word

a. Gioco sempre a pallone _____ é divertente

[I always play football because it is fun]

b. Penso che il nuoto è _____

[I think that swimming is tiring]

c. A volte vado allo stadio perché è _____

[I sometimes go to the stadium because it's exciting]

d. A mio_____ è facile. *[In my opinion it's easy]*

e. _____ me è noioso. *[According to me it's boring]*

f. Gioco con i miei amici perché è _____

[I play with my friends because it's fantastic]

g. Caterina suona il violino _____ ____ è difficile

[Caterina plays the violin even if it's difficult]

h. Faccio sci perché è a_____

[I go skiing because it's thrilling]

3. Translate into English

a. Perché è facile

b. A mio parere è noioso

c. Secondo me è divertente

d. Anche se è faticoso

e. Penso che è dinamico

f. Mi piace molto perché è

appassionante

g. Non mi piace perché é difficile

4. Anagrams [adjectives]

a. fotisaco

b. vertedinte

c. nappantessioa

d. cifdifile

e. sonoio

f. zioemontena

g. cilefa

h. namidico

i. sticofanta

j. ressaintente

k. santerilas

l. loperisoco

5. Broken words

a. S_____ i_ p_____ a_____ s_ è f_____
[I play the piano even if it's tiring]

b. M___ z____ F_____ g_____ a c_____
[My aunt Franca plays cards]

c. V_____ i_ b___ p_____ è d_____
[I go on the bike because it's fun]

d. L_____ v___ a_ p_____ c___ i s_____ a_____
[Lina goes to the park with her friends]

e. M___ p_____p_____ è d_____
[I like it because it is dynamic]

f. N___ m___p_____ il n_____ p_____ è p_____
[I don't like swimming because it's dangerous]

6. Complete

a. Faccio _____ *[I go cycling]*

b. Mario _____ai videogiochi
[Mario plays videogames]

c. Lui _____ nuoto *[He does swimming]*

d. Vado ____ palestra *[I go to the gym]*

e. _____ in piscina *[I go to the pool]*

f. _____che è facile *[I think it's easy]*

g. Prendo il_____*[I sunbathe]*

h. _____me è pericolosa
[According to me it's dangerous]

i. A mio _____ *[in my opinion]*

Unit 15. Talking about free time and giving opinions: READING

Mi chiamo Pietro. Sono italiano. Ho dodici anni. Sono molto sportivo. Nel mio tempo libero faccio molto sport perché è fantastico! Di solito gioco a rugby o pallacanestro. Una volta alla settimana faccio arrampicata anche se, secondo me, è pericolosa! La domenica vado in palestra e indosso una tuta e delle scarpe da ginnastica. A volte però è un po' faticoso.

Ciao, mi chiamo Isabella e sono di Roma. Ho quindici anni. Nel mio tempo libero, quando fa freddo, vado in palestra perché è salutare. Quando fa caldo, invece, vado in bici o faccio una passeggiata. Tutti i giorni però faccio i compiti anche se è noioso! Poi guardo Netflix o ascolto musica, mi piace molto perché è emozionante. A casa di solito indosso jeans, o una tuta, quando leggo un libro nella mia camera.

Salve, mi chiamo Ana Laura. Vivo in Brasile. Ho sedici anni. Nel mio tempo libero amo cantare perché è emozionante. Il fine settimana vado al centro commerciale con le mie amiche. Quando esco di solito indosso una giacca sportiva e una minigonna. A volte vado al cinema con mia sorella. Mi piace perché, a mio parere, guardare un film é sempre interessante.

Mi chiamo Chloé. Sono francese. Ho quattordici anni. Durante le vacanze vado in spiaggia e faccio nuoto. La mattina, a volte, prendo il sole con mia sorella perché è rilassante. Nel pomeriggio leggo un libro o ascolto la musica. La sera vado al ristorante ed esco con i miei amici. Quando vado in discoteca indosso dei pantaloncini e una maglietta. Mi piace ballare in discoteca perché è emozionante. Mia sorella invece, in estate, gioca sempre a carte!

1. Find the Italian for the following in Pietro's text

a. I am Italian

b. I am 12

c. I am very sporty

d. in my free time

e. usually I play

f. I go to the park

g. according to me

h. it's dangerous

i. trainers

j. a bit tiring

2. Find the Italian for the following in Chloe's text

a. during the holidays

c. I swim

d. I go to the beach

e. it is relaxing

f. I go to a restaurant

g. a t-shirt

h. I wear shorts

i. it's exciting

j. instead

k. she always plays

3. Complete the following statements about Isabella's text

a. She is _____ years old
b. In her free time, when it_____ , she goes to the _____
c. When it's hot, instead, she _____ or goes for a walk
d. When it's stormy she plays _____ or _____ with her _____ brother
e. Isabella does not like _____ weather
f. Her pet can _____ Italian

4. Answer in Italian the questions below about Ana Laura

a. Dove vive Ana Laura?

b. Quanti anni ha?

c. Cosa fa nel suo tempo libero?

d. Dove va il fine settimana?

e. Cosa indossa?

f. Perché le piace guardare un film?

5. Find someone who...

a. reads a book in her bedroom _____

b. is from France _____

c. is very sporty _____

d. wears a miniskirt _____

e. does rock climbing _____

f. likes sunbathing _____

g. loves singing _____

Unit 15. Talking about free time and opinions: WRITING

1. Split sentences

Nel mio tempo	interessante
Durante le	il piano
Il fine	vacanze vado al mare
Vado allo	libero faccio corsa
La domenica gioco	stadio con mio fratello
A volte suono	è fantastico
Penso che è	settimana
A mio parere	a tennis

2. Complete with the correct option

a. Il fine _____ il mio amico va allo stadio.

b. Spesso _____ il piano perché è rilassante.

c. Durante le _____ faccio nuoto con i miei amici.

d. In inverno _____ un maglione e una _____.

e. A ____ parere andare in palestra è faticoso.

f. _____ i giorni leggo un libro o gioco a carte.

g. La domenica la mia _____ Sara va ___cinema.

h. Non faccio mai arrampicata perché è _____

vacanze	indosso	suono	tutti	sciarpa
pericolosa	settimana	mio	amica	al

3. Spot and correct the grammar and spelling mistakes [note: in several cases a word is missing]

a. In inverno vado palestre con mia sorella

b. Durante le vacance vado in spiagia

c. Mi piace perché e interessante

d. A mio parere il ciclismo ha faticoso

e. Guardo la tele tutto i giorni in salotto.

f. La domenica facio colazione in cucina con madre.

g. Spesso guardo Netflix, penso que è appassionante.

h. Di solito indosso un vestito nera perché e elegante

i. Nel mia tempo libero ascoltare musica.

4. Guided writing – write 3 short paragraphs in the first person [I] using the details below

Name	Lives	Activity	With	Opinion
Stefano	Leeds	I go to the gym	my friend	exciting but tiring
Santino	Napoli	I play tennis	my brother	dynamic
Luciana	Glasgow	I listen to music	dog	fantastic

5. Describe this person in Italian using the 3rd person [he/she]

Name: Steven

Lives in: New York

Age : 13

Pet: a white dog

Weather: sunny and good weather

Always: goes to the park and does cycling

Opinion: because it is fun and relaxing

Grammar Time 13: Giocare, Fare, Andare + Essere and Avere

Giocare [to play]		
(io) gioco *[I play]*	**(noi) giochiamo** *[we play]*	**a carte** *[cards]*
(tu) giochi *[you play]*	**(voi) giocate** *[you all play]*	**a calcio/pallone** *[football]*
(lui/lei) gioca *[he/she plays]*	**(loro) giocano** *[they play]*	**a pallacanestro** *[basketball]*
		a scacchi *[chess]*

Fare [to do]		
(io) faccio *[I do]*	**(noi) facciamo** *[we do]*	**ciclismo** *[cycling]*
(tu) fai *[you do]*	**(voi) fate** *[you all do]*	**i compiti** *[homework]*
(lui/lei) fa *[he/she does]*	**(loro) fanno** *[they do]*	**una passeggiata** *[a walk]*

Andare [to go]		
(io) vado *[I go]*	**(noi) andiamo** *[we go]*	**al parco** *[to the park]*
(tu) vai *[you go]*	**(voi) andate** *[you all go]*	**al cinema** *[to the cinema]*
(lui/lei) va *[he/she goes]*	**(loro) vanno** *[they go]*	**in bicicletta** *[on a bike ride]*
		in piscina *[to the pool]*

Essere [to be]			
(io) sono *[I am]*	**(noi) siamo** *[we are]*	***Singular***	***Plural***
(tu) sei *[you are]*	**(voi) siete** *[you all are]*	**alto/a** **alti/e** *[tall]*	
		bello(a) **belli/e** *[beautiful]*	
(lui/lei) è *[he/she is]*	**(loro) sono** *[they are]*	**inglese** **inglesi** *[English]*	
		italiano/a **italiani/e** *[Italian]*	

Avere [to have]		
(io) ho *[I have]*	**(noi) abbiamo** *[we have]*	**due fratelli** *[2 brothers]*
		gli occhi scuri *[dark eyes]*
(tu) hai *[you have]*	**(voi) avete** *[you all have]*	**i capelli castani** *[brown hair]*
		undici anni *[11 years old]*
(lui/lei) ha *[he/she has]*	**(loro) hanno** *[they have]*	**un cane** *[a dog]*

*Author's note: the subject pronouns *"io"*, *"tu"*, *"lui"*, *"lei"*, *"noi"*, *"voi"*, *"loro"* are optional! They are useful to:
1) Add emphasis
2) Help know who we are talking about in the third person (he/she)

1. Complete with the one of the following verbs: *Ho – Vado – Sono – Gioco – Faccio*

a. _____ sport

b. _____ al parco

c. _____ un gatto

d. _____ a calcio

e. _____ a carte

f. _____ un cane

g. _____ quindici anni

h. _____ due animali

i. _____ al cinema

j. _____ arrampicata

k. _____ ciclismo

l. _____ a scacchi

m. _____ a pallacanestro

n. _____ gli occhi scuri

o. _____ i capelli biondi

2. Rewrite the sentences in the first column in the third person singular

io	lui , lei
gioco a tennis	
vado al cinema	
ho un gatto	
sono alta	
faccio nuoto	

3. Translate into English

a. Facciamo ciclismo

b. Giochiamo a scacchi

c. Lei non fa niente

d. Loro vanno allo stadio

e. Abbiamo due cani

f. Siamo francesi

g. Non ha fratelli

h. Non sono di Londra

i. Non faccio niente

4. Complete

a. Io non v_____ mai in piscina

b. Mia madre a volte v_____ in chiesa

c. (Noi) A_____ spesso al centro sportivo

d. Mio fratello h___ un gatto

e. Noi s_____ inglesi, tu s___ italiano

f. Io h___ i capelli rossi

g. Mio fratello ed io f_____ nuoto

6. Translate into Italian

a. I never play tennis with my dad

b. My mother never goes to church

c. My brother is tall and slim. He has blond hair and blue eyes

d. My uncle is forty years old

e. My sister goes to the gym every day

f. They never go to the swimming pool

g. My friends are generous and fun

5. Complete with the appropriate verb

a. (Io) Non _____ al cinema con i miei genitori

b. Mia sorella ed io _____ al parco

c. Mia madre _____ quaranta anni

d. Mio cugino _____ molto alto e bello

e. I miei fratelli _____ sempre alla Xbox

f. (Lui) spesso _____ sport

g. Quando fa bel tempo Anna _____ al mare

Revision Quickie 4: Clothes/Free time/Opinions

1. Match

1. Faccio i compiti	a. I go to church
2. Faccio sport	b. I go to the swimming pool
3. Gioco a pallacanestro	c. I go to the gym
4. Gioco a carte	d. I play volleyball
5. Vado in chiesa	e. I do the homework
6. Vado in piscina	f. I go swimming
7. Vado in palestra	g. I do rock climbing
8. Gioco a pallavolo	h. I do sport
9. Faccio nuoto	i. I go horse-riding
10. Faccio equitazione	j. I go to the beach
11. Vado in spiaggia	k. I play cards
12. Faccio arrampicata	l. I play basketball

2. Opinions – Complete

a. A mio p _ _ _ _ _

b. S _ _ _ _ _ _ me

c. P _ _ _ o c _ _ è...

d. N _ _ m _ p _ _ _ _

e. A _ _ _ _ se...

f. È fa _ _ _ _ _ _ _ o

g. È ap _ _ _ _ _ _ _ _ _ e

h. Mi p _ _ _ _

i. Pr _ _ _ _ _ sco

3. Fill in the gaps in Italian

a. Il fine s_____ normalmente faccio e_____ *[At the weekend I usually go horseriding]*

b. In i_____ la mia a_____ Lea v___ in p_____ *[In the winter my friend Leas goes to the gym]*

c. Non f_____ s___ perché a m___ p_____ è p_____ *[I don't do skiing because in my opinion it is dangerous]*

d. Quando v_____ al parco, p_____ una t_____ *[When I go to the park I wear a tracksuit]*

e. Q_____ fa c_____, vado i_ p_____ *[When it is hot I go to the swimming pool]*

f. La d_____ mio f _____ g_____ a tennis *[On Sunday my brother plays tennis]*

g. Quando h__ t_____ v_____ i___ p_____ *[When I have time I go to the pool]*

4. Translate into Italian

a. At the weekend:

b. During my holidays:

c. I play basketball:

d. I do my homework:

e. I go rock climbing:

f. My friend plays videogames:

g. I go to the swimming-pool:

h. I go to the gym:

5. Translate to Italian

a. I wear a coat

b. We wear a uniform

c. They play basketball

d. She goes rock climbing

e. When I have free time

f. They go swimming

g. My parents do sport

h. She plays football often

Question Skills 3: Clothes/Free time/Opinions

1. Translate into English

a. Cosa indossi d'estate?

b. Quando vai al cinema?

c. Cosa fai nel tuo tempo libero?

d. Ti piace giocare con i tuoi amici?

e. Con chi giochi a pallacanestro?

f. Perché non ti piace il calcio?

g. Dove fai nuoto?

h. Qual è il tuo sport preferito?

i. Ti piace ascoltare la musica?

2. Complete with the missing question word:

a. _____ vivi?

b. _____ sport fai?

c. Ti _____ il ciclismo ?

d. _____ vai allo stadio?

e. _____ indossi per andare a scuola?

f. Con _____ giochi a tennis?

g. _____ ti chiami?

h. _____ non leggi un libro?

come	cosa	chi	quando
perché	dove	piace	che

3. Split questions

Dove vai la	in inverno?
Con chi	andare in bici?
Perché	nel tuo tempo libero?
Quando fai	domenica?
Ti piace	giochi a scacchi?
Qual è	i compiti?
Cosa indossi	non ti piace il tennis?
Cosa fai	il tuo sport preferito?

4. Translate into Italian

a. What? _____

b. Where? _____

c. How? _____

d. When? _____

e. Who? _____

f. Who with? _____

g. Do you like? _____

h. Why? _____

5. Write the questions to these answers

a. Indosso una giacca quando fa freddo

b. Faccio sport il fine settimana

c. Vado in piscina la domenica

d. Mi piace uscire con i miei amici

e. Guardo la televisione con mia madre

f. Indosso un'uniforme: camicia bianca e cravatta

g. Raramente faccio sci, spesso faccio corsa

6. Translate into Italian

a. Where do you play tennis?

b. What do you do in your free time?

c. What do you wear to go to school?

d. What is your favourite sport?

e. Do you do like jogging?

f. When do you do your homework?

g. Why don't you play golf?

THE LANGUAGE GYM

UNIT 16
Talking about my
daily routine

In this unit you will learn how to say:

- What you do every day
- At what time you do it
- Sequencing events/actions (e.g. using 'then', 'finally')

You will revisit:
- Numbers
- Free time activities
- Nationalities
- Clothes
- Hair and eyes
- Food
- Jobs

UNIT 16
Talking about my daily routine
'Cosa fai di solito durante il giorno?'
[What do usually do during the day?]

| Di solito [Usually]

Normalmente [Normally]

La mattina [In the morning]

Il pomeriggio [In the afternoon]

La sera [In the evening]

Lunedì [On Monday]

Martedì [On Tuesday]

Mercoledì [On Wednesday]

Giovedì [On Thursday]

Venerdì [On Friday]

Sabato [On Saturday]

Domenica [On Sunday] | ceno [I have dinner]

esco di casa [I leave my house]
faccio colazione [I have breakfast]
faccio i compiti [I do my homework]
faccio la doccia [I shower]
gioco sul telefonino [I play on the phone]
guardo la televisione [I watch tv] | colspan | of | time | table |

UNIT 16
Talking about my daily routine
'Cosa fai di solito durante il giorno?'
[What do usually do during the day?]

Di solito *[Usually]* **Normalmente** *[Normally]* **La mattina** *[In the morning]* **Il pomeriggio** *[In the afternoon]* **La sera** *[In the evening]* **Lunedì** *[On Monday]* **Martedì** *[On Tuesday]* **Mercoledì** *[On Wednesday]* **Giovedì** *[On Thursday]* **Venerdì** *[On Friday]* **Sabato** *[On Saturday]* **Domenica** *[On Sunday]*	**ceno** *[I have dinner]* **esco di casa** *[I leave my house]* **faccio colazione** *[I have breakfast]* **faccio i compiti** *[I do my homework]* **faccio la doccia** *[I shower]* **gioco sul telefonino** *[I play on the phone]* **guardo la televisione** *[I watch tv]*	all'una			

* all'una [1]

alle *[at]* **verso le** *[around]* **dalle...alle** *[from...to]* **poi** *[then]*	**due** [2] **cinque** [5] **sei** [6] **sette** [7] **otto** [8] **nove** [9] **dieci** [10] **undici** [11] **dodici** [12]	**e** *[past]* **meno** *[to]*	**cinque** [5] **dieci** [10] **un quarto** *[quarter]* **venti** [20] **venticinque** [25] **mezza** *[half]*
		in punto *[o' clock]*	

mi alzo *[I get up]* **mi riposo** *[I relax]* **pranzo** *[I have lunch]* **torno a casa** *[I go back home]* **vado a lavoro** *[I go to work]* **vado a letto** *[I go to bed]* **vado a scuola** *[I go to school]*	**a** *[at]*	**mezzogiorno** *[12pm]* **mezzanotte** *[12 am]*

Author's note: * before *una* (1 o'clock) *la* shortens to *l'* before vowel. This means that in Italian you would say: *all'una (at 1) / verso l'una (at about 1) / dalle dodici all'una... (from 12 until 1 p.m.)*

Unit 16. Talking about my daily routine: VOCAB BUILDING (Part 1)

1. Match up

1. Mi alzo	a. I have lunch
2. Vado a scuola	b. I have dinner
3. Vado a letto	c. I get up
4. Pranzo	d. I have breakfast
5. Ceno	e. I do my homework
6. Faccio colazione	f. I go to school
7. Faccio i compiti	g. I go back home
8. Torno a casa	h. I go to bed

2. Translate into English

a. Mi alzo alle sei del mattino

b. Vado a letto alle undici della sera

c. Pranzo a mezzogiorno

d. Faccio colazione alle sette

e. Torno a casa alle tre e mezza del pomeriggio

f. Ceno verso le nove e poi mi riposo

g. Guardo la televisione verso le quattro

h. Vado a scuola alle otto

i. Vado a lavoro verso le otto e un quarto

3. Complete with the missing words

a. _____ a scuola [I go to school]

b. _____ di casa [I leave the house]

c. _____ a casa [I come back home]

d. _____ la tele [I watch telly]

e. _____ i compiti [I do my homework]

f. _____ lavoro [I go to work]

g. _____ sul telefonino [I play on the phone]

h. _____ all'una [I have lunch at one]

4. Complete with the missing letters

a. ____ccio la doccia [I have a shower]

b. ____rno a ___asa [I go back home]

c. ____oco sul _____nino [I play on the phone]

d. ____nzo [I have lunch]

e. ____eno [I have dinner]

f. ____do a scuola [I go to school]

g. Mi ____zo [I get up]

h. Va ___ a le_____ [I go to bed]

i. _____rdo la televisione [I watch tv]

5. Faulty translation – spot and correct any translation mistakes. Not all translations are wrong.

a. Mi alzo sempre alle sei : I always shower at 6am

b. Vado a letto a mezzanotte: I go to bed at noon

c. Lunedì faccio i compiti : I do my homework on Tuesday

d. Pranzo: I have lunch

e. Vado a scuola: I come back from school

f. Torno a casa: I leave the house

g. Guardo la tele: I watch telly

h. Esco di casa: I leave school

i. Sabato suono il piano: On Friday I play music.

6. Translate the following days and times into Italian

a. Monday at 6.30am

b. Thursday at 7.30am

c. Sunday at 8.20pm

d. Wednesday at midday

e. Friday at 9.20am

f. Tuesday at 11.00pm

g. Saturday at midnight

h. Today at 5.15pm

Unit 16. Talking about my daily routine: VOCAB BUILDING (Part 2)

1. Complete the table

Vado a letto	
	I relax
Mi alzo	
	I go back home
Alle otto e un quarto	
Pranzo	
	I have dinner
Gioco sul telefonino	
	I leave the house
Faccio colazione	
Vado a scuola	
	I do my homework
Mi vesto	

2. Complete the sentences using the words in the table below

a. Alle sette e _____ [at seven thirty]

b. _____ le cinque [around five o'clock]

c. Alle_____ del mattino[at 8am]

d. A _____ [at noon]

e. Alle _____ e un quarto [at 11.15]

f. Verso le tre _____ venti [at about 2.40]

g. A _____ [at midnight]

h. Verso _____ quattro [at about four o'clock]

i. _____ sette e venti [at 7.20]

j. Alle otto meno cinque _____ [at 7.55]

cinque	mezza	alle	otto	mezzogiorno
undici	le	meno	verso	mezzanotte

3. Translate into English (numerical)

a. Alle otto e mezza = At 8.30

b. Alle nove e un quarto = _____

c. Alle dieci meno cinque = _____

d. A mezzogiorno = _____

e. A mezzanotte = _____

f. Alle undici meno cinque = _____

g. Alle dodici e venti = _____

h. Alle sei e mezza = _____

4. Complete

a. Al____ c_____ e m_____ [at 5.30]

b. Ve_____ l__ o_____ e u__ q_____
[at around 8.15]

c. A m_____ [at noon]

d. Verso l__ o_____ m_____ un q_____ [at 7.45]

e. A m_____ [at midnight]

f. A____ u_____ e m_____ [at 11.30]

g. Dal_____ t_____ alle qu_____
[from 3 to 4]

5. Translate the following into Italian

a. I go to school at around 8 _____

b. I come back home at around 4 _____

c. I have dinner at 7.30 _____

d. I do my homework at around 5.30 _____

e. I have breakfast at 6.45 _____

f. I go to bed at midnight _____

g. I have lunch at midday_____

Unit 16. Talking about my daily routine: READING (Part 1)

Mi chiamo Hiroto. Sono giapponese. Di solito durante il giorno faccio questo. Mi alzo verso le sei e faccio la doccia. Dopo, faccio colazione con mio padre e mio fratello minore. Poi, mi lavo i denti e mi pettino. Verso le sette e mezza esco di casa e vado a scuola. Torno a casa verso le quattro e guardo la tele. Poi, vado al parco con i miei amici fino alle sei. Mi piace perché è divertente! La sera, dalle sei alle sette e mezza faccio i compiti e verso le otto, ceno con la mia famiglia. Non mangio molto. Solo un hamburger. Poi, guardo un film in tv e verso le undici, vado a letto.

Mi chiamo Raúl. Sono messicano. Di solito, mi alzo alle sei e un quarto. Poi faccio la doccia e faccio colazione con i miei fratelli. Dopo mi lavo i denti e preparo lo zaino. Verso le sette vado a scuola a piedi. Torno a casa verso le tre e mezza. Dopo mi riposo un po'. Normalmente navigo su internet, guardo una serie su Netflix o chatto con i miei amici su WhatsApp o Snapchat. Dalle cinque alle sei faccio i compiti. Secondo me è noioso. Ceno alle sette e mezza. Mangio riso o insalata. Poi guardo la tele e,verso le undici e mezza vado a letto.

Mi chiamo Andreas. Sono tedesco. Questa è la mia giornata tipica. Di solito, mi alzo **presto** [early], verso le cinque. Faccio una corsa e poi faccio la doccia e mi vesto. Dopo, verso le sei e mezza, faccio colazione con mia madre e mia sorella. Mangio frutta. Poi mi lavo i denti e preparo lo zaino. Verso le sette e un quarto vado a scuola. Torno a casa verso le tre e mezza. Nel pomeriggio di solito guardo la tele o chatto con i miei amici su internet. Dalle sei alle otto faccio i compiti. Poi, alle otto e un quarto, ceno con la mia famiglia. Dopo cena, gioco alla playstation fino a mezzanotte. A mio parere, é appassionante. Ma a mia madre non piace! Infine, vado a **dormire** [sleep].

1. Answer the following questions about Hiroto

a. Where is he from?

b. At what time does he get up?

c. Who does he have breakfast with?

d. At what time does he leave the house?

e. Until what time does he stay at the park?

f. Why does he like it?

2. Find the Italian for the phrases below in Hiroto's text

a. At around eleven

b. With my friends

c. I go by bike

d. I go to the park

e. I shower and get dressed

f. I don't eat much

g. From six to seven

h. I do my homework

3. Complete the statements below about Andreas' text

a. He gets up at _____ around_____

b. He comes back from school at _____

c. For breakfast he eats _____

d. He has breakfast with _____and_____

e. After getting up he _____ and then showers

f. Then he brushes histeeth and prepares _____

_____ . Around 7.15 he _____ .

g. Usually he _____ until midnight,

but his mum _____.

4. Find the Italian for the following chunks in Raúl's text

a. I am Mexican

b. I shower

c. with my brothers

d. I relax a bit

e. I eat rice or salad

f. I surf the internet

g. I have dinner at half past seven

Unit 16. Talking about my daily routine: READING (Part 2)

Mi chiamo Yang. Ho dodici anni. Sono cinese. Questa è la mia giornata tipica. Di solito, mi alzo verso le sei e mezza. Poi faccio una doccia e mi vesto. Poi, faccio colazione con mia madre e mio fratello, Li Wei. Dopo mi lavo i denti e preparo lo zaino. Verso le sette e mezza esco di casa e vado a scuola. Torno a casa verso le quattro e riposo un po'. Nel pomeriggio guardo la tele, ascolto musica o gioco con il telefono perché penso che è rilassante. Dalle sei alle sette e mezza faccio i compiti. Dopo, alle otto, ceno con la mia famiglia. Non mangio molto. Infine guardo un film e verso le undici vado a letto.

Mi chiamo Kim, sono inglese. Ho quindici anni. La mia routine quotidiana è molto semplice. Normalmente, mi sveglio presto, verso le cinque e mezza. Faccio una corsa e poi mi lavo e mi vesto. Dopo, verso le sette, faccio colazione con mia madre e la mia sorellastra. Poi, mi lavo i denti e preparo lo zaino. Verso le sette e mezza esco di casa e vado a scuola. Torno a casa dopo le tre. Poi, riposo un po'. Di solito, ascolto musica o chatto con i miei amici su WhatsApp. Dalle sei alle otto faccio i compiti. Alle otto e un quarto, ceno con la mia famiglia. Dopo, guardo un film in tv **fino a** [until] mezzanotte. Infine, vado a letto.

Mi chiamo Anna. Sono italiana. La mia routine quotidiana è molto semplice. Di solito, mi alzo alle sei e un quarto. Poi faccio colazione con mia sorella maggiore. Dopo mi lavo i denti e preparo lo zaino. Verso le sette vado a scuola in autobus. Torno a casa verso le due e mezza. Nel pomeriggio navigo su internet, guardo la tele o leggo riviste di moda. A mio parere è fantastico! Verso le otto ceno con la mia famiglia. Mangio frutta o un'insalata. Poi leggo un libro o gioco sul tablet e, verso le undici e mezza, vado a letto.

1. Find the Italian for the following in Yang's text

a. I am Chinese

b. my typical day

c. I shower

d. I prepare my bag

e. at around 7.30

f. I don't eat much

g. I watch telly

h. I go to school

i. I do my homework

j. from six to seven thirty

k. I watch a movie

2. Translate these items from Kim's text

a. I am English

b. normally

c. around 5.30

d. with my mum and stepsister

e. I go back home

f. at about three

g. I have dinner with my family

h. I rest a bit

i. I brush my teeth

j. I go for a run

4. Find someone who...

a. has breakfast with their older sister

b. doesn't watch telly at night

c. reads fashion magazines

d. gets up at 5.30am

e. has breakfast with their brother and mother

f. chats with their friends on the internet after school

g. does exercise in the morning

3. Answer the following questions on Anna's text

a. What nationality is Anna?

b. At what time does she get up?

c. What three things does she do after school?

d. How does she go to school?

e. Who does she have breakfast with?

f. At what time does she go to bed?

g. What does she eat for dinner?

h. What does she do before going to bed?

THE LANGUAGE GYM

Unit 16. Talking about my daily routine: WRITING

1. Split sentences

Vado a scuola	casa
Torno a	compiti
Faccio i	in autobus
Guardo	il telefono
Gioco con	alle dieci e mezza
Mi alzo	di casa
Vado a letto	verso le sei
Esco	la tele

2. Complete with the correct option

a. Mi alzo _____ sette del mattino

b. Faccio _____ compiti

c. Guardo _____ tele

d. _____ con il telefono

e. Vado a _____ alle undici

f. Torno _____ casa

g. Esco di _____

h. Vado a scuola _____ autobus

a	letto	alle	in
la	i	casa	gioco

3. Spot and correct the grammar and spelling mistakes [in several cases a word is missing]

a. Vado a squola in bici

b. Mi alzo a sette e mezza

c. Esco casa alle otto

d. Torno al casa

e. Vado scuola in autobus

f. Vado di letto verso le dieci

g. Ceno alle oto meno quarto

h. Faccio mio compiti alle cinque mezza

4. Complete the words

a. qu_____ [quarter]

b. me_____ [half]

c. al____ di____ [at 10]

d. v_____ l__ s____ [at around six]

e. al____ o_____ [at 8]

f. ve_____ [twenty]

g. l_____ [then]

h. p_____ [I have lunch]

i. e_____ [I leave]

j. g_____ [I play]

5. Guided writing – write 3 short paragraphs in the first person [I] using the details below

Person	Gets up	Showers	Goes to school	Comes back home	Watches telly	Has dinner	Goes to bed
June	6.30	7.00	8.05	3.30	6.00	8.10	11.10
Frank	6.40	7.10	7.40	4.00	6.30	8.15	12.00
Anita	7.15	7.30	8.00	3.15	6.40	8.20	11.30

Describe your daily routine using reflexive verbs.
'Qual'è la tua routine quotidiana?'
[What is your daily routine?]

A volte [From time to time]	**mi alzo** [I get up]	**all'** [at]	**una**	**e** [past]	**cinque**[5]
	mi asciugo i capelli [I dry my hair]	**alle** [at]	**due**		**dieci** [10] **quarto** [quarter]
Una volta alla settimana [Once a week]	**mi lavo i denti** [I brush my teeth]		**tre**		
Due volte alla settimana [Twice a week]	**mi faccio una doccia** [I have a shower]		**quattro** **cinque**	**meno** [to]	**venti** [20] **venticinque** [25]
Durante la settimana [During the week]	**mi faccio un bagno** [I have a bath]	**verso le** [around]	**sei** **sette**		**mezza** [half]
Il fine settimana [At the weekend)	**mi metto l'uniforme** [I put on my uniform]		**otto**		
Ogni giorno [Every morning]	**mi pettino i capelli** [I brush my hair]		**nove** **dieci**	**in punto** ['o clock]	
Tutti i giorni [Every day]	**mi preparo** [I get ready]		**undici**		
Sempre [Always]	**mi riposo** [I relax]		**dodici**		
Quando posso [When I can]	**mi sveglio** [I wake up]				
	mi trucco [I put make-up on]	a **mezzogiorno** [at midday]			
	mi vesto [I get dressed]	a **mezzanotte** [at midnight]			

Unit 16. Daily routine with reflexive verbs: Translation

Paragraph 1	Tick a box each time you spot the correct translation in the text				Write the translation
Hi, my name is Roberto. Every day I wake up at half past six, I have a shower and I put on my uniform. I have breakfast and I go to school at eight o'clock. From time to time I go back home at four because I go to my friends' house. Every afternoon I relax a bit in the sofa. I always go to bed at ten.	alle dieci	perché vado	mi metto l'uniforme	sempre	_____
	alle quattro	mi sveglio	Faccio colazione	vado a scuola	_____
	alle otto in punto	alle sei e mezza	Ogni giorno	torno a casa	_____
	Ciao, mi chiamo Roberto	mi faccio la doccia	a casa dei miei amici	un po' sul sofa	_____
	Ogni pomeriggio	mi riposo	Vado a letto	ogni tanto	_____

Paragraph 2					
Good morning, my name is Karen. During the week I always get up at quarter past seven. I have a bath at quarter to eight, I dry my hair and I brush my teeth. I go out at nine o'clock and I go to school by bus. Every day, I go back home at three, I play with the PlayStation, I relax and I go to bed.	sempre	mi riposo	alle tre	in autobus	_____
	torno a casa	esco di casa	mi lavo i denti	mi sveglio	_____
	mi asciugo i capelli	alle nove in punto	mi faccio il bagno	Buongiorno	_____
	alle sette e un quarto	durante la settimana	mi chiamo Karen	tutti i giorni	_____
	gioco con la PS	alle otto meno un quarto	mi lavo i denti	vado a scuola	_____

Paragraph 3					
Hi, my name is Emma. Twice a week, during the week end, I relax and I get up at ten since I don't go to school. Five times a week, when I go to school, I wake up at seven o'clock and I brush my hair. I get back home at four, I relax and I play with my brother and my dog.	alle dieci	mi sveglio	mi riposo	alle quattro	_____
	vado a scuola	alle sette in punto	mi pettino i capelli	Due volte alla settimana	_____
	Torno a casa	durante il fine settimana	Ciao, mi chiamo Emma	cinque volte alla settimana	_____
	e il mio cane	non vado a scuola	quando	con mio fratello	_____
	perché	alle otto	e gioco	mi alzo	_____

Grammar Time 14: Reflexive verbs

USEFUL VOCABULARY

Alzarsi	to get up
Chiamarsi	to be called
Farsi un bagno	to bathe
Farsi la barba	to shave
Farsi la doccia	to shower
Lavarsi	to wash
Lavarsi i denti	to brush your teeth
Riposarsi	to rest
Pettinarsi	to comb your hair
Prepararsi	to get ready
Truccarsi	To put make up on

Present Indicative of ARE verbs ending in -SI

	Alzarsi	**Farsi la doccia**
(io)	**mi** alzo *[I get up]*	**mi** faccio la doccia *[I have a shower]*
(tu)	**ti** alzi *[you get up]*	**ti** fai la doccia *[you have a shower]*
(lui) (lei)	**si** alza *[he/she gets up]*	**si** fa la doccia *[he/she has a shower]*
(noi)	**ci** alziamo *[we get up]*	**ci** facciamo la doccia *[we have a shower]*
(voi)	**vi** alzate *[you all get up]*	**vi** fate la doccia *[you all have a shower]*
(loro/ essi)	**si** alzano *[they get up]*	**si** fanno la doccia *[they have a shower]*

1. Complete with mi, si or ci

a. (loro) _____ svegliano

b. (io) _____ faccio la doccia

c. (lei) _____ pettina

d. (noi) _____ laviamo

e. (lui) _____ lava i denti

f. (noi) _____ pettiniamo

g. (loro) _____ preparano

h. (tu) _____ alzi

2. Complete with the correct form of the verb

a. Lei (lavarsi) s____ l_____ i denti

b. Noi (farsi la doccia) c__ f_____l_d_____ nel bagno

c. Lui (preparasi) s___ p_____ tutte le mattine

d. Lui (farsi la barba) s___ f____ l__ b_____ in camera

e. Lei (truccarsi) _____ _____

f. Loro(alzarsi) _____ _____ presto

3. Translate into English

a. Mi sveglio verso le sei, peró mio fratello si sveglia alle sette. Mi faccio la doccia poco dopo.

b. Mia sorella si riposa prima di andare a scuola. Lei si pettina sempre e si trucca.

c. Mi faccio la barba tutti i giorni, mentre mio padre si fa la doccia tutti i giorni.

d. I miei genitori si svegliano presto. Dopo si lavano e fanno colazione prima di noi.

e. Mio padre é pelato*[bald]* quindi, non si pettina mai.

f. Mia madre ha i capelli rossi. Lei si pettina e si trucca un'ora prima di uscire di uscire di casa.

g. Non abbiamo una vasca da bagno in casa. Quindi, ci facciamo la doccia.

h. Mi lavo i denti cinque volte al giorno. Invece, mio fratello si lava i denti solo una volta al giorno.

 **THE LANGUAGE GYM**

Io mi alzo mezz'ora dopo mio padre, alle sei e mezza. Mi lavo il viso, mi faccio la doccia, mi faccio la barba, mi pettino e per ultimo mi vesto e vado in cucina. Faccio colazione da solo. Mangio latte e cereali, un toast con marmellata e bevo caffè con latte. Dopo, mi lavo i denti, e mi preparo per andare a scuola, e verso le sette esco di casa. (Mario, 16)

5. Find in Mario's text the Italian for:

a. I get up

b. I wash my face

c. I comb my hair

d. I brush my teeth

e. I get ready

f. I shave

g. I shower

h. I drink

i. I leave the house

6. Complete

a. Mi facci__ la doccia [I shower]

b. Si prepar__ [She prepares herself]

c. Ci facci__ _ _ la doccia [We shower]

d. Vi lav__ _ _ [You guys wash]

e. Mi prepar__ [I prepare myself]

f. Si pettina__ _ [They comb their hair]

g. Mi lav__ i dienti [I brush my teeth]

h. Si fan__ _ il bagno [They bathe]

8. Translate

a. Normally, I shower at seven o'clock

b. He never brushes his teeth

c. We shave three times a week

d. They get up early

e. He never combs his hair

f. I put make up on

g. We prepare ourselves for school

h. They relax in the living room

4. Find in Chiara's text below the Italian for:

a. They wake up

b. My father gets up

c. He showers

d. He gets ready

e. My mother gets up

f. He leaves the house

g. He shaves

h. He combs his hair

I miei genitori si svegliano molto presto. Mia madre si alza verso le cinque e mezza, per preparare la colazione a me e a mio padre. Prima di preparare la colazione, si veste, si prepara e prende un caffè guardando la televisione. Mio padre si sveglia mezz'ora piú tardi. Si fa la doccia, si fa la barba, si pettina, e dopo fa colazione con mia madre in cucina. Lui esce di casa alle sette. (Chiara, 12)

7. Complete

a. _____ _____ alle sei
[They get up at six]

b. _____ _____la barba alle sette
[They shave at seven]

c. _____ _____ presto
[I get up early]

d. Non _____ _____ la barba
[He doesn't shave hiself]

e. _____ _____ i denti dopo aver mangiato
[We brush our teeth after eating]

f. Sempre _____ _____
[She always puts make up on]

Revision Quickie 5: Clothes/ Food / Free Time /Jobs

1. Clothes – Match up

Una sciarpa (1)	A baseball cap
Un completo	A skirt
Una cappello	A dress
Una cravatta	A shirt
Una gonna	A t-shirt
Un vestito	boots
Una maglietta	A suit
Una camicia	Socks
Stivali	Trousers
Calzini	A scarf (1)
Pantaloni	A tie

2. Food – Provide a word for each of the cues below

A fruit starting with **M**	la mela
A vegetable starting with **P**	
A dairy product starting with **F**	
A meat starting with **P**	
A drink starting with **S**	
A drink made using lemons **L**	
A sweet dessert starting with **G**	
A fruit starting with **A**	

3. Complete the translations below

a. Shoes : sca_____

b. Hat: cap_____

c. Hair: cape_____

d. Curly: ric_____

e. Grey: gri_____

f. Milk: la_____

g. Water: ac_____

h. Drink: bib_____

i. Job: lav_____

j. Clothes: ves_____

4. Clothes, Colours, Food, Jobs – Categories

Vestiti	Colori	Lavori	Cibo

camicia	azzurro	professoressa	operaio
carne	marrone	avvocato	pollo
gonna	cuoco	formaggio	cravatta
arancia	cappello	riso	rosso

5. Match questions and answers

Che lavoro fa tuo padre?	Indosso una tuta
Quale colore ti piace?	Alle otto e mezza
Quale tipo di carne non ti piace?	È avvocato
Di solito, cosa indossi per andare in palestra?	Gioco a scacchi
A che ora vai a scuola?	Il blu
Qual è la tua bibita preferita?	Non mi piace l'agnello.
Cosa fai nel tempo libero?	Il succo di frutta

6. (Free time) Complete with *faccio, vado* or *gioco* as appropriate

a. Non _____ sport

b. Mai _____ a pallacanestro

c. Spesso _____ in palestra

d. _____ ginnastica tutti i giorni

e. Sempre _____ con la playstation

f. Oggi non _____ in piscina

 **THE LANGUAGE GYM**

7. Complete with the missing verb, choosing from the list below

a. _____ tanto succo di frutta.

b. _____ le fragole perché sono buone.

c. Nel pomeriggio, _____ al centro sportivo o _____ con i videogiochi.

d. _____ molto sport perché é salutare.

e. La mattina non _____ molto a colazione. Solo dei cereali.

f. Mio padre _____ come ingegnere. Io non _____ perché _____ studente.

g. Non mi _____ giocare sul telefono. _____ guardare una serie su Netflix.

h. La mattina, mi _____ verso le sei.

alzo	gioco	adoro	lavoro
vado	faccio	preferisco	sono
lavora	bevo	piace	mangio

11. Translate into Italian

a. I play tennis every day

_____

b. I wear a jacket sometimes

_____

c. I go to the gym often

_____

d. I don't watch cartoons

_____

e. I get up at around six a.m.

_____

f. I shower twice a day

_____

g. I prefer fruit and vegetables

_____

h. I drink coffee every day

_____

8. Time markers – Translate

a. Mai:

b. A volte:

c. Sempre:

d. Tutti i giorni:

e. Raramente:

f. Una volta alla settimana:

g. Due volte al mese:

9. Split sentences

Mi piace giocare	piace nuotare
Non mi	videogiochi
I miei genitori	a pallavolo
A colazione	libero leggo un libro
Mia sorella sempre	sono severi
Il mio professore	bevo un caffè
A scuola porto	indossa i legging
A cena mangio	è simpatico
Nel mio tempo	una camicia bianca
Lui gioca spesso ai	tanta verdura

10. Complete the translation

a. Mio fratello _____ pane tostato a colazione [My brother eats toast for brekfast]

b. Non _____. Sono _____ [I don't work. I am a student]

c. A volte _____ al cinema con mio padre [From time to time I go to the cinema with my father]

d. Non _____ mai la televisione [I never watch tv]

e. _____ i miei professori [I love my teachers]

f. I miei genitori sono _____ [My parents are strict]

g. Non _____ mai jogging [I never go jogging]

148

UNIT 17
Describing my house, where it is located and saying what I like/dislike about it

In this unit you will learn how to say in Italian

- Where your house/apartment is located
- What your favourite room is
- What you like to do in each room
- The present indicative of key reflexive verbs in -ARE

You will revisit:
- Adjectives to describe places
- Frequency markers
- Countries

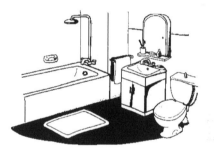

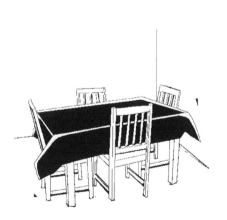

UNIT 17
Describing my house
'Ti piace la tua casa? - Dove si trova?'
[Do you like your house? - Where is it located?]

			Nella mia casa ci sono due/tre/quattro stanze *[in my house there are 2/3/4 rooms]*	
Vivo in una casa *[I live in a house]*	**bella** *[pretty]* **brutta** *[ugly]* **grande** *[big]* **nuova** *[new]* **piccola** *[small]* **vecchia** *[old]*	**che si trova** *[which is located]* **in campagna** *[in the countryside]* **in montagna** *[in the mountains]* **in periferia** *[on the outskirts]* **in una zona residenziale** *[in a residential area]*	**La mia stanza preferita è** *[my favourite room is]*	**il bagno** *[the bathroom]* **il giardino** *[the garden]* **il salotto** *[the living room]* **la cucina** *[the kitchen]*
Vivo in un appartamento *[I live in a flat]*	**bello** *[pretty]* **brutto** *[ugly]* **grande** *[big]* **nuovo** *[new]* **piccolo** *[small]* **vecchio** *[old]*	**nel centro della città** *[in the city centre]* **sulla costa** *[on the coast]*		**la mia camera da letto** *[my bedroom]* **la sala da pranzo** *[the dining room]* **la terrazza** *[the terrace]*

Unit 17. Describing my house: VOCABULARY BUILDING [PART 1]

1. Match up

vivo in	a flat
una casa	new
un appartamento	residential
grande	area
nuovo	I live in
la campagna	a house
zona	big
residenziale	the countryside

2. Translate into English

a. Vivo in una casa piccola e vecchia.

b. Vivo in un appartamento grande e nuovo.

c. Il mio appartamento si trova in periferia.

d. La mia casa si trova in campagna.

e. La mia stanza preferita è la camera da letto.

f. Mi piace la cucina.

g. Mi piace mangiare in cucina.

h. Sempre mi riposo in salotto

3. Complete with the missing words

a. Vivo _____ costa *[I live on the coast]*

b. Mi _____ la mia casa *[I like my house]*

c. _____ in una casa vecchia peró _____
[I live in an old but pretty house]

d. Mi piace il mio _____
[I like my living room]

e. La mia _____ si trova nella _____
[My house is on the outskirts]

f. Non mangio mai nella mia _____ da
_____ *[I never eat in the bedroom]*

4. Complete the words (about 'una casa')

a. una s_____ *[a room]*   g. la c_____ *[the coast]*

b. b_____ *[ugly]*   h. la p_____ *[the outskirts]*

c. n_____ *[new]*   i. il c_____ *[the centre]*

d. v_____ *[old]*   j. il g_____ *[the garden]*

e. g_____ *[big]*   k. la t_____ *[the terrace]*

f. la mia c_____ da_____ *[my bedroom]*

5. Classify the words/phrases below in the table below

a. sempre	i. grande
b. mangiare	j. a volte
c. mai	k. camera da letto
d. bello	l. campagna
e. nuovo	m. piccolo
f. montagna	n. cucina
g. si trova	o. costa
h. cucina	p. vivo

Time phrases	Nouns	Verbs	Adjectives
a.			

6. Translate into Italian

1. I live in an old flat

2. I live in a new house

3. In the town centre

4. I like my garden

5. In the living room

6. I live in a residential area

7. My favourite room is the kitchen

8. My house is located in a residential area

THE LANGUAGE GYM

Unit 17. Describing my house: VOCABULARY BUILDING [PART 2]

1. Match up

Si trova	costa
una casa sulla	residenziale
vivo in	la mia casa
un appartamento…	in centro
nel…	moderno
una zona	una casa grande
Mi piace	centro

2. Complete with the missing word

a. Non mi piace la mia_____ [I don't like my kitchen]

b. È piccolo però _____ [It is small but pretty]

c. Si trova nel _____ della città [It is in the town centre]

d. Si trova nella _____ [It is on the outskirts]

e. Vivo in una _____ grande [I live in a big house]

f. In una _____ residenziale [In a residential area]

g. La mia _____preferita è… [my favourite room is…]

h. Mi rilasso nel _____ [I relax in the garden]

i. Studio nel _____ [I study in the living room]

j. Ci _____ quattro stanze [There are four rooms]

zona	cucina	ci sono	centro	giardino
casa	salotto	bello	stanza	periferia

3. Translate into English

a. Vivo en una casa piccola

b. Si trova sulla costa

c. Un appartamento grande ma brutto

d. Si trova in una zona residenziale

e. Nella mia casa ci sono tre stanze

f. Mi piace studiare in salotto

g. mi piace mangiare in cucina

h. Vivo in una villa sulla costa

i. Vivo nella periferia della cittá

4. Broken words

a. Mi piace il mio g_____ [I like my garden]

b. Vivo nella m_____ [I live in the mountains]

c. Nel centro della c_____ [In the city centre]

d. Studio nella mia s_____ [I study in my room]

e. Una zona re_____ [A residential area]

f. La mia stanza pr_____ é… [my favourite room is…]

5. Il or 'La'

a. ___La___ costa

b. _____ campagna

c. _____ sala da pranzo

d. _____ salotto

e. _____ città

f. _____ giardino

g. _____ bagno

h. _____ stanza

i. _____ periferia

j. _____ zona

6. Bad translation – spot any translation errors and fix them

a. Vivo in una casa alla costa [I live in a flat on the coast]

b. La mia stanza preferita é la cucina
[My favourite room is the dining room]

c. Mi piace mangiare nella sala da pranzo
[I like to eat in my bedroom]

d. Vivo in un appartamento in una zona residenziale
[I live in a house in a residential area]

e. Mi piace la mia casa perché è grande e bella
[I don't like my house because it is big and ugly]

f. Mi piace mangiare in cucina [I like to work in a canteen]

Unit 17. Describing my house: READING

Mi chiamo Dante. Sono italiano, di Verona. Vivo in una casa grande e bella sulla costa. Mi piace molto. Nella mia casa ci sono dieci stanze e la mia stanza preferita è la cucina. Mi piace **cucinare** *[to cook]* in cucina con mia madre. Mi sveglio e mi lavo la faccia, dopo mi vesto nella mia stanza da letto.

Il mio amico Paolo vive in una casa piccola nella montagna. Paolo é molto simpatico e lavoratore. Non gli piace la sua casa perché è piccola.

Mi chiamo Giovanna e sono di Bolzano, però vivo a Roma , nel Lazio. La mia casa si trova nel centro della cittá, vivo in un appartamento. In casa parlo italiano e tedesco. Il tedesco è una lingua molto bella ma difficile. Vivo in una casa piccola, nuova e molto bella. Ci sono sei stanze e anche un giardino grande. Il mio cane vive nel giardino e si chiama Bruno, è molto affettuoso. La mia stanza preferita è la sala da pranzo perché mi piace molto mangiare. Mi piace rilassarmi e non fare niente. Guardo sempre i cartoni animati e una serie su Netflix. Mi piace anche ascoltare musica e passare il mio tempo libero nella mia camera da letto.

Mi chiamo Lenny. Sono rumeno e vivo in una casa molto vecchia però bella, nella campagna, in Italia. Adoro la mia casa. Nella mia casa ci sono cinque stanze però la mia preferita é la mia stanza da letto. Tutti i giorni, dopo la scuola mi piace rilassarmi in salotto e guardo la televisione con mia sorella. Non mi piace il bagno perché è piccolo e sempre sporco.

Mi chiamo Ariella. Sono di Milano. Mi sveglio sempre alle cinque di mattina perché vivo **lontano** *[far]* dalla scuola, nella periferia della cittá. Vivo in un appartamento in un edificio molto antico. L'appartamento è molto vecchio e un po' brutto, però mi piace. Mi piace riposarmi nella mia stanza da letto. A volte leggo libri oppure ascolto musica su Spotify. La camera da letto è la mia stanza preferita.

1. Answer the following questions about Dante

a. Where is he from?

b. What is his house like?

c. How many rooms are there in his house?

d. Which is his favourite room?

e. Where does he get dressed?

f. Where does Paolo live?

g. Does he like his house? Why?

2. Find the Italian or the phrases below in Giovanna's text

a. my house is in the centre

b. I live in a flat

c. I speak Italian and German

d. I also have a garden

e. I really like to eat

f. he lives in the garden

g. I like to relax

h. I like to spend my time

4. Find the Italian for the following phrases/sentences in Ariella's text

a. I am from Milan

b. I always wake up at 5

c. I live far from school

d. the flat is very old

e. and a bit ugly

f. but I like it

g. Sometimes I read books

3. Find Someone Who – which person...

a. Lives far from school

b. Speaks two languages

c. Has a really big house

d. He lives in an old building

e. Has a pet that lives outside the house

f. Has a dirty bathroom

g. Is a foodie (loves food)

h. Listens to music on a streaming platform

i. Watches TV with their sister

Unit 17. Describing my house: TRANSLATION

1. Gapped translation

a. Vivo in periferia *[I live on the _____]*

b. La mia casa è molto grande peró un po' brutta
[My house is _____ big but __ _____ ugly]

c. Si _____ nella... *[It is located in the ...]*

d. Vivo nel centro _____ _____
[I live in the city centre]

e. Nella mia casa __ _____ cinque stanze
[In my house there are five rooms]

f. Non mi piace molto la _____ perché è _____
[I don't really like the kitchen because it's ugly]

2. Translate to English

a. la costa

b. un appartamento

c. vivo in

d. il centro

e. della cittá

f. la mia stanza preferita

g. mi piace cucinare

h. la mia camera da letto

i. il salotto

3. Translate into English

a. Vivo in un appartamento piccolo e brutto.

b. La casa è moderna ma abbastanza piccola.

c. Il mio appartamento è vecchio però mi piace molto.

d. Vivo in una casa sulla costa.

e. Nella mia casa ci sono cinque stanze.

f. La mia stanza preferita è la camera da letto.

4. Translate into Italian

a. Big: G_____

b. Small: P_____

c. Outskirts: P_____

d. Coast: C_____

e. Area: Z_____

f. Residential: R_____

g. Ugly (m): B_____

h. Room: S_____

i. There are: C____ s_____

j. Old (f): V_____

5. Translate into Italian

a. I live in a small house

b. in the city centre

c. in my house there are...

d. seven rooms

e. my favourite room is...

f. the living room

g. I like to relax in my bedroom

h. and I like to work in the living room

i. I live in a small and old flat

j. in a residential area

Grammar Time 15: VIVERE – to live

				MASC
(Io) vivo [I live] **(Tu) vivi** [You live] **(Lui) vive** [He lives] **(Lei) vive** [She lives] **(Noi) viviamo** [We live] **(Voi) vivete** [You all live] **(Loro) vivono** [They live]	**in un appartamento**	**in campagna** [in the countryside] **in periferia** [on the outskirts] **in una zona residenziale** [in a residential area]	**Mi piace perché è** [I like it because it is] **Mi piace molto perché è** [I really like it because it is]	**accogliente** [cosy] **bello** [pretty] **brutto** [ugly] **grande** [big] **nuovo** [new] **piccolo** [small] **spazioso** [spacious] **vecchio** [old]
				FEM
	in una casa **in una villa**	**nel centro della cittá** [in the city centre] **nella montagna** [in the mountains] **sulla costa** [on the coast]	**Non mi piace perché è** [I don't like it because it is] **Non mi piace per nulla perché è** [I dont' like it at all]	**accogliente** [cosy] **bella** [pretty] **brutta** [ugly] **grande** [big] **nuova** [new] **piccola** [small] **spaziosa** [spacious] **vecchia** [old]

1. Match

vivono	I live
viviamo	You live
vive	She lives
vivo	We live
vivete	You guys live
vivi	They live

2. Complete with the correct form of 'vivere'

a._____ in una casa bella
[I live in a beautiful house]

b. Dove _____ ? *[Where do you live?]*

c. _____ a Londra da tre anni
[We have been living in London for three years]

d. _____ in una casa sulla costa
[She lives in a house on the coast]

e. _____ in una casa o in un appartamento?
[Do you live in a house or in a flat?]

f. _____ in un appartamento vecchio
[They live in an old flat]

g. _____ in periferia
[We live on the outskirts]

h. Mio padre _____ in una fattoria
[My father lives on a farm]

3. Complete with the correct form of 'vivere'

a. Mia madre ed io _____ a

Barcellona. Mio padre _____ a

Madrid.

b. (voi) Dove _____?

c. Io _____ a Londra. Mio fratello

_____ a Roma.

d. I miei zii _____ in America.

e. Mia sorella non _____ qui.

f. (Io) _____ in una casa molto grande

in periferia

g. (tu) _____ in una casa enorme!

4. Spot and correct the errors

a. (Io) Non vivi nel centro della città

b. I miei genitori viviamo qui

c. Mia sorella vivono in una casa nella costa

d. Mia madre ed io vivete in una zona residenziale

e. I miei fratelli non vive a Roma.

f. Mio nonno vivi a Milano.

5. Complete the translation

a. My siblings live in the countryside

= *I miei fratelli* _____ *in* _____

b. I live in a flat = _____ *in un* _____

c. My mother doesn't live with my father

= *Mia madre non* _____ _____ *mi padre*

d. We live on the outskirts

= _____ *nella* _____

e. Where do you live? = *Dove* _____?

f. They live in a small house

= _____ *in una* _____ _____ .

6. Translate into Italian

a. My parents and I live in a cosy house

b. My mother lives in a small house on the coast

c. My cousins live in a beautiful house in the countryside

d. My girlfriend lives in a modern flat in the centre

e. My sisters live in an old flat on the outskirts

f. My best friend Paolo lives in a spacious flat near the town centre

UNIT 18
Saying what I do at home in my spare time, how often and where

In this unit you will learn how to provide a more detailed account of your daily activities.

You will revisit:
- Time markers
- Reflexive verbs
- Parts of the house
- Description of people and places
- Telling the time
- Nationalities
- The verbs 'fare', 'giocare' and 'andare'

THE LANGUAGE GYM

Unit 18
Saying what I do at home in my spare time, how often and where
'Cosa fai a casa nel tuo tempo libero?'
[What do you do at home in your free time?]

A volte *[Sometimes]*	**ascolto musica** *[I listen to music]*	**in cucina** *[in the kitchen]*
	carico foto su Instagram *[I upload pics to Instagram]*	
Di solito *[Usually]*	**faccio i compiti** *[I do my homework]*	**in sala da pranzo** *[in the dining room]*
	gioco alla playstation *[I play PlayStation]*	
Due volte alla settimana *[Twice a week]*	**guardo Youtube** *[I watch Youtube]*	
	guardo una serie su Netflix *[I watch series on Netflix]*	**nella mia camera** *[in my bedroom]*
Il fine settimana *[At the weekend]*	**leggo un libro** *[I read a book]*	
	parlo al telefono *[I talk on the phone]*	**nella camera di mio fratello** *[in my brother's bedroom]*
	preparo la cena *[I prepare dinner]*	
Quando ho tempo *[When I have time]*	**mi riposo** *[I rest]*	
	mi rilasso *[I relax]*	**in giardino** *[in the garden]*
	scarico canzoni *[I download songs]*	
	suono la chitarra *[I play the guitar]*	
Sempre *[Always]*		**nella sala giochi** *[in the games room]*
Tutti i giorni *[Every day]*	**mi piace** *[I like]*	
	non mi piace *[I don't like]* → **ascoltare musica** *[listening to music]* / **caricare foto** *[uploading photos]* / **parlare al telefono** *[talking on the phone]*	**in salotto** *[in the living room]*
	mi piace molto *[I really like]* → **leggere un libro** *[reading a book]* / **scaricare canzoni** *[downloading songs]* / **guardare YouTube** *[watching YouTube]*	**in terrazza** *[in the terrace]*
	amo *[I love]*	
	preferisco *[I prefer]*	

158

Unit 18. Saying what I do at home: VOCABULARY BUILDING [PART 1]

1. Match up

1. Leggo fumetti	a. I talk
2. Guardo un film	b. I wash my hands
3. Preparo la cena	c. I watch a movie
4. Leggo un libro	d. I prepare dinner
5. Mi vesto	e. I read a book
6. Parlo	f. I shower
7. Mi lavo le mani	g. I get dressed
8. Faccio la doccia	h. I read comics

2. Complete with the missing words

a. Mi _____ [I get dressed]

b. Leggo _____ [I read comics]

c. _____ al telefono [I talk on the phone]

d. Mi lavo i _____ [I wash my teeth]

e. Faccio una _____ [I shower]

f. _____ la cena [I prepare dinner]

g. _____ su Internet [I go on the Net]

h. Ascolto _____ [I listen to music]

i. _____ foto su Instagram
[I upload photos onto Instagram]

3. Translate into English

a. Di solito faccio la doccia verso le sei del mattino

b. Il venerdi sera guardo sempre un film

c. Normalmente leggo fumetti in salotto

d. Faccio colazione verso le sette nella sala da pranzo

e. Di tanto in tanto parlo con mia madre in cucina

f. A volte faccio colazione in cucina

g. Raramente gioco alla playstation con mio fratello

h. Esco sempre di casa verso le otto del mattino

i. Mi lavo sempre le mani **prima di** [before]
preparare la cena

4. Complete the words

a. A _____ [I listen]	g. Mi ve____ [I get dressed]
b. L_____ [I read]	h. G_____ [I play]
c. P_____ [I talk]	i. E_____ [I leave]
d. P_____ [I prepare]	j. F_____ [I do]
e. C_____ [I upload]	k. M__ r_____ [I rest]
f. Mi l_____ [I wash]	l. G_____ [I watch, see]

5. Classify the words/phrases below in the table below

a. verso le sei	i. faccio colazione
b. sempre	j. a volte
c. mai	k. tutti i giorni
d. camera da letto	l. ascolto musica
e. guardo la tele	m. leggo fumetti
f. gioco alla Play	n. vado in bici
g. preparo la cena	o. due volte alla settimana
h. carico foto su Instagram	p. chatto su Skype

Time phrases	Rooms in the house	Things you do in the kitchen	Free-time activities
a.			

6. Fill in the table with what activities you do in which room

Gioco con Xbox	camera da letto
Guardo la tele	
Faccio la doccia	
Faccio i compiti	
Mi lavo i denti	
Mi riposo	
Preparo la cena	

Unit 18. Saying what I do at home: VOCABULARY BUILDING [PART 2]

7. Complete the table

English	Italiano
I get dressed	
I shower	
	Faccio i compiti
I upload photos	
	Esco di casa
	Parlo al telefono
I rest	

8. Multiple choice quiz

	Option a	Option b	Option c
Mai	always	never	sometimes
A volte	sometimes	always	every day
Sempre	never	often	always
Mi lavo	I shave	I wash	I go out
La mattina	morning	afternoon	evening
Mi rilasso	I go out	I watch	I rest
Giardino	garden	garage	kitchen
Cucina	bedroom	lounge	kitchen
Gioco	I rest	I play	I prepare
Leggo	I watch	I read	I play
Esco	I go out	I rest	I read
Camera da letto	bathroom	bedroom	dining room

9. Anagrams: Italian-English

1. aMi = *mai* = *never*

2. ciCuna =

3. sEco =

4. oeLgg =

5. emSpre =

6. aricoC=

7. voste iM =

10. Broken words

a. La cu_____ [kitchen]

b. M_____ [never]

c. A vo_____ [sometimes]

d. Se_____ [always]

e. Sp_____ [often]

f. I fum_____ [comics]

g. La mia cam_____ [my bedroom]

h. Es_____ [I go out]

i. Ch_____ [I chat]

11. Complete based on the translation in brackets

a. V_____ l__ s_____ e mezza, m__ l_____ i d_____ [Around seven thirty, I brush my teeth]

b. F_____ c_____ a_____ o_____ e un q_____ [I have breakfast at quarter past eight]

c. A v_____ p_____ l__ c_____ [Sometimes I prepare the dinner]

d. S_____ g_____ l__ t_____ n___ s_____ [I always watch telly in the living room]

e. D__ s_____ e_____ d__ c_____ a____ o_____ e mezza [I usually leave the house at eight thirty]

f. L_____ f_____ r_____ [I read comics rarely]

g. F_____ i c_____ v_____ l_____ c_____ [I do my homework at around five]

12. Gap-fill from memory

a. A volte _____ fumetti

b. Sempre mi _____ i denti

c. Spesso_____ una serie su Netflix

d. Non _____ mai libri sul tablet

e. Il pomeriggio _____ i compiti

f. _____ foto su Instagram tutti i giorni

g. Il fine settimana _____ in bici

h. _____ di casa verso le otto

i. Spesso_____ musica rock perché mi piace.

Mi chiamo Fabio. Sono di Gibilterra e ho un cane nero. Mi sveglio sempre presto, verso le cinque e un quarto. Dopo, vado un'ora in palestra e poi faccio una doccia. Mio fratello Joe, invece, è molto pigro e inattivo. Lui non gioca mai a calcio, né fa altri sport. Per questo motivo è un po' grasso. Nel pomeriggio di solito leggo fumetti o ascolto musica nella mia camera. In settimana, quando torno a casa dopo scuola, faccio i compiti con mia madre. Lei mi piace perché è intelligente e mi aiuta sempre. La sera vado a letto verso le nove.

Salve, mi chiamo Ilaria e vivo in Danimarca. Tutti i giorni mi alzo alle cinque. Poi mi lavo e faccio colazione in giardino. Esco di casa alla sette e vado a scuola a cavallo. Quando torno a casa chatto su Skype con la mia famiglia in Inghilterra e vado su Internet nella mia camera. Poi vado in bici o gioco in giardino con il cane. A volte guardo video su YouTube o carico foto su Instagram. Mio fratello Samuel carica video su TikTok di nuovi balli. Vado d'accordo con mio fratello perché è divertente e dinamico. Balla molto bene! Parliamo sempre o giochiamo a carte. Samuel è il mio migliore amico.

Ciao, sono Valentino e sono italiano. Mi sveglio sempre presto, verso le sei e mezza. Poi faccio la doccia e mi lavo i denti in bagno. Non faccio mai colazione, invece mia sorella Valeria mangia cereali in sala da pranzo. Vado a scuola a piedi. Torno a casa verso le tre e mezza e mi rilasso un po'. Di solito guardo la tele in salotto. Navigo su internet, guardo una serie su Netflix o video su TikTok nella mia camera. Poi, verso le otto, preparo la cena in cucina con mia madre. Amo preparare insalate perché, a mio parere, sono deliziose e sane. Normalmente vado a letto alle dieci.

1. Answer the following questions about Fabio

a. Where is he from?

b. What animal does he have?

c. What time does he wake up? What does he do after?

d. Why is Joe fat?

e. Where does he do his homework on weekdays?

f. Who helps him with his homework?

g. When does he go to bed?

2. Find the Italian for the phrases below in Ilaria's text

a. I get up

b. Then I shower

c. I go to school

d. by horse

e. I go on the internet

f. Uploads videos to TikTok

g. New dances

h. I always chat

3. Find Someone Who – which person...

a. Wakes up earliest

b. Has a family member that likes to dance

c. Likes to watch videos of people dancing

d. Has nothing for breakfast

e. Has a really lazy brother

f. Likes to prepare healthy food

g. Has a family member that is their best friend

h. Goes to school in the most exciting way

4. Find the Italian for the following phrases/sentences in Valentino's text

a. I am Italian

b. I wake up early

c. I have nothing for breakfast

d. Valeria eats cereals

e. in the dining room

f. in the living room

g. I watch TikTok videos

 THE LANGUAGE GYM

Unit 18. Saying what I do at home in my free time: WRITING

1. Split sentences

1. Parlo	a. cena
2. Mi rilasso nella	b. presto
3. Preparo la	c. con mia madre
4. Carico foto	d. mia camera
5. Faccio i	e. videogiochi
6. Mi sveglio	f. su Instagram
7. Gioco ai	g. i denti
8. Mi lavo	h. compiti

2. Complete with the correct option

a. Mi alzo alle sei del _____

b. Gioco a pallone in _____

c. Vedo la tele in _____

d. Ascolto musica nella mia _____

e. Preparo la _____ con mio padre

f. Mi _____ i denti

g. _____ una serie su Netflix

h. _____ a scuola in autobus

salotto	mattino	lavo	camera
vado	cena	guardo	giardino

3. Spot and correct the grammar and spelling mistakes [note: in several cases a word is missing]

a. facio la doccia verso sette

b. faccio colazione in coocina

c. nel mia camera da letto

d. gioco al viodegiochi

e. esco di cassa

f. lego un libro

g. veddo una serie a Netflix

h. vado a schuola in autobus

i. la camera di mio fratella

4. Complete the words

a. faccio co_____ [I have breakfast]

b. la cu_____ [the kitchen]

c. la mia _____da _____ [my bedroom]

d. il _____ [the garage]

e. e_____ di c_____ [I leave the house]

f. nel _____ [in the living room]

g. nella _____ da _____ [in the dining room]

h. nel _____ [in the bathroom]

i. g_____f_____n_____c_____d__m__ f_____ [I watch films in my brother's bedroom]

5. Guided writing –write 3 short paragraphs in the first person [I] using the details below

Person	When	Gets up	Has breakfast	Goes to school	Evening activity 1	Evening activity 2
Elaine	every day	6.15	kitchen	with sister	read a book	prepare dinner
Mauro	usually	7.30	living room	with brother	go to the gym	talk to family on Skype
Claire	sometimes	6.45	dining room	with mother	listen to music in garden	talk to my sister on the phone

Grammar Time 16: GIOCARE, (Part 3) FARE (Part 3) ANDARE (Part 2)

1. Complete with 'Faccio', 'Gioco' or 'Vado'

a. _____ la doccia

b. _____ a scacchi

c. _____ in Spagna

d. _____ in piscina

e. _____ ai videogiochi

f. _____ nuoto

g. _____ a rugby

h. Non _____ niente

3. Complete with the appropriate verb

a. Mia madre ____ in chiesa la domenica

b. Mia sorella non _____ mai i compiti

c. (noi) _____ a pallacanestro tutti i giorni

d. I miei genitori non _____ molto sport

e. I miei amici spesso _____ a pallone

f. La mia ragazza ed io _____ al cinema

g. Cosa _____ tu?

h. (voi) Dove _____?

i. Che lavoro _____ tu?

j. Mio zio _____ il professore.

k. I miei cugini _____ allo stadio il fine settimana

l. Mio padre _____ a tennis due volte a settimana

m. In estate noi_____ in spiaggia

n. Il fine settimana io e mio fratello non _____ niente

o. A che ora voi _____ a scuola?

2. Complete with the missing forms of the present indicative of the verbs below

	Fare	Andare	Giocare
io [I]		vado	gioco
tu [you]	fai		
Lui/lei [he/she]			
noi [we]			
voi [you all]	fate		giocate
loro [they]		vanno	

4. Complete with the 'noi' form of giocare/fare/andare

a. _____ a rugby

b. _____ a scuola

c. _____ a calcio

d. _____ in chiesa

e. _____ a hockey

f. _____ al parco

g. _____ a cricket

h. _____ in piscina

i. _____ sport

j. _____ ciclismo

k. _____ footing

l. _____ a scacchi

5. Complete with the 'loro' form of the verbs

a. _____ a tennis

b. _____ allo stadio

c. _____ arrampicata

d. _____ i compiti

e. _____ nuoto

f. _____ in spiaggia

g. _____ a casa

h. _____ a pallavolo

i. _____ a golf

j. _____ footing

k. _____ la spesa

l. _____ in montagna

 **THE LANGUAGE GYM**

UNIT 19
My holiday plans
(Talking about future plans for holidays)

In this unit you will learn how to talk about:

- What you intend to do in future holidays
- Where you are going to go
- Where you are going to stay
- Who you are going to travel with
- How it will be
- Means of transport

You will revisit:
- The verb 'andare'
- Free-time activities
- Previously seen adjectives

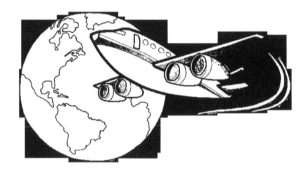

UNIT 19
My holiday plans
'Dove andrai in vacanza?'
[Where are you going on holiday?]

Quest'estate [This summer] **Quest'inverno** *[This winter]* **Il prossimo anno** *[Next year]* **A Natale** *[This Christmas]* **Tra due settimane** *[In two weeks]*	**andrò in vacanza in** *[I am going to go on holiday to]* **andremo in** *[we're going to go to]*	Australia Francia Italia Grecia Spagna Liguria Puglia Toscana	**in aereo** *[by plane]* **in autobus** *[by coach]* **in camper** *[by campervan]* **in macchina** *[by car]* **in nave** *[by boat]* **in treno** *[by train]*	**ballerò** *[I will dance]* **dormirò** *[I will sleep]* **farò immersioni** *[I will go diving]* **farò spese** *[I will go shopping]* **mangerò** *[I am going to eat]*
	passerò *[I will spend]* **passeremo** *[we will spend]*	**una settimana** *[1 week]* **due settimane** *[2 weeks]*	**lì** *[there]* **con la mia famiglia** *[with my family]*	**non vedo l'ora!** *[I can't wait!]* **riposerò** *[I am going to rest]*
	starò *[I am going to stay]* **staremo** *[we are going to stay]*	**nella casa di famiglia** *[in the family home]* **in un campeggio** *[in a campsite]* **in un hotel economico** *[a cheap hotel]* **in un hotel di lusso** *[a luxury hotel]*		**sarà divertente** *[it will be fun]*
	mi piacerebbe... *[I would like to...]* **ci piacerebbe...** *[we would like to...]*	**ballare** *[dance]* **fare spese** *[do shopping]* **fare immersioni** *[go diving]* **fare un giro turistico** *[go sightseeing]* **mangiare e dormire** *[eat and sleep]* **prendere il sole** *[sunbathe]* **riposare** *[rest]* **suonare l'ukulele** *[play the ukulele]* **viaggiare** *[travel]* **uscire in centro** *[go out into town]*		**sarà fantastico** *[it will be fantastic]* **sarà noioso** *[it will be boring]*

Author's notes: a. *Questo/questa means 'this'. When it is followed by a word starting with a vowel it becomes* **quest'** *like in* **quest'estate**. *Elision is very common in Italian :* l'acqua/ un'insalata...
b. *Have you noticed the verbs:* and**rò**/ mang**erò**/ ripos**erò**. *What does this ending suggest you? These verbs in the future can be translated both as 'I will...' or 'I am going to...'*

THE LANGUAGE GYM

Unit 19. My holiday plans: VOCABULARY BUILDING

1. Match up

1. andrò	a. I will eat
2. mangerò	b. a campsite
3. starò	c. I'm going to go
4. un hotel economico	d. it will be fun
5. un campeggio	e. I'm going to stay
6. mi piacerebbe	f. to rest
7. riposare	g. a cheap hotel
8. sarà divertente	h. I would like to

3. Translate into English

a. Quest'estate andrò in Grecia

b. Viaggerò in nave

c. Andrò a Cuba in aereo

d. Farò spese

e. Mi piacerebbe fare un giro turistico

f. Riposerò tutti i giorni

g. Ci piacerebbe mangiare e dormire

h. A volte farò immersioni

i. Andremo in vacanza in Spagna

2. Complete with the missing word

a. Mangiare e _____ [To eat and sleep]

b. _____ tanto [I will rest a lot]

c. Mi_____ andare a... [I would like to go to...]

d. _____ l'ukulele [I will play the ukulele]

e. Prenderò ___ _____ [I will sunbathe]

f. _____ noioso [It will be boring]

g. Passeremo ____ _____ in Italia
[We are going to spend 2 weeks in Italy]

h. Viaggerò in_____ [I'm going to travel by plane]

i. Alloggeremo in un hotel ___ _____
[We will stay in a luxury hotel]

4. Complete with the missing words

a. M_____ e dormire [To eat and sleep]

b. _____ in un campeggio
[We will stay in a campsite]

c. _____una settimana
[I am going to spend 1 week]

d. Mi_____ andare [I would like to go to]

e. Andare in_____ [To go to the beach]

f. Fare un giro_____ [To go sightseeing]

g. _____ il sole [To sunbathe]

h. Non vedo l'_____ [I can't wait]

5. Broken words

a. Andr_____ [I will go]

b. Andre_____ [we will to go]

c. Vacan_____ [holiday]

d. Camp_____ [campsite]

e. Immers_____ [diving]

f. In a_____ [by plane]

g. I__ b_____ [by boat]

h. Ball_____ [to dance]

i. Mang_____ [to eat]

j. Ripos_____ [to rest]

6. Bad translation – spot any translation errors and fix them

a. Il prossimo anno andrò: *Next summer I will go*

b. Andrò in Argentina in aereo: *I am going to go to Argentina by boat*

c. Mangerò e dormirò: *I am going to drink and sleep*

d. Mi piacerebbe riposare tanto: *I would like to rest a bit*

e. Staremo in un hotel: *I am going to stay in a hotel*

f. Passerò due settimane lì: *I am going to spend one week here*

g. Viaggeremo in autobus: *I am going to travel by train*

h. Staremo a casa della mia famiglia: *We will stay in my family's house*

Unit 19. My holiday plans: READING (Part 1)

Mi chiamo Hugo. Sono di Oviedo ma vivo a Madrid. Quest'estate andrò in vacanza nel sud della Spagna, in Andalusia. Viaggerò in macchina con il mio ragazzo Alejandro. Passeremo quattro settimane lì. Andremo in spiaggia tutti i giorni e mangeremo cibi deliziosi. Non farò un giro turistico, a mio parere è faticoso. Preferisco prendere il sole e ballare!

Mi chiamo Deryk e vivo in Canada. Nella mia famiglia siamo in quattro. Quest'estate andremo in Inghilterra e poi in Quebec, in Canada. Durante le vacanze riposerò e leggerò un libro. Penso che andrò anche a sciare con i miei amici in Canada. Mi piacerebbe mangiare cibi deliziosi, come 'poutine' (simile a patate fritte con formaggio). Sarà fantastico!

Mi chiamo Dino. Sono italiano ma vivo in Cina. Tra due settimane andrò in Svizzera in aereo. Passerò quindici giorni lì, da solo, e starò in un camper in montagna. Mi piacerebbe vedere il lago di Ginevra. Penso che visiterò anche musei. Non mi piace molto lo sport, preferisco **scoprire** [discover] la cultura del posto. Sarà interessante!

Mi chiamo Diana, sono polacca ma vivo in Germania. Il prossimo anno andrò a Roma con la mia amica, Natasha. Viaggerò in aereo e poi in macchina, perché ho molto tempo. Passerò cinque settimane lì e starò in una casa di famiglia, in campagna. Non vedo l'ora di andare in centro e visitare il Vaticano. Non mi piace fare spese, secondo me è noioso. Preferisco andare a cena fuori, in un ristorante o in una pizzeria.

1. Find the Italian for the following in Hugo's text

a. I am from

b. but I live in

c. I am going to travel by

d. with my boyfriend

e. four weeks

f. we will go

g. in my opinion

h. I prefer to sunbathe

2. Find the Italian for the following in Diana's text

a. next year

b. by car

c. I have a lot of time

d. I am going to spend

e. in the family home

f. in the morning

g. according to me

3. Complete the following statements about Deryk

a. He is from _____

b. There are _____ people in his family

c. They will travel to _____ and _____

d. Deryk is going to _____ and _____

e. He thinks that is going to _____with his friends

f. "Poutine" is made up of _____and _____

4. List any 8 details about Dino (in 3rd person) in English

1.

2.

3.

4.

5.

6.

7.

8.

5. Find someone who...

a. ...is going to England this summer

b. ...loves learning about culture

c. ...prefers the sun to sightseeing

d. ...who is going on holiday to Europe

e. ... is going to travel by car

 **THE LANGUAGE GYM**

Mi chiamo Berta. Sono tedesca. Ho una tartaruga in casa. È grossa e molto buffa ed è la mia migliore amica. Quest'estate andrò in vacanza in Italia, con la mia famiglia. Viaggerò in aereo e poi in macchina. Passerò due settimane sul Lago di Garda e starò in un hotel di lusso. Non vedo l'ora! Poi andremo tre giorni a Verona. Penso che vedremo monumenti famosi, come l'Arena di Verona (un antico anfiteatro romano), dove fanno Opera e concerti di musica. Tutti i giorni mangerò tanti cibi deliziosi e gelati. Mi piacerebbe fare spese e comprare vestiti italiani firmati, se avro' **soldi!** [*money*]

Mi chiamo Oliver. Sono di Sidney, in Australia . Il prossimo anno andrò in vacanza in Toscana con mio fratello. Viaggeremo in aereo e passeremo tre settimane lì. In Toscana visiteremo tanti posti. Non vedo l'ora di andare a Firenze, famosa per musei e momumenti, e visitare il Duomo. Poi andremo a Siena per vedere il *Palio* (antico festival dei cavalli), penso che sarà emozionante. Infine, riposerò qualche giorno in campagna, in una villa con piscina e un grande giardino. Sicuramente mangerò tanti cibi locali come la *ribollita* (zuppa di pane e verdure) e tanti salumi.

Mi chiamo Catrina, ho dodici anni e vivo a Genova. Quest'estate andrò in vacanza ad Amalfi, nel sud dell'Italia per dieci giorni. Viaggerò in macchina con mio padre e mia nonna. Staremo in un hotel economico, **a pochi metri** [*a few metres away*] dalla spiaggia. Andrò al mare tutti i giorni e prenderò il sole. La costa lì è spettacolare! Farò lunghe passeggiate e mangerò tanti gelati. Faremo anche un giro turistico a Napoli e andremo a vedere Pompei, famosa per il sito archeologico. Ho un'amica che vive a Sorrento, vicino Amalfi, si chiama Anna. Mi piacerebbe giocare con lei e fare immersioni. Sarà divertente, non vedo l'ora!

1. Answer the following questions about Berta

a. Where is she from?

b. What does she say about her pet?

c. Who will she go on holiday with? How will they travel?

d. Where will they stay?

e. What are they going to visit?

f. What is the "Arena" in Verona?

g. What will she do every day?

h. What would she like to buy?

2. Find the Italian in Catrina's text

a. this summer

b. for 10 days

c. the coast

d. long walks

e. famous for

f. I have a friend

g. to go diving

h. sunbathe together

i. I can't wait

3. Find Someone Who – which person...

a. Is going to travel south?

b. would like to buy Italian clothes?

c. Has a funny pet?

d. Is going to be staying in a villa with pool?

e. Is going to see a spectacular coast?

f. Is travelling from Australia?

g. Is going to visit an archeological site?

h. Is planning to eat ice-cream every day?

4. Find the Italian for the following phrases/sentences in Oliver's text

a. next year

b. famous for its museums

c. old horse festival

d. it will be exciting

e. finally

f. a few days in the countryside

g. with a swimming pool

h. local food

Unit 19. My holiday plans: TRANSLATION/WRITING

1. Gapped translation

a. *I am going to go on holiday:* Andrò in _____

b. *I am going to travel by car:* Viaggerò in _____

c. *We are going to spend one week there:*

_____ una settimana _____

d. *I am going to stay in a cheap hotel:*

Starò in un hotel _____

e. *We are going to eat and sleep every day:*

Mangeremo e _____ tutti i giorni

f. *When the weather is nice I am going to go to the beach:*
Quando fa bel tempo _____ _____ spiaggia

g. *I am going to go shopping:* Farò _____

2. Translate to English

a. Mangiare

b. Comprare

c. Riposare

d. Fare un giro turistico

e. Andare in spiaggia

f. Tutti i giorni

g. In aereo

h. Fare immersioni

i. Andare in centro

j. Fare spese

3. Spot and correct the grammar and spelling mistakes [note: in several cases a word is missing]

a. Faro imersioni

b. Passerò una setimana li

c. Starò in hotel lusso

d. Staremo in un hotel a centro

e. Mi piacerebbe farò spese

f. Viaggerò con aereo e machina

g. Andrò vacanza per due settimana

h. Suonerò l'ukulele e sara divartento

i. Mangerro cibi delizioso

4. Categories: Positive or Negative? Write P or N

a. Sará divertente: **P**

b. Sará noioso:

c. Sará piacevole:

d. Sará rilassante:

e. Sará interessante:

f. Sará terribile:

g. Sará spettacolare:

h. Sará faticoso:

i. Sará affascinante:

j. Sará impressionante:

5. Translate into Italian

a. I am going to rest

b. I will go diving

c. We will go to the beach

d. I will sunbathe

e. I would like to go sightseeing

f. I will stay in...

g. a cheap hotel

h. We are going to spend 2 weeks

i. I will go by plane

j. It will be fun

Revision Quickie 6: Daily Routine/House/Home life/Holidays

1. Match-up

In periferia	In the garden
In bagno	In the living room
In cucina	In my bedroom
A casa	In my house
In giardino	In the shower
Nella mia camera	In the dining room
In sala da pranzo	In the bathroom
Nella doccia	In the kitchen
In salotto	On the outskirts

2. Complete with the missing letters

a. Faccio la _____ [I shower]

b. Mi sve_____ [I wake up]

c. Gu_____ la tele [I watch telly]

d. Le_____ fumetti [I read comics]

e. E_____ di casa [I leave home]

f. V_____ a scuola [I go at school]

g. Pre_____ l'autobus [I catch the bus]

h. Mi ve_____ [I get dressed]

i. Faccio co_____ [I have breakfast]

3. Spot and correct any of the sentences below which do not make sense

a. Faccio la doccia in cucina

b. Pranzo in bagno

c. Preparo il pranzo nella camera da letto

d. Mi lavo i capelli in salone

e. Vado nella mia camera in autobus

f. Gioco a ping-pong col mio cane

g. Mi lavo le mani in salotto

h. Guardo la tele in giardino

i. Dormo nell'armadio

j. Faccio colazione in bagno

4. Split sentences

1. Guardo	a. l'autobus
2. Ascolto	b. colazione
3. Leggo	c. la tele
4. Prendo	d. un caffè
5. Faccio	e. musica
6. Vado in Giappone	f. fumetti
7. Bevo	g. compiti
8. Carico foto	h. in aereo
9. Faccio i miei	i. su Instagram
10. Arreglo	j. a carte
11. Lavoro con	k. mi dormitorio
12. Gioco	l. il computer

5. Match the opposites

a. buono	1. malsano
b. simpatico	2. cattivo
c. facile	3. bello
d. divertente	4. antipatico
e. sano	5. difficile
f. brutto	6. noioso
g. caro	7. rapido
h. lento	8. alto
i. spesso	9. economico
j. mai	10. raramente
k. basso	11. sempre

6. Complete with the missing words

a. Andrò in Giappone _____ aereo.

b. Andrò in Italia _____ i miei genitori.

c. Non gioco mai _____ calcio.

d. Odio ____ nuoto.

e. Alloggio in un hotel ____ lusso

f. Vado al parco una volta ____ settimana

g. Guardo una serie ____ Netflix

h. Carico foto _____ Instagram

7. Draw a line in between each word

a. Mipiacemoltogiocareapallacanestro

b. Guardolateleeascoltomusica

c. Nelmiotempoliberogiococonivideogiochi

d. AndròinGermaniainmacchina

e. Staròinunalbergodilusso

f. Lamattinaandròinspiaggia

g. Questestateandròinvacanza

h. Avoltevadoinpalestra

8. Spot the translation mistakes and correct them

a. Mi alzo presto: *I go to bed early*

b. Odio la pallacanestro: *I hate volleyball*

c. Andrò in piscina: *I will go to the beach*

d. Mangeremo e dormiremo: *We will rest and dance*

e. Nuoterò tutti i giorni: *I am going to run every day*

f. Viaggerò in macchina: *I will travel by plane*

g. Alloggerò in un caravan: *I will stay in a cheap hotel*

h. Prenderò il sole in spiaggia: *I will sunbathe in the pool*

i. A volte faccio una passeggiata: *Sometimes I go to the gym*

9. Translate into English

a. Prendo l'aereo

b. Andrò

c. Alloggerò

d. Mi lavo

e. Suono il violino

f. Preparo la cena

g. Mangio verdure

h. Vado a scuola

i. Non faccio niente

j. Faccio i compiti sul tablet

10. Translate into Italian

a. I have dinner: C_ _ _

b. I watch: G_ _ _ _ _

c. I do: F_ _ _ _ _

d. I shower: M_ l_ _ _

e. I read: L_ _ _ _

f. I work: L_ _ _ _ _

g. I rest: R_ _ _ _ _

h. I play (sport): G_ _ _ _

i. I play (instrument): S_ _ _ _

j. I upload: C_ _ _ _ _

k. I eat: M _ _ _ _ _

11. Translate into Italian

a. I shower then I have breakfast

b. Tomorrow I am going to go to Japan

c. I brush my teeth every day

d. I never play basketball

e. I get up early

f. I have dinner at six

g. I am going to go to Italy by car

h. In my free time I play chess and read books

i. I spend many hours on the Internet

Question Skills 4: Daily routine/House/Home life/Holidays

1. Complete the questions with the correct option

Dove	A che	Quante	Cosa
Perché	Qual	Quando	Con chi

a. _____ ora ti alzi?

b. _____ fai nel tuo tempo libero?

c. _____ è il tuo compleanno?

d. _____ ore passi davanti al computer?

e. _____ ____ giochi alla playstation?

f. _____ non fai mai sport?

g. _____ vai il venerdì sera?

h. _____ è la tua stanza preferita?

2. Split questions

A che ora	non giochi a pallone con noi?
Cosa mangi	starai in Italia?
Cosa fai	esci di casa?
Con	sei?
Perché	a colazione?
Quante settimane	chi giochi a scacchi?
Di dove	nel tuo tempo libero?
Ti piace	in vacanza?
Dove andrai	suonare la chitarra?

3. Match each statement below to one of the questions included in activity 1 above

a. Due o tre

b. Gioco a tennis o suono la chitarra

c. Con mio fratello minore

d. Verso le sei

e. Vado al cinema con un amico

f. Il dodici aprile

g. Perché sono pigro e non ho tempo

h. La mia camera da letto, ovvio!

4. Translate into Italian

a. Who?

b. When?

c. Who with?

d. Why?

e. How many?

f. How much?

g. Which ones?

h. Where to?

i. Do you like…?

j. Can you…?

k. Where is…?

l. How many hours?

m. How many people?

n. What is your favourite…?

5. Translate into Italian

a. Where is your room?

b. Where do you go after school?

c. What do you do in your free time?

d. Until what time do you study?

e. How long do you spend on the Internet?

f. What is your favourite past time?

g. What do you do to help in the house?

h. Do you like doing sport?

VOCABULARY TESTS

On the following pages you will find one vocabulary test for every unit in the book. You could set them as class assessments or as homeworks at the end of a unit. Students could also use them to practice independently.

1a. Translate the following sentences (worth one point each) into Italian

Hello, I am well	Ciao! Sto bene
Hello, I am very well because I am happy	Ciao sto molto bene perché sono felice
How old are you?	Quanti anni hai?
I am five years old	Ho cinque anni
I am seven years old	Ho sette anni
I am nine years old	Ho nove anni
Good morning, I am feeling great.	Buongiorno, mi siento molto bene
What is your name?	Come ti chiami?
My name is Paolo	Mi chiamo Paolo
Good morning, I feel bad because I am sad	Buongiorno, mi siento male perché sono triste
Score	**/10**

1b. Translate the following sentences (worth two points each) into Italian

What is your brother called?	Come si chiama tuo fratello?
What is your sister called?	Come si chiama tua sorella?
My brother is called Mario	Mio fratello si chiama Mario
My sister is fourteen years old	Mia sorella ~~si chiama~~ ha quatordici anni
My brother is fifteen years old	Mio fratello ha quindici anni
I don't have any siblings	Non ho fratelli o sorelle
My name is Jean and I am French	Mi chiamo Jean e sono francese
I have a brother who is called Alfie	Ho un fratello che si chiama Alfie.
I live in the capital of Japan	Vivo/habito nel capital di Japon
I live in the capital of Italy	Vivo " " " di Italia
Score	**/20**

1a. Translate the following sentences (worth one point each) into Italian

My name is Sergio	
I am eleven years old	
I am fifteen years old	
Where are you from?	
I am English. I speak a little Italian	
I am Scottish. I speak Spanish quite well.	
My friend is Polish. He speaks German fluently.	
The 6th September	
The 10th October	
The 8th July	
Score	**/10**

1b. Translate the following sentences (worth two points each) into Italian

I am 17. My birthday is on 21st June	
My brother is called Joe. He is 19	
My sister is called Maria. She is 22	
My brother's birthday is on 23rd March	
My name is Felipe. I am 15. My birthday is on 27th July	
I live in Venice.	
We live in Rome	
I do not like my town because it is rather noisy	
I love my city because it is very pretty	
Is your birthday in May or June?	
Score	**/20**

1a. Translate the following sentences (worth one point each) into Italian

Black hair	
Brown eyes	
Blonde hair	
Blue eyes	
My name is Gabriella	
I am 12 years old	
I have long hair	
I have short hair	
I have green eyes	
I have brown eyes	
Score	**/10**

1b. Translate the following sentences (worth two points each) into Italian

I have grey hair and grey eyes	
I have red straight hair	
I have curly white hair	
I have brown hair and brown eyes	
I wear glasses and have spiky hair	
I don't wear glasses and I have a beard	
My brother has blond hair and has a moustache	
My brother is 22 years old and has a crew cut	
Do you wear glasses?	
My sister has blue eyes and wavy black hair	
Score	**/20**

1a. Translate the following sentences (worth one point each) into Italian

My name is	
I am from	
I live in	
In a house	
In a modern building	
In an old building	
On the outskirts	
In the centre	
On the coast	
In Rome	
Score	/10

1b. Translate the following sentences (worth two points each) into Italian

My brother is called Marco	
My sister is called Anna	
I live in an old building	
I live in a modern building	
I live in a beautiful house on the coast	
I live in an ugly house in the centre	
I am from Milan but I live in an apartment in the centre of Glasgow	
I am 15 years old and I am Italian	
I am Spanish, from Madrid but I live in Florence, in Tuscany	
I live in Switzerland in a small villa in the countryside	
Score	/20

1a. Translate the following sentences (worth one point each) into Italian

My younger brother	
My older brother	
My older sister	
My younger sister	
My father	
My mother	
My uncle	
My auntie	
My male cousin	
My female cousin	
Score	**/10**

1b. Translate the following sentences (worth two points each) into Italian

In my family there are four people	
My father, my mother and two brothers	
I don't get along with my older brother	
My older sister is 15	
My younger sister is 8	
My grandfather is 78	
My grandmother is 67	
My uncle is 54	
My auntie is 44	
My female cousin is 17	
Score	**/20**

1a. Translate the following sentences (worth one point each) into Italian

Tall (masculine)	
Short (feminine)	
Ugly (masculine)	
Good-looking (masculine)	
Generous (masculine)	
Boring (feminine)	
Intelligent (masculine)	
Sporty (masculine)	
Good (feminine)	
Slim (feminine)	
Score	/10

1b. Translate the following sentences (worth two points each) into Italian

My mother is strict and boring	
My father is stubborn and unfriendly	
My older sister is intelligent and hard-working	
My younger sister is sporty	
In my family I have five people	
I get along with my older sister because she is nice	
I don't get along with my younger sister because she is annoying	
I love my grandparents because they are funny and generous	
What are your parents like?	
My uncle and auntie are fifty and I don't get along with them	
Score	/20

THE LANGUAGE GYM

1a. Translate the following sentences (worth one point each) into Italian

A horse	
A rabbit	
A dog	
A turtle	
A bird	
A parrot	
A duck	
A guinea pig	
A cat	
A mouse	
Score	**/10**

1b. Translate the following sentences (worth three points each) into Italian

I have a white horse	
I have a green turtle	
At home we have two fish	
My sister has a spider	
I don't have pets	
My friend Pedro has a blue bird	
My cat is very fat	
I have a snake that is called Adam	
My duck is funny and noisy	
How many pets do you have at home?	
Score	**/30**

1a. Translate the following sentences (worth one point each) into Italian

He is a male cook	
He is a journalist	
She is a waitress	
She is a nurse	
He is a househusband	
She is a doctor	
He is a teacher	
She is a businesswoman	
He is a hairdresser	
She is an engineer	
Score	**/10**

1b. Translate the following sentences (worth three points each) into Italian

My uncle is a cook	
My mother is a nurse	
My grandparents don't work	
My sister works as a teacher	
My auntie is an actress	
My (male) cousin is a student	
My cousins are lawyers	
He doesn't like it because it is hard	
He likes it because it is gratifying	
He hates it because it is stressful	
Score	**/30**

1a. Translate the following sentences (worth two points each) into Italian

He is taller than me	
He is more generous than her	
She is less intelligent than him	
He is more friendly than her	
She is better looking than him	
She is more talkative than me	
I am more funny than him	
My dog is less noisy	
My rabbit is more fun	
She is as talkative as me	
Score	**/20**

1b. Translate the following sentences (worth 3 points each) into Italian

My brother is stronger than me	
My mother is shorter than my father	
My uncle is better looking than my father	
My older sister is more talkative than my younger sister	
My sister and I are taller than my cousins	
My grandfather is less strict than my grandmother	
Paolo is more generous than Fabio	
My rabbit is quieter than my duck	
My cat is fatter than my dog	
My mouse is faster than my turtle	
Score	**/30**

1a. Translate the following sentences (worth one point each) into Italian

I have a pen	
I have a ruler	
I have a rubber	
In my bag	
In my pencil case	
My friend Luigi	
Pietro has	
I don't have	
A purple exercise book	
A yellow pencil sharpener	
Score	**/10**

1b. Translate the following sentences (worth three points each) into Italian

In my schoolbag I have four books	
I have a yellow pencil case	
I have a red schoolbag	
I don't have black markers	
There are two blue pens	
Lucia has a pencil sharpener	
Do you guys have a rubber?	
Do you have a red pen?	
Is there a ruler in your pencil case?	
What is there in your schoolbag?	
Score	**/30**

1a. Translate the following sentences (worth three points each) into Italian

I don't like milk	
I love meat	
I don't like fish much	
I hate chicken	
Fruit is good	
Honey is healthy	
I prefer mineral water	
Milk is disgusting	
Chocolate is delicious	
Cheese is unhealthy	
Score	**/30**

1b. Translate the following sentences (worth five points each) into Italian

I love chocolate because it is delicious	
I like apples a lot because they are healthy	
I don't like red meat because it is unhealthy	
I don't like sausages because they are unhealthy	
I love fish with potatoes	
I hate seafood because it is disgusting	
I like fruit because it is light and delicious	
I like spicy chicken with vegetables	
I like eggs because they are rich in protein	
Roast chicken is tastier than fried fish	
Score	**/50**

1a. Translate the following sentences (worth one point each) into Italian

I have breakfast	
I have lunch	
I have 'snack'	
I have dinner	
Delicious	
Light	
Disgusting	
Refreshing	
Hard	
Sweet	
Score	**/10**

1b. Translate the following sentences (worth three points each) into Italian

I eat eggs and coffee for breakfast	
I have seafood for lunch	
I never have dinner	
For snack I have two 'toasts'	
In the morning I usually eat fruit	
I love meat because it is tasty	
From time to time I eat cheese	
In the evening I eat little	
We eat a lot of meat and fish	
I don't eat sweets often	
Score	**/30**

1a. Translate the following sentences (worth two points each) into Italian

A red skirt	
A blue suit	
A green scarf	
Black trousers	
A white shirt	
A brown hat	
A yellow T-shirt	
Blue jeans	
A purple tie	
Grey shoes	
Score	**/20**

1b. Translate the following sentences (worth three points each) into Italian

I often wear a black baseball cap	
At home I wear a blue track suit	
At school we wear a green uniform	
At the beach I wear a red bathing suit	
My sister always wears jeans	
My brother never wears a watch	
My mother wears branded clothes	
I very rarely wear suits	
My girlfriend wears a pretty dress	
My brothers always wears trainers	
Score	**/30**

1a. Translate the following sentences (worth two points each) into Italian

I do my homework	
I play football	
I go rock climbing	
I go cycling	
I do weights	
I go to the swimming pool	
I do sport	
I go horse riding	
I play tennis	
I go to the beach	
Score	**/20**

1b. Translate the following sentences (worth five points each) into Italian

I never play basketball because it is boring	
I play PlayStation with my friends	
My father and I go fishing from time to time	
My brother and I go to the gym every day	
I do weights and go jogging every day	
When the weather is nice, we go hiking	
When the weather is bad, I play chess	
My father goes swimming at the weekend	
My younger brothers go to the park after school	
In my free time, I go rock climbing or to my friend's house	
Score	**/50**

1a. Translate the following sentences (worth two points each) into Italian

In my free time	
Every day	
On Sunday	
During my holidays	
In the summer	
I go swimming	
I play with my friends	
I go to the stadium	
I go to the gym	
I go on a bike ride	
Score	**/20**

1b. Translate the following sentences (worth four points each) into Italian

At the weekend I go cycling	
According to me it is exciting	
I do skiing, I think that it is fun	
I do rock climbing. In my opinion it is dangerous	
I often go jogging. I like it because it is relaxing	
In the winter we stay at home and play cards	
Every day I play videogames even if it tiring	
I play football with my friends because it is dynamic	
We never do sport. We play on the computer or on PlayStation	
In my free time I go on a bike ride because it is thrilling	
Score	**/40**

1a. Translate the following sentences (worth one point each) into Italian

I get up	
I have breakfast	
I eat	
I drink	
I go to bed	
Around six o' clock	
I rest	
At noon	
At midnight	
I do my homework	
Score	/10

1b. Translate the following sentences (worth three points each) into Italian

Around 7.00 in the morning I have breakfast	
I shower then I get dressed	
I eat then I brush my teeth	
Around 8 o'clock in the evening I have dinner	
I go to school by bus	
I watch television in my room	
I go back home at 4.30	
From 6 to 7 I play on the computer	
Afterwards, around 11.30, I go to bed	
My daily routine is simple	
Score	/30

THE LANGUAGE GYM

1a. Translate the following sentences (worth one point each) into Italian

I live	
In a new house	
In an old house	
In a small house	
In a big house	
On the coast	
In the mountains	
In an ugly apartment	
On the outskirts	
In the centre of town	
Score	**/10**

1b. Translate the following sentences (worth three points each) into Italian

In my house there are four rooms	
My favourite room is the kitchen	
I enjoy relaxing in the living room	
In my apartment there are seven rooms	
My parents live in a big house	
My uncle lives in a small house	
We live near the coast	
My friend Martina lives on a farm	
My cousins live in Barcelona	
My parents and I live in a cosy house	
Score	**/30**

1a. Translate the following sentences (worth one point each) into Italian

I chat with my mother	
I play on the PlayStation	
I read magazines	
I read comics	
I watch films	
I listen to music	
I rest	
I do my homework	
I go on a bike ride	
I leave the house	
Score	/10

1b. Translate the following sentences (worth three points each) into Italian

Usually I read a book in my room	
Twice a week I play the guitar	
I like downloading songs	
I upload many photos onto Instagram	
Every day I watch series on Netflix	
I always watch videos on YouTube	
After school I rest in the garden	
When I have time, I play with my brother	
I don't like talking on the phone	
I prefer uploading photos on Facebook.	
Score	/30

1a. Translate the following sentences (worth two points each) into Italian

I am going to go	
I am going to stay	
I am going to play	
I am going to eat	
I am going to drink	
I am going to rest	
I am going to go sightseeing	
I am going to go to the beach	
I am going to do sport	
I am going to dance	
Score	/20

1b. Translate the following sentences (worth five points each) into Italian

We are going to buy souvenirs and clothes	
I am going to stay in a cheap hotel near the beach	
We are going to stay there for three weeks	
I am going to spend two weeks there with my family	
We are going to go on holiday to Argentina tomorrow	
We are going to Spain for two weeks and we are going to travel by plane	
I would like to do sport, go to the beach and dance	
We are going to spend three weeks in Italy, we will stay in a caravan	
We are going to go stay in a luxury hotel near the beach	
We are going to go sightseeing and shopping every day	
Score	/50

The End

We hope you have enjoyed using this workbook and found it useful!

As many of you will appreciate, the penguin is a fantastic animal. At Language Gym, we hold it as a symbol of resilience, bravery and good humour; able to thrive in the harshest possible environments, and with, arguably the best gait in the animal kingdom (black panther or penguin, you choose). There are several hidden penguins (pictures)in this book, did you spot them all?

Printed in Great Britain
by Amazon